Minor Omissions

Living in Latin America

Robert M. Levine
Series Editor

Minor Omissions

Children in Latin American History and Society

Edited by
Tobias Hecht

THE UNIVERSITY OF WISCONSIN PRESS

The University of Wisconsin Press
1930 Monroe Street
Madison, Wisconsin 53711

www.wisc.edu/wisconsinpress/

3 Henrietta Street
London WC2E 8LU, England

5   4   3   2   1

Printed in the United States of America

Library of Congress Cataloging-in-Publication Data
Minor omissions : children in Latin American history and society /
edited by Tobias Hecht.
p. cm. — (Living in Latin America)
Includes bibliographical references.
ISBN 0-299-18030-1 (cloth : alk. paper) — ISBN 0-299-18034-4 (pbk. :
alk. paper)
1. Children—Latin America—History. I. Hecht, Tobias, 1964– II.
Series.
HQ792.L3 M56 2002
305.23′098—dc21
2002003993

For Irene Hecht

Table of Contents

Acknowledgments

This book would never have come into being without the encouragement of Robert M. Levine. My thanks go first to him.

Isabel Balseiro and Keith Hart, my toughest critics, were spot on, as usual. Anonymous readers for the press offered helpful suggestions on the first draft, and Paul Wise made the final manuscript a better read. Nara Milanich gave invaluable advice at every stage.

I am very grateful to the National Endowment for the Humanities, which supported my work on this book through a one-year research fellowship for independent scholars.

Although I am just one among many contributors to this volume, I think it is fair to say that we all have an intellectual debt to scholars of childhood and the family in Latin America whose work is not represented here. In particular, I wish to thank Lewis Aptekar, Claudia Fonseca, Pilar Gonzalbo Aizpuru, Elizabeth Anne Kuznesof, Asunción Lavrin, María Emma Mannarelli, Maria Luiza Marcilio, Patricia Márquez, Mary Del Priore, Mark Szuchman, and Ann Twinam. Readers are encouraged to turn to the work of these authors to find some of the treasures regrettably omitted here.

Minor Omissions

Introduction

Tobias Hecht

Over the last five centuries, the vast majority of children in Latin America left no written accounts of their lives. Nearly all records about them were authored by adults and reflect perspectives that may be very different from those of the children themselves.[1]

The problem is a familiar one to anyone who has examined black history in the Americas, or women's history, or the history of any socially repressed and silenced group. Yet slave narratives do exist, and women have been writing for as long as men have, if less prolifically and publicly. First-hand historical records of children's lives in Latin America, on the other hand, are exceedingly rare.[2] What is more, where children's writings have been used by historians, the records tend to say as much about what adults expected and taught children to write as they do about the everyday lives of their young authors (Steedman 1982; Calvert 1992: 4–5). On what sort of a foundation, then, could a history of childhood in Latin America be built? And more important, would such a foundation ultimately tell us anything new about Latin American history and society?

A few historians of Latin America from earlier generations, most notably Gilberto Freyre,[3] did write about children, but it is probably safe to say that the historiography of childhood in Latin America began in earnest only some time after its European and North American counterparts were established. And the history of childhood has a surprisingly short history. The field can be said to have been opened with the 1960 work by French historian Philippe Ariès, published in English translation as *Centuries of Childhood* (1962). Although Ariès never wrote about children in Latin America, some of the debates he introduced are relevant here.

Ariès sidestepped the lack of primary sources by children and even about their day-to-day experiences in medieval and early modern Europe by shifting attention to childhood, that is, to a socially constructed and malleable set of ideas. He relied extensively on the analysis of medieval art, arguing that European children were portrayed as tiny adults, with nothing distinctive about the representation of their features except for the scale. Their clothing, he claimed, was likewise identical to that used by adults, except that it was fashioned for small bodies, and he observed that children played the same games as their elders. From this sort of evidence, Ariès (1962: 128) concludes that, "In medieval society, the idea of childhood did not exist: this is not to suggest that children were neglected, forsaken or despised. The idea of childhood is not to be confused with affection for children: it corresponds to an awareness of the particular nature of childhood, that particular nature which distinguishes the child from the adult, even the young adult. In medieval society this awareness was lacking."

Ariès's somewhat confusing chronologies, his selective use of sources, his tendency to employ present-day conceptions of childhood as the sole gauge by which he judged childhood's existence or nonexistence during earlier historical periods, and the categorical and sometimes farfetched nature of his conclusions have been criticized by subsequent scholars (see, for instance, Archard 1993; Pollack 1983; and La Fontaine 1986).

Notwithstanding this criticism, Ariès left indelible marks on the subsequent study of childhood and opened a vast and nearly uncharted subfield of family and social history. Whereas a scholar could state in 1948 (cited in deMause 1974: 2) that "the history of childhood has never been written, and there is some doubt whether it ever can be written [because] of the dearth of historical data bearing on childhood," since *Centuries of Childhood* was published few historians would dare to make such a claim. Although Ariès's object of study was not narrowly the lived experiences of real children but rather the idea of childhood, his work had the effect of wresting the study of children from the developmental psychologists who, since the second half of the nineteenth century, had been virtually the only scholars with an enduring interest in them (Archard 1993; also Jenks 1996: especially 22–29). Ariès not only opened the way for historians to study childhood; other scholars, especially sociologists and anthropologists, soon followed, if in small numbers.[4]

Whereas the methodological debates and also the important distinction that Ariès made between the study of childhood and that of children have relevance for historians of Latin America, the particular focus of research in Europe and North America has only partly set the tone for the study of childhood in Latin America. The central concern of much of the European and North American research, particularly from the 1960s through the 1980s, is sentiment, that is, whether parents loved their children.[5] One of the problems with this debate, as Hugh Cunningham (1995: 2–3), has pointed out, is that such writing "has actually been more to do with parents than with children. Did parents in the past . . . love their children? . . . The question as posed is impossible to answer, partly because we simply do not know, and can never know, very much about the intimacies of relationships between parents and children, and partly because it assumes that we would recognize love if we saw it, and record its absence if it was not there, as though it were a material object."

Aside from sentiment, there are other important topics of research on European and North American childhood, but most do concern the treatments of children at the hands of adults. These include children's rights (Hawes 1991; Archard 1993), sexual abuse and exploitation (for instance Kinkaid 1998; Kitzinger 1990; Ennew 1986), child labor (for an overview of the field see Miljeteig, White, and Williams 1999), and infant abandonment (for a recent assessment, see Panter-Brick and Smith 2000). Many of these subjects concern processes or experiences that, while not divorced from larger historical forces, are still rather narrowly related to children.

If the history of childhood in Europe and in North America is a late developer,[6] the history and sociology of childhood in Latin America are truly in their infancy. One need look no further than the conference programs of the Latin American Studies Association to appreciate this lack of interest in children: of the more than three thousand papers presented at recent LASA meetings, scarcely a handful concern any aspect of childhood.

Yet the panorama is beginning to change. Just as scholars now take for granted that history is crosscut by the categories of class, gender, and race, they increasingly highlight the relevance of age to social experience. A small but growing number of scholars are now researching the lives of Latin American children, and it is interesting to note that the emphasis of their work is somewhat different from that of scholars of European and North American childhood. The concern of historical research on Latin American children—as opposed to some of the anthropological work (for instance Scheper-Hughes 1992)—is not so much sentiment or even parenting; as Asunción Lavrin (1991: 421) noted in an introduction to a study of childhood in Mexico, "The memory of childhood [in Latin America] has been assimilated to that of education or welfare, and the works that have dealt with children in that manner have used an institutional approach in which they [children] have remained ancillary rather than the centerpiece of the research." While Lavrin's assessment may have been intended as a criticism of the limited scope of research on children in Latin America, the promise of such a "memory," as this book aims to demonstrate, is that it situates the study of children squarely within the larger forces of history from which it cannot usefully be divorced.

As Donna Guy notes in this volume, historians of childhood in Latin America have also tended to treat children in relation to themes closely linked to and emerging from the history of women. Thus, illegitimacy, tied to notions of honor and to family history more generally, has been one of the more thoroughly researched topics involving children in colonial Latin America (for two important points of departure, see Mannarelli 1993; and Twinam 1999).

In the introduction to a special issue of the *Journal of Family History* dedicated to children in Latin America, Sonya Lipsett-Rivera (1998: 223) lamented that "Early accounts of children [in the region] are often more prescriptive than descriptive." Yet it is also true that these prescriptive sources, such as manuals about the proper upbringing of children, are fundamental to any history of childhood. The dearth of primary sources left by children only highlights the need to corroborate normative ideas about how children's lives ought to be with evidence that attests to their lived experiences.

When one begins to look for them, references to Latin American children are surprisingly plentiful. Children figure in letters, memoirs, biographies, travel journals, medical records, wills, divorce proceedings, laws, edicts, pronouncements, administrative books, ecclesiastical records, murals, sculptures, canvasses, poems, songs, and countless artifacts. And, like slaves who spoke not only with the aid of words but also through "rebellion, flight, suicide, and even crime" (Mattoso 1991),[7] or peasants, who may find ways of expressing themselves through "foot dragging, dissimulation, desertion, false compliance, pilfering, feigned ignorance, slander, arson, [and] sabotage" (Scott 1985: xvi), children speak through their games and lore (Opie and Opie 1959, 1969), their labor, their consumption habits (Seiter 1993), their own pernicious practices of social exclusion (James 1993), their use of violence (Asquith 1996), and myriad other means.

Even the silence about children in certain contexts is telling. In an article about sex between adults and children in colonial Brazil, Luiz Mott (1991: 46) argues that "Pedophilia in itself never came to be considered a specific crime under the [Luso-Brazilian] Inquisition." For example, in cases of teachers who abused their pupils, the fact that the act was committed between a man and a boy (thus constituting homosexuality) was of far greater concern than the disparate ages of those involved, a detail that tended not to be highlighted by authorities. The silence until late in the nineteenth century about child labor and child mortality is likewise telling.

But if it is accepted that there are primary sources about children and childhood worth studying, there remains a second and more important question: would such a study tell us anything new about Latin American society? Are children merely forgotten relics from the past, curios and anecdotes in an otherwise well-understood history? I would argue, on the contrary, that "adult society" cannot easily or usefully be disentangled from childhood. Insights from fields other than history serve as a useful analogy for illustrating this point.

Until the 1970s anthropologists and sociologists rarely wrote about children.[8] When they did they tended to be concerned with how children reproduced adult values and behavior. In a radical departure from this form of inquiry, Enid Schildkrout (1978: 112), in her ethnography of a Nigerian city, studied children as "independent and mutually interacting variables." The result, she found, was that adults can be seen to depend on children for their own social roles. She argued that "'sex roles' in Hausa society could not be defined as they are without children performing certain roles which are distinct from and complementary to adult roles" (114). Children, in other words, far from being mere incipient adults, empty vessels of social reproduction, were instrumental to the social roles of grown-ups. Similarly, in studying the lives of children residing illegally at a men's hostel in South Africa, Sean Jones (1993) uncovered a dimension of apartheid that spoke of the ravages of a system that clearly affected South Africans of all ages.

Treating the study of children as indispensable to the understanding of society at large has proven fruitful in Latin America as well. For instance, in research on fosterage in Southern Brazil, anthropologist Claudia Fonseca (1995) found that many of the people she studied claimed to have more than one mother: in addition to their biological mother they had one or various foster mothers who took care of them during different periods of their life and whom they also referred to as mothers. The practice of sharing offspring—and motherhood—can be seen as "a basic element of the organization of kinship" (15) in these low-income communities. Taking in and fostering out children created strong networks among adults, and children themselves were essential in the efforts of the newly married to "consolidate their status as adults as soon as possible. . . . The young bride will request to 'borrow' a nephew to take care of until her own baby is born. Old women will seek a grandson or granddaughter to 'keep them company.' Infertile couples will be on the lookout for any 'excess' babies [algum nenê 'sobrando'], that is, ones who came at a bad moment for the parents" (25).

It is useful to keep in mind the impossibility of understanding certain phenomena when children are factored out of the equation. The historical record suggests that the labor of children has been indispensable to the larger economy in every context from slavery to peasant farming, from agroindustry to the urban informal sector. Similarly, although children's patterns of consumption have escaped the notice of all but the ever-astute marketing professionals, Latin American children, notwithstanding the poverty in which so many of them live, are formidable consumers, and their preferences transform cultural practices. Consumer fads are taken to such extremes that, as one observer of impoverished children in Caracas has argued, boys in that city are more likely to murder for a pair of Nikes than for food to fill their empty stomachs (Márquez 1998).

The absence, until recently, of virtually any consideration of children in the history of Latin America is, I argue, a reflection more of the concerns and preoccupations of those writing history than of a lack of material worthy of scrutiny. The exceptions to the rule illustrate how history can be read differently if children are seen to be part of it. In *Order, Family, and Community in Buenos Aires, 1810–1860*, by no means a narrow study of childhood, Mark Szuchman (1988) examines the links between familial and larger sociopolitical orders. Rather than focusing on the household's "internal dynamics . . . its productive capabilities, its patterns of consumption, its procreative strategies, and so forth" (15), his emphasis is on how the workings of the family interacted with those of the polity at large. Children are vital to his analysis because they were vital to debates about social control and about "the extent to which [liberals and conservatives] believed the state should become responsible for reforming the forthcoming generations through the instrument of education" (228). Children were also vital to Argentinian notions of authority and nationhood.

A recent book about childhood in Brazil (Del Priore 1999) demonstrates the extent to which children are enmeshed in almost all aspects of Latin American history. Surely the most ambitious—and successful—attempt to deal with children as part of a national history in Latin America, the volume treats them in relation to religion, labor, crime, maritime history, and other topics, and permits a partial reinterpretation of Brazilian social history.

The argument that familiar aspects of Latin American history can be seen in a new light through an examination of the experiences of children and notions about childhood is compelling. The Conquest as we know it, I would argue, might not have occurred had it not been for the role of boys on the transatlantic voyages. Brought on board as pages, cabin boys, and apprentices, boys would often constitute 40 percent or more of crews during the sixteenth century. Pages, as the maritime historian Pablo Pérez Mallaína (1998: 75–79) records, began working at the age of eight or ten. They kept track of time by watching over and turning the hour glasses, swabbed the decks, called the crew to meals, and performed a religious role to which adult mariners were not deemed well suited: "the pages . . . watched over the divine cult on board, because at the end of the afternoon they recited the tenets and principal prayers of the Christian faith. Their youth required religious formation, and their almost infantile innocence was considered a better vehicle for the transmission of prayers to the Lord than the crudeness of the veteran soldiers" (77).

Yet boys were not merely the helpers of the adult mariners: without them there would have been no qualified sailors. As Juan de Escalante de Mendoza (1985 [1575]: 47), the sixteenth-century general and historian, wrote, the most important characteristic of a sailor, beyond "being of sound health and disabled not in his feet, hands, or any of his extremities, is to have made use of the sea from his early childhood *(haber usado el mar desde su tierna edad)*." All of Iberia's adult mariners had themselves first entered into service as boys and their training was the hands-on experience of sailing from a very young age.[9]

For sixteenth-century Europeans, uncertain how to interpret the nature and ways of the original inhabitants of the Americas, competing Iberian notions about childhood served as a sort of lens through which they scrutinized questions that for them were quite puzzling, such as whether Amerindians possessed souls, whether it was morally acceptable to wage war against them and enslave them, and whether Indians could be converted to Christianity. For example, in 1539 the Spanish theologian Francisco de Vitoria delivered a set of influential lectures in which he argued that the condition of the Indian was "similar to that of children, who, in Aristotle's definition, were only potentially, but not actually, rational beings" (Pagden 1991: xxv–xxvi). In likening the Amerindians to children, Vitoria was clearly suggesting not that they were incapable of surviving on their own but that, "given the supposed stupidity which those who lived among them report of them, and which they say is much greater than that of children and madmen among other nations," they might be better off under the tutelage of Spain, at least "for as long as they remained children" (Vitoria 1991: 291). Juan Ginés de Sepúlveda, the humanist scholar and royal historian, made a similar argument: the Conquest was just, even necessary, for "in prudence, talent, virtue, and humanity they [the Indians] are as inferior to the Spaniards as children to adults" (cited in Hanke 1974: 84).

Such claims about the Amerindians were countered by Bartolomé de Las Casas, the combative Dominican theologian. Las Casas's prolific writings are sprinkled with references to children, mostly descriptions of the horrors that befell the youngest native inhabitants of the Americas. Elsewhere, though, he portrays the Amerindians as possessing, in a more metaphorical sense, a childlike innocence and gentleness. "The sons of [European] nobles among us, brought up in the enjoyments of life's refinements, are no more delicate than are these Indians," he writes in *The Devastation of the Indies* (1992 [1552]: 28). In the same volume he argues that the fighting among Indians ought not to concern the Spaniards: "The wars of the Indians against each other are little more than games played by children" (33). In the case of those few Indians who were, to his mind, "hardhearted and impetuous . . . their hardness and impetuosity would be that of children, of boys ten or twelve years old" (40–41). It was precisely the childlikeness of the Indians, Las Casas, argued, that made them particularly suited for receiving the Christian faith.

Seen as more malleable than adults, children were pivotal in the work of early Catholic missionaries in the Americas.[10] The sixteenth-century civil servant and historian Gonzalo Fernández de Oviedo y Valdés (1959 [1514–1557]: 67) even dared to suggest that God had put the Indians in the New World and forgotten about them for a very long time; when he remembered them and saw "the evil there was across the land [he] allowed only that the innocent few, especially baptized children, be saved and that the rest pay [for their sins]."

Children were a sort of ground zero for the colonial encounter, a point of entry through which Europeans not only interpreted the nature of the indigenous societies but gained access to and sought to change them. In colonial Latin America the adage *"gobernar es poblar"* (to govern is to populate) belied Iberian insecurities about competing claims to New World lands from other European powers. The New World was, of course, populated when Columbus arrived, and, despite the demographic calamity that ensued when Old World diseases and war ravaged entire civilizations, it continued to be home to a population. Nevertheless, the production of new subjects with an allegiance to the colonial order was of the utmost importance to a secure empire.

The elements of production available to the Iberian monarchies proved problematic, however. Most of the early European colonists in the Americas were men, and the Spanish crown was initially concerned about the effect of interracial unions between its male subjects and Indian or (subsequently) African women. But the monarchy's ultimate acquiescence to the inevitable—even coming to encourage the strategically convenient unions of Spaniards with the daughters of *caciques,* or native lords—implied a concomitant acceptance that the family was not going to be exported from Spain to America, but rather reinvented (Urquidi 1991). The colonial subject, likewise, had to be invented, and children were the one indispensable raw material for this invention.

Before moving on to discuss the contents of this book, it is worthwhile considering, in demographic terms, why the study of children is crucial to any understanding of Latin America. In 1996, fully one third of Latin Americans were just fourteen or younger (UN 1998). A few decades earlier, those under the age of eighteen even represented a demographic majority in some countries. For example, in 1974, 48 percent of the population of Honduras was aged fourteen or younger, and 59 percent was nineteen or younger; a mere 25 percent of the country's population was above the age of twenty-nine.

Latin American history, the stuff of wars, elections, conquests, inventions, colonization, and all those other events and processes invariably associated with adults—most of them men—was also lived and partially forged by children. This book aims to explore how the "minor omission" of children from Latin American history may in fact be no small matter. It should be pointed out, though, that this book, like any edited work, has its own omissions. While it touches on more than five hundred years of history, it gives short shrift to certain periods, such as early-nineteenth-century liberalism, and to certain topics, such as education.[11] Eclectic rather than encyclopedic, this is a book concerned both with ideal notions of childhood and with the experience of actual children. The authors come from diverse disciplines, predominantly history but also literature, religion, anthropology, and art.

The Contents of This Book

Both the colonized peoples of the Americas and the Iberian invaders had elaborate ideas about how children were to behave and how they formed part of society. The first two chapters of this volume examine childhood as a contested site of encounter between these competing sets of beliefs.

In chapter 1, Carolyn Dean explores images of children in a series of canvases by anonymous Andean artists of the seventeenth century, illustrating how "pictorial children served as visual metaphors for Andean adults, who did not always behave according to the needs and desires of colonial authorities." But the interpretation of these images by contemporary (seventeenth-century) viewers would have turned on a shared notion of what a child is, and this, she suggests, did not exist. To the common Andeans, the primary audience of the paintings, "the equation of a child's irrationality to an adult's misbehavior is of doubtful significance." Thus, in this chapter, which brings together the interpretive tools of art history and social history, the canvases become a point of departure for exploring differences between Andean and European concepts of childhood.

In chapter 2, "Model Children and Models for Children in Early Mexico," Sonya Lipsett-Rivera focuses on the differences—as well as some surprising similarities—between Aztec and Iberian notions about what constituted an ideal childhood. Relying on a rich tapestry of sources, including transcriptions of *huehuetlatolli* (speeches by Aztec elders), Spanish manuals about proper behavior on the part of children, and court records, the chapter also examines the inevitable collisions between these norms and the recorded behavior of actual children.

Historically, rates of illegitimacy in Latin America have been very high. But how did society regard illegitimate children? What did it mean to be born illegitimate? In the third chapter, "Historical Perspectives on Illegitimacy and Illegitimates in Latin America," Nara Milanich explores filiation, or an individual's birth status as legitimate or illegitimate, as an important variable that conditions experiences of childhood in Latin America. One important dimension of illegitimacy analyzed here is the circulation of children, that is, the widespread practice whereby youngsters, especially illegitimate ones, were reared outside of their natal homes by people other than their biological parents. Because filiation was always and everywhere mediated by class status and racial or ethnic identity, it is difficult to generalize about the experiences of illegitimates; what is clear is that, like class or race, filiation is a cultural construct that has been fundamental to the production of social hierarchy in Latin America, from the dawn of the colonial enterprise to the dawn of the twenty-first century. This chapter suggests that illegitimacy has endured as a significant cultural category because the discriminatory distinction between illegitimate and legitimate offspring has been perceived as integral to the existence of the family, and family order has in turn been perceived as essential to social order.

Abandoned children in Latin America tend to bring to mind the specter of contemporary youngsters living by their wits and sleeping in the streets of such cities as Bogotá and Rio de Janeiro, but the phenomenon was already of concern in colonial times. In chapter 4, "Down and Out in Havana," Ondina González reveals the workings of an eighteenth-century foundling home known as Casa Joseph that took in infants left at its doorstep. Such babies were granted the not unimportant social right of being assumed to be legitimate, if of unknown parentage, and white babies were even bestowed with the "privilege of nobility." But civil and ecclesiastic officials endeavored to avoid their respective responsibilities toward the home's charges, and the results of this early experiment in child welfare proved calamitous.

Bianca Premo, in "Minor Offenses" (a turn of phrase that inspired the title of this volume), examines crime in eighteenth-century Lima as it relates to larger notions of childhood, discipline, and the state, on the one hand, and race, class, and gender, on the other. She argues that the state sought to defend society against the forces of disorder, including the criminal activities of the young, and, in a slightly contradictory way, saw itself as a merciful patriarch charged with reforming wayward youths. This dual charge was part of an overarching notion of *patria potestad*, or paternal right, in which, just as a man had authority over his children, so too did "a master over his slave, . . . a bishop over his priests, and . . . the king over his subjects—these were the interrelated hierarchies on which a civil order was founded." Yet in examining how punishment was meted out and clemency granted, she finds that patterns of discipline and reform were mediated by other hierarchies of colonial society, namely those of race, class, and gender, with the result that accusations had different implications and were subject to different interpretations, depending on the identity of the accused and the accuser.

The late nineteenth and early twentieth centuries were an era of enormous import for the history of children in Latin America. This was the moment when infant mortality was first recognized as a problem, when separate judicial and penal facilities were established for children, and when children came to figure prominently in debates about poverty, urban disorder, and the future of the nation. Chapters 6 and 7 treat this era.

Donna Guy, in "The State, Family, and Marginal Children in Latin America," examines delinquent and abandoned children and their treatment in this period. In the nineteenth century, childhood was enmeshed in notions of patriarchal property rights based on principles set forth in the Napoleonic Code. Fathers had a series of responsibilities in relation to their children—to feed, clothe, and educate them to the best of their abilities—and also important rights, such as imposing discipline, selecting their professions, approving of their spouses, and benefiting from the fruits of their unremunerated labor. "The patriarchal right was a double-edged sword. It meant that men had to acknowledge paternity in order to have a legal heir, and at the same time . . . support their offspring. Single mothers were left with all the stigma and responsibilities of raising a child unrecognized by the father." But what was the fate of children abandoned by their parents or accused of crimes? With special reference to Argentina, Guy explores how public officials contended with wayward, abandoned, and criminal children and youths. She finds not only that their treatment varied considerably according to gender but that policies adopted under welfare programs around the time of the global depression undermined paternal authority.

In chapter 7, Irene Rizzini draws our attention to the complexities of this era in Latin America's largest country, Brazil. Through an examination of records left by Brazilian jurists, doctors, and social reformers, children are shown to have been represented as an ambiguous social problem, as at once endangered and dangerous. Brazil's "child-saving movement" of the late nineteenth and early twentieth centuries, inspired by contemporary efforts in North America and Europe, sought to protect children who were abandoned or else being raised by families deemed unfit to care for them. Yet the philanthropic movement obeyed a political logic through which the country's leaders sought to make of Brazil a modern, civilized country. Rather than aiming to alter the social conditions that so divided rich and poor, this movement was concerned primarily with preserving its inherited privileges. The challenge such reformers set for themselves was to protect the poor and protect the wealthy from the poor—without otherwise altering class relations.

Chapter 8 returns our attention to the relationships between society, art, and childhood. In "How Haitian Artists Disclose Childhood of All Ages," LeGrace Benson examines works by artists of diverse backgrounds and sensibilities who interweave images of children with Haiti's

European, African, and New World heritages. These images—from daily life and dreams—echo what the author calls a "Long Conversation" from Brittany and the Slave Coast, Paris, Philadelphia, Hollywood and beyond.

In the second half of the twentieth century, civil wars wreaked havoc across much of Central America. In chapter 9, Anna L. Peterson and Kay Almere Read explore how children have suffered, fought, survived, and died in the wars in El Salvador, Guatemala, and Nicaragua. The suffering of children at the hands of the enemy has been emphasized by all sides in these conflicts; less known is the extent to which children have been active, sometimes willing, participants in these conflicts. The authors ask how children's multiple forms of participation in political violence might influence both their eligibility for aid and the upholding—even defining—of their rights.

Chapter 10 may offer historians of future generations attempting to understand twentieth-century childhoods spent in the streets of Latin America an important primary source. The first part of the chapter consists of diary entries by Bruna Veríssimo, a young person who has lived in the streets of Recife, Brazil since the age of nine. The author, who never attended school, taught herself to read and write by studying street signs. The second part of the chapter is an interview conducted by Veríssimo with a younger, formerly homeless friend.

Chapter 11 turns to discussions of children in contemporary Latin America. I argue here that children tend to attract the attention of researchers primarily when they are victims or perpetrators of violence. Almost wholly ignored, however, are the nearly one half million Latin American children who die each year, mostly as a result of hunger and treatable diseases. The chapter also discusses the enormous gap between the sort of childhood lived by poor children in Latin America and that experienced by the offspring of the rich.

Literature is sometimes a step ahead of reality, and this book ends with a short story, "The Children's Rebellion," a tale that is frightening, hopeful, and prescient in approximately equal proportions. This is a story about two children who, having been taken away from their leftist parents, meet at an art exhibit attended by members of their country's military and civilian elite. The children ultimately challenge the expected relations of power between adults and children, between the authorities and those with art, language, and human ingenuity as their

only weapons. One of Uruguayan-born Cristina Peri Rossi's most famous short stories (though never before published in English translation), the tale was written in 1972. This was a year before the consolidation of Uruguay's slow coup, four years before the rise of neighboring
Argentina's military dictatorship, well before *disappear* came to be accepted in English as a transitive verb; it would be even longer before
the truth was known about the missing children of a generation of Ar-
gentinean and Uruguayan leftists who had hoped for a better future.

Notes

1. For discussions of this problem, see Russakoff (1998: 29), Hardman
(1973), and Jenks (1996).
2. An important exception from just after the establishment of the Republic
in Brazil is the diary by "Helena Morley" (1957) covering the years 1893–1895,
when the author was aged twelve through fifteen.
3. See, for example, *The Masters and the Slaves* (1963 [1933]) and *The
Mansions and the Shanties* (1968 [1936]).
4. For an excellent assessment of the sociological study of childhood, see
Prout and James (1990).
5. For a discussion of the focus on sentiment in the history of childhood,
see Cunningham (1995: Introduction). For some of the most important examples of such work, see deMause (1974), Shorter (1975), and Pollack (1983).
6. A term applied by Benthall (1992) to the ethnography of childhood.
7. Here and elsewhere in this book, quotations in English from reference
works listed in other languages have been translated by the authors of the chapters concerned.
8. Two important exceptions are Margaret Mead (e.g., 1977 [1928]) and
Ruth Benedict (e.g., 1938).
9. For a discussion of children on Portuguese vessels, see Ramos (1999).
10. For an excellent introduction to the relevance of this topic in the history
of Brazil, see Chambouleyron (1999) and Del Priore (1991).
11. Readers can find an outstanding treatment of youth culture, education,
and liberalism in Andrew Kirkendall's (2002) *Class Mates: Male Student Culture and the Making of a Political Class in Nineteenth-Century Brazil.*

References

Archard, David. 1993. *Children: Rights and childhood.* London: Routledge.
Ariès, Philippe. 1962. *Centuries of childhood: A social history of family life.*
     Translated by R. Baldick. New York: Random House.
Asquith, Stewart. 1996. When children kill children. *Childhood* 3 (1): 99–116.

Benedict, Ruth. 1938. Continuities and discontinuities in cultural conditioning. *Psychiatry* 1 (2): 161–67.

Benthall, Jonathan. 1992. A late developer? The ethnography of children. *Anthropology Today* 8 (2): 1.

Calvert, Karin. 1992. *Children in the house: The material culture of early childhood, 1600–1900.* Boston: Northeastern University Press.

Chambouleyron, Rafael. 1999. Jesuítas e as crianças no Brasil quinhentista. In *História das crianças no Brasil,* edited by M. Del Priore. São Paulo: Contexto.

Cunningham, Hugh. 1995. *Children and childhood in Western society since 1500.* London: Longman.

Del Priore, Mary, ed. 1991. *História da criança no Brasil.* São Paulo: Contexto.

———. 1999. *História das crianças no Brasil.* São Paulo: Contexto.

deMause, Lloyd. 1974. *The history of childhood.* New York: Psychohistory Press.

Ennew, Judith. 1986. *The sexual exploitation of children.* Cambridge: Polity Press.

Escalante de Mendoza, Juan de. 1985 [1575]. *Itinerario de navegación de los mares y tierras occidentales.* Madrid: Museo Naval.

Fernández de Oviedo y Valdés, Gonzalo. 1959 [1514–1557]. *Historia general y natural de las Indias.* Edited by J. Pérez de Tudela y Bueso. Biblioteca de autores españoles, vols. 117–21. Madrid: Ediciones Atlas.

Fonseca, Claudia. 1995. *Caminhos da adoção.* São Paulo: Cortez.

Freyre, Gilberto. 1963 [1933]. *The masters and the slaves: A study in the formation of Brazilian society.* Translated by S. Putnam. London: Weidenfeld & Nicolson.

———. 1968 [1936]. *The mansions and the shanties: The making of modern Brazil.* Translated by H. de Onís. London: Weidenfeld & Nicolson.

Hanke, Lewis. 1974. *All mankind is one: A study of the disputation between Bartolomé de Las Casas and Juan Ginés de Sepúlveda in 1550 on the intellectual and religious capacity of the American Indians.* DeKalb: Northern Illinois University Press.

Hardman, Charlotte. 1973. Can there be an anthropology of children? *Journal of the Anthropological Society of Oxford* 4 (11): 85–99.

Hawes, Joseph M. 1991. *The children's rights movement: A history of advocacy and protection.* Boston: Twayne.

James, Allison. 1993. *Childhood identities: Self and social relationships in the experience of the child.* Edinburgh: Edinburgh University Press.

Jenks, Chris. 1996. *Childhood.* New York: Routledge.

Jones, Sean. 1993. *Assaulting childhood: Children's experiences of migrancy and hostel life in South Africa.* Johannesburg: Witwatersrand University Press.

Kinkaid, James R. 1998. *Erotic innocence: The culture of child molesting.* Durham: Duke University Press.

Kirkendall, Andrew J. 2002. *Class mates: Male student culture and the making of a political class in nineteenth-century Brazil.* Lincoln: University of Nebraska Press.

Kitzinger, Jenny. 1990. Children, power and the struggle against sexual abuse. In *Constructing and deconstructing childhood: Contemporary issues in the sociological study of childhood,* edited by A. James and A. Prout. London: Falmer Press.

La Fontaine, Jean. 1986. An anthropological perspective on children in social worlds. In *Children of social worlds,* edited by M. Richards and P. Light. Cambridge: Polity Press.

Las Casas, Bartolomé de. 1992 [1552]. *The devastation of the Indies: A brief account.* Translated by H. Briffault. Baltimore: Johns Hopkins University Press.

Lavrin, Asunción. 1991. Mexico. In *Children in historical and comparative perspective,* edited by J. H. Hawes and R. Hiner. New York: Greenwood.

Lipsett-Rivera, Sonya, ed. 1998. Special issue on children in the history of Latin America. *Journal of Family History* 23 (3).

Mannarelli, María Emma. 1993. *Pecados públicos: La ilegitimidad en Lima, siglo XVII.* Lima: Flora Tristán.

Márquez, Patricia C. 1998. *The street is my home: Youth and violence in Caracas.* Stanford: Stanford University Press.

Mattoso, Kátia de Queiros. 1991. O filho da escrava. In *História da criança no Brasil,* edited by M. Del Priore. São Paulo: Contexto.

Mead, Margaret. 1977 [1928]. *Coming of age in Samoa: A study of adolescence and sex in primitive societies.* London: Penguin.

Miljeteig, Per, Ben White, and Christopher Williams, eds. 1999. Special issue entitled "Understanding child labour." *Childhood* 6 (1).

Morley, Helena [Alice Dayrell Brant]. 1957. *The diary of "Helena Morley."* Translated by E. Bishop. New York: Farrar, Straus.

Mott, Luiz. 1991. Pedofilia e pederastia no Brasil antigo. In *História da criança no Brasil,* edited by M. Del Priore. São Paulo: Contexto.

Opie, Iona, and Peter Opie. 1959. *The lore and language of school children.* Oxford: Oxford University Press.

———. 1969. *Children's games in street and playground.* Oxford: Oxford University Press.

Pagden, Anthony. 1991. Introduction. In *Francisco de Vitoria, political writings,* edited by A. Pagden. Cambridge: Cambridge University Press.

Panter-Brick, Catherine, and Malcolm T. Smith, eds. 2000. *Abandoned children.* Cambridge: Cambridge University Press.

Pérez Mallaína, Pablo E. 1998. *Spain's men of the sea.* Translated by C. R. Phillips. Baltimore: Johns Hopkins University Press.

Pollack, L. 1983. *Forgotten children: Parent–children relations from 1500 to 1900.* Cambridge: Cambridge University Press.

Prout, Alan, and Allison James. 1990. A new paradigm for the sociology of childhood? In *Constructing and deconstructing childhood: Contemporary issues in the sociological study of childhood,* edited by A. James and A. Prout. London: Falmer Press.

Ramos, Fábio Pestana. 1999. A história trágico-marítima das crianças nas embarcações portuguesas do século XVI. In *História das crianças no Brasil,* edited by M. Del Priore. São Paulo: Contexto.

Russakoff, Dale. 1998. Through children's eyes: On campuses all across the country, a new academic movement is picking up steam. *Washington Post,* 23 November.

Scheper-Hughes, Nancy. 1992. *Death without weeping: The violence of everyday life in Brazil.* Berkeley: University of California Press.

Schildkrout, Enid. 1978. Roles of children in urban Kano. In *Sex and age as principles of social differentiation,* edited by J. La Fontaine. London: Academic Press.

Scott, James C. 1985. *Weapons of the weak: Everyday forms of peasant resistance.* New Haven: Yale University Press.

Seiter, Ellen. 1993. *Sold separately: Children and parents in consumer culture.* New Brunswick, N.J.: Rutgers University Press.

Shorter, Edward. 1975. *The making of the modern family.* New York: Basic Books.

Steedman, Carolyn. 1982. *The tidy house: Little girls writing.* London: Virago.

Szuchman, Mark D. 1988. *Order, family, and community in Buenos Aires, 1810–1860.* Stanford: Stanford University Press.

Twinam, Ann. 1999. *Public lives, private secrets: Gender, honor, sexuality, and illegitimacy in colonial Spanish America.* Stanford: Stanford University Press.

UN (United Nations). 1998. *1996 Demographic yearbook.* New York: United Nations.

Urquidi, María. 1991. De la "familia interrumpida" a la familia novohispana. Formación y transformación de la familia Urquidi de Chihuaha. In *Familias novohispanas, Siglos XVI al XIX,* edited by P. Gonzalbo Aizpuru. Mexico City: Colegio de México.

Vitoria, Francisco de. 1991. On the American Indians [*De Indis*]. In *Francisco de Vitoria, political writings,* edited by A. Pagden. Cambridge: Cambridge University Press.

1

Sketches of Childhood

Children in Colonial Andean Art and Society

Carolyn Dean

Colonizers commonly compare the people they have conquered and colonized to children. In the viceroyalty of Peru, for example, Hispanic authorities—both state and ecclesiastical—frequently characterized native Andeans as childlike or even childish. Infantilizing analogies not only justified paternalistic attitudes on the part of the colonizer but also legitimized political domination; children, after all, do not have the same social rights as grown-ups and can (and frequently ought to) be controlled by adults. Thus the often-alleged arrested intellect and childlike behavior of the colonized shifted the focus from the initial relationship of European to Andean to the secondary, less problematic, relationship of parent to child.[1]

The analogy of Peruvian Indians to children not only depended upon the belief that children ought to be controlled in certain ways, but, even more fundamentally, assumed a shared sense of what a child is. Here I explore how native Andean notions of children differed from those of Europeans and the interpretative chasm that opened in colonial Peru as a result. As a case study, I will focus on a particular set of images of children, showing, first, how pictorial children served as visual metaphors for Andean adults, who did not always behave according to the needs and desires of colonial authorities in midcolonial Cuzco, Peru, and, second, how any interpretation of these pictorial children depends upon a common notion of what a child is. From this specific example, we can suggest some more general conclusions about how "children" were every bit as much social constructions as they were biological beings in the Spanish colonies of Peru.

The Colonized as Children

In their encounter with native Americans, Europeans confronted cultural patterns that were alien, incomprehensible to them, and therefore, from a European perspective, irrational. Despite the Papal Bull of 1537, which recognized the natives of the Americas as rational humans, ensuing debate about the nature of the "Indian" revolved around his or her ability to reason. Indian "irrationality" was frequently explained by analogy with other creatures already defined by Europeans as irrational—the most common being beasts, barbarians, and children. Indigenous Americans, at various times and for various reasons, were compared to all three groups. By the midcolonial period (the seventeenth century), beasts and barbarians usually described *indios de guerra* (hostile Indians), Amazonian dwellers, and others who inhabited the Spanish frontiers and continued to oppose colonization and harass the colonizers. In contrast, the comparison of the colonized to children emerged as the most frequently employed analogy for those natives who had been integrated into the Spanish colonial system. It is useful, then, to explore, at least briefly, what the Spaniards of the seventeenth century meant when they described the colonized as childlike or, more generally, what they understood a child to be.

In early-modern Catholic Europe the notion that a child was naturally inclined to misbehave was articulated in the doctrine of infant depravity, which held that childhood folly was a manifestation of original sin. Children were thus as much, if not more, a product of their imperfect mental and spiritual states as of their immature physical condition. Children were seen to be capable of reason from age seven onward, but reason had to be actively encouraged by both schoolmasters and parents (Ariès 1965 [1960]: 102). While scholars of the history of European childhood disagree about when and why this abstract notion of childhood as a separate mental state emerged, there is general agreement in the literature that, by the seventeenth century, European intellectuals were devoting considerable attention to the mental development of children and the positive impact of education on molding a well-behaved, productive adult.[2] One aspect of the European assessment of childhood was that "childish" behavior, not acceptable in an adult, was acceptable and even expected in children.

In seventeenth-century Europe, those of low social status were commonly described as childish. Moralists and pedagogues blamed the often-unacceptable behavior of both groups on their lack of education and inherent moral weakness (Ariès 1965 [1960]: 102, 262). Children, then, became convenient symbols of the unsocialized or less acculturated elements of society. Of course, seventeenth-century Europeans are not the only people to have likened diverse social groups to children in order to justify "paternalistic" control. The notion that Indians of the Spanish colonies possessed the temporarily irrational mental condition of European children was evoked in particular by many members of the religious community who proposed that although neither Indians nor children regulated their lives by the laws of reason, the behavior of both could be "improved" through Christian education. Because priests and friars were the educators of the Indians, analogies of their native wards to children were useful. The familial language of the church, whose representatives were addressed as "father," predisposed the European to this line of reasoning.

Various writings by members of religious orders evangelizing in Peru include numerous comparisons of native Americans to children. The Jesuits were prominent proponents of the likening of Indians to children in that they saw themselves as the religious order especially devoted to education. In the sixteenth century, Jesuit José de Acosta (1985 [1558]: 224–25) wrote, "Such are the miseries that many Indians have lived in, and do to this day, for the devil abuses them like children, with many foolish illusions"; he adds that their "childish behavior" *(niñerías)*, which is how he describes various "idolatrous" practices, ought not to be condemned but rather that the Andeans ought to be pitied, as such "childishness" was the consequence of their lack of education. Bernabé Cobo (1983 [1653]: 32) tells us that native Americans "are extremely puerile in their behavior" and compares them to Spanish children in their love of play and trickery. The seventeenth-century extirpator of idolatry, Pablo Joseph de Arriaga (1968 [1621]: 128), wrote that priests should tell their native charges that their offenses against Christian teachings would be punished corporally for, like a mother, the Church would castigate her disobedient children.

Indeed, punishment of American natives was similar to that of European schoolboys, as described by Ariès (1965 [1960]: 262). The offender was first admonished; then, if the offenses were repeated, corporal punishment was administered. Arriaga (1968 [1621]: 101) mandates that known sorcerers be taught doctrine in the church in the morning and afternoon "as children are." He also dictates that for the vice of drunkenness, commoners ought to be admonished; if a second offense occurred, they were to be flogged. For a third offense the hair was to be cropped (Arriaga 1968 [1621]: 172). Andeans were acutely sensitive to this latter punishment, as short hair was characteristic of native children (Molina 1873 [c. 1584]: 53; Guaman Poma 1988 [c. 1615]: 201). Priests and friars thus made their native charges physically more like children so as to underscore the ideational equation and make clear that so-called misbehavior on the part of adults would not be tolerated.

For the most part, we think of the analogy of native Andeans to children as a verbal and textual matter. The sermons and writings of colonial authorities were not the only venues in which Indians were compared to children, however. Some of the most powerful "statements" evoking the colonized-as-children analogy are pictorial. Images of children created in seventeenth-century Peru offer eloquent testimony about how the colonizer wielded the analogy of Indians to children as a part of the process of colonization. Images converted the spoken or written analogy into a metaphor by visualizing the equation. What is more, publicly displayed paintings—unlike ephemeral sermons and texts, unread by the largely illiterate masses—made the comparisons of Indians to children both permanent and accessible, especially when those paintings decorated the walls of the churches that indigenous Andeans attended in large numbers.

Children in Imagery

Although few scholars have focused specifically on the meaning and function of images of children in art, it is clear that youngsters commonly served as symbolic referents to adult concerns in seventeenth-century Europe. Mary Frances Durantini (1983), in her exemplary study of images of children in Dutch art of this period, concludes that the artists of the seventeenth century consistently used images of children to address adult problems, vices, and preoccupations. While the Protestant Dutch and the Catholic Spaniards certainly differed in many regards, they shared the notion that childhood is a distinct mental state, one that requires substantial educational efforts if the outcome is to be a well-socialized adult. The perceived innocence of children and their apparent lack of calculated (that is, socialized) responses render them ideal didactic pictorial devices.

To examine how pictorial children were used to address Andean behavior, I will focus on a single series of canvases, dating 1674–1680, by anonymous indigenous Andean artists that depict the Corpus Christi procession in Cuzco (Dean 1999: 77–78). Among the most renowned paintings of colonial Peru, they offer a record of colonial Andean society that is unique in both scope and detail. Today, only sixteen of the original eighteen canvases, which once adorned the walls of Cuzco's parish church of Santa Ana, can be securely identified.[3] Portrayed are members of seventeenth-century Cuzco's various racial, social, religious, and political groups as they participated in, or witnessed, the Corpus Christi procession. The series colorfully documents Cuzco at a time when its population was numerically dominated by indigenous Andeans but governed by a minority of Spanish descent; Africans and those of mixed ethnicity are depicted as well.

In the paintings, Cuzqueño society is organized into distinct horizontal planes, stacked one upon another, that help the viewer differentiate between various social groups. Of the sixteen canvases, eleven are arranged in three planes.[4] Those participating in the procession—the municipal council, the ecclesiastical council, various religious orders, and numerous local sodalities—occupy the centers of the canvases. Because each canvas of the series focuses on a distinct segment of the procession, they can be referred to by naming the central parading group or groups (for example, the canvas of the Franciscan friars or that of the sodality of San Cristóbal). The majority of people situated above and behind the cortege are Cuzco's nonparticipating elites and their retainers; below and in front are viewers of the middle and lower sectors of Cuzqueño society. These spatial planes contain a spectrum of ethnic types, with people of Andean, African, and European descent clearly identifiable in all three zones.

Each plane is characterized by behavioral similarities among its constituents that serve to relate these members of the shared space, while segregating one plane from another. In general, those located in the upper plane watch the procession respectfully or discuss the proceedings with their neighbors. Their hands are folded over their waists or in gestures of prayer or rest on balcony railings or windowsills; some men have removed their hats as the religious images pass. Heads incline toward one another to indicate unobtrusive conversation; for the most part, gesturing remains subdued with hands kept close to the bodies. The comportment of those in this upper plane of the canvases matches that of the participants who occupy the central sector, walking erect from right to left in a dignified manner. Some participants engage in conversation with coparticipants or acknowledge the celebrants in the upper quadrant. Those in the cortege do not interact with the commoners, who occupy the lower sector of the canvases. As in the upper plane, activity in the center is generally restrained; facial expressions are serious.

In contrast to the upper and middle zones, the lower plane, occupied primarily by Cuzqueño commoners and dominated numerically by native Andeans, is characterized by more diversified behavior. Although many individuals, their backs to us, watch the procession, numerous others engage in animated discussions. Many are inattentive, if not disrespectful. In this plane we find men smoking and eating; facial expressions are less restrained and activity more pronounced. In general, the figures are stacked one upon another in a way that suggests a crowd, if not a throng, with bodies positioned at various angles to the procession. In contrast, bodies in the middle and upper sectors are more evenly spaced and more consistently face the procession.

The canvases thus depict adults of Cuzco's upper classes as differentiated in appearance, demeanor, and behavior from their lower class compatriots. In contrast, children of different classes, while distinguished by appearance, are not behaviorally differentiated. A number of children found in the upper and middle spatial planes do not conform to the behavioral characteristics associated with their elders. In fact, misbehaving youngsters appear in all three sectors. Whereas adult elites attend the procession respectfully, a number of their children are disruptive; they behave like many commoners of all ages who are similarly disrespectful, or at least inattentive.

In the foreground of the canvas featuring friars of the Mercedarian Order, for example, a child aims a peashooter at a nearby celebrant (see figures 1.1 and 1.2). Similarly, in the foreground of the canvas of the parading Dominican friars, two children with pea shooters pester a man

Fig. 1.1. Anon., 1674–80, *Mercedarian Friars*. Corpus Christi series, Cuzco, Peru (Museo del Arzobispo, Cuzco).

of African descent while a third prepares to join in by loading his mouth with small projectiles (figure 1.3). In another of the paintings a child, leaning over a balcony in the upper background, aims a peashooter at a group of musicians who are riding in the processional cart of the Virgin of the Purification (La Candelaria). A second child, located in another balcony, aims his shooter at the first child. In the canvas of the parading Franciscans, a child in indigenous dress, located at the far left, aims his peashooter at the procession of friars (figure 1.4). In figure 1.5, the painting featuring Cuzco's magistrate (the *corregidor*) in procession, a child in the right background aims a peashooter at some target off the canvas. Because all those around him are kneeling, an action performed in the presence of the Holy Sacrament (the focus of the Corpus Christi celebration), his target can only be the approaching bishop with the monstrance who is the subject of another canvas in the series. One final example of misbehaving youth can be found in the central zone of the canvas of the parish of San Sebastián where a child attempts to catch a ride on the back of the processional cart (figure 1.6). What are we

Fig. 1.2. Anon., 1674–80, *Mercedarian Friars*. Detail of central portion with boy and pea-shooter.

Fig. 1.3. Anon., 1674–80, *Dominican Friars*. Detail drawing of two children with peashooters. Corpus Christi series, Cuzco, Peru (Private Collection, Santiago de Chile).

Fig. 1.4. Anon., 1674–80, *Franciscan Friars*. Detail drawing of child with peashooter. Corpus Christi series, Cuzco, Peru (Private Collection, Santiago de Chile).

Fig. 1.5. Anon., 1674–80, *Corregidor Pérez*. Detail of background including child with pea-shooter (middle right). Corpus Christi series, Cuzco, Peru (Museo del Arzobispo, Cuzco).

Fig. 1.6. Anon., 1674–80, *San Sebastián Parish.* Corpus Christi series, Cuzco, Peru (Museo del Arzobispo, Cuzco).

to make of these remarkable children who are pictorially allied with Cuzco's lower classes?

The pictured misbehavior on the part of children runs contrary to the otherwise highly structured formal arrangement of these paintings, wherein people's actions are prescribed according to their locations within the canvases. That children, as shown in the Corpus Christi series, act according to age group rather than class affiliation echoes the prevailing European paradigm regarding the nature and behavior of youngsters as outlined above. The European assessment of childhood as a state of mind as well as body allowed a symbolic pictorial linkage between children and adults whose behavior was deemed "childish." Consequently, the Corpus Christi children can be seen to behave (or misbehave, as the case may be) according to European expectations, and, indeed, no adults move to correct the youngsters' disruptive activities. Misbehavior on the part of some children is thus pictorially characterized as normal and customary.

According to these paintings, members of the primarily indigenous lower classes also misbehave: they are visually described as childlike. Both children and the lower classes, as portrayed in this series of canvases, are distinguished from society's elites by either their ignorance of correct behavior or their refusal to conduct themselves in a respectful manner when in the presence of religious and/or civic authority. Implicitly, then, images such as these reflected, propagated, and justified paternalistic attitudes on the part of their Hispanic or Hispanicized viewers. The Corpus Christi children demonstrated the "naturalness" of extant social inequality and simultaneously offered reassuring interpretations of contemporary social conditions to an implicitly paternalistic and authoritative Hispanic or Hispanicized audience.

However, aside from the indigenous elites, who were responsible for the parish's entry in the Corpus Christi procession, the Andean parishioners of Santa Ana—the primary audience of these works—would have identified with those portrayed in the lower zone of the canvases. Consequently, these paintings informed their audience of their separateness from Cuzco's elites by emphasizing not only the physical distance between the classes but difference in appearance, manner, and behavior. The link between misbehaving members of the lower plane and children encodes an encouragement to refrain from disrespectful or childish behavior and to emulate the elites and those associated with them. The artists of the series have employed a paradigm, familiar to Europeans and the Europeanized elements of Cuzqueño society, that was thought to accurately characterize the mental state and consequential behavior patterns of children, European lower classes, and unacculturated Andeans (most of whom, in urban Cuzco, were lower class as well).

It is worth noting that while the intellectuals who helped forge the European notion of the separateness of childhood referred to children in general, their observations were applied only to boys (Ariès 1965 [1960]: 60–61). Unlike boys, whose need for education was stressed, young girls remained in the home, receiving training in domestic tasks from their mothers. This androcentrism has its corollary in the Corpus Christi paintings, where we see only male children transgressing. Female children, where distinguishable, behave properly, as do most female adults.

While children were expected to behave irrationally, that is, misbe-have—and the Corpus Christi series portrays many boys doing just that—we also see children whose behavior is unremarkable or who even surpass adults in demonstrating respect. These respectful children, who display the instinctual spirituality that was also associated with young-sters, were undoubtedly meant to encourage similar behavior on the part of the adult audience. In figure 1.7, the canvas of Cuzco's bishop

Fig. 1.7. Anon., 1674–80, *Bishop Mollinedo leaving the Cathedral.* Corpus Christi series, Cuzco, Peru (Museo del Arzobispo, Cuzco).

(Don Manuel de Mollinedo y Angulo), who carries the monstrance, a kneeling child serves as a model of religious devotion. The child is placed above, and separated from, the rest of the crowd, clearly serving as an example to all. In the canvas of the magistrate's procession, two well-dressed Andean boys appear as patrons, hands folded in prayer. A number of male youths, old enough to have learned "rational" behavior, have been incorporated into the ceremonial activity. Boys in white surplices bear the candles that flank the high cross in six of the canvases (see, for example, figure 1.6). In another canvas, a native youth bears the traditional crown of the native leader of a cathedral sodality. In this same canvas Charles II, the teenage Spanish king, is present in the central scene of the altar in which he defends the Eucharist against the Turks (figure 1.8). The child Christ, wise beyond his years, is the subject of another processional altar constructed outside the Jesuit church.[5] These exemplary children, though fewer in number, provide a counterpoint to their misbehaving fellows. By including children so prominently in this series of canvases, the exceptional nature of youth is underscored, and these youngsters are thus able to address the audience in a didactic and moralizing fashion. To the European and Europeanized viewer, the Corpus Christi children, both misbehaving and well behaved, would have been easily apprehended visual metaphors for inappropriate (irrational) and appropriate (rational) adult behavior.

It is likely that the artists of the Corpus Christi series, like their European counterparts, deliberately featured children in the canvases, as the activities of youngsters are among the most remarkable and humorous elements in these crowded compositions. The prominent presence of children can hardly be written off as a mere anecdotal diversion from the primary processional activity, however. The artist's intentionality can be seen most clearly in the canvas of the sodality of Saint Sebastian (figure 1.6). The processional carriage of the saint, representing the local parish of San Sebastián, was copied from an engraving in a seventeenth-century Valencian festivity book composed by Juan Bautista Valda (1663), as were all of the carriages in the Corpus Christi series.[6] In Valda (1663: 534), the carriage belongs to the Valencian tailor's guild and the engraving is signed by the artist José Caudí (figure 1.9). Caudí's image has been reversed in the canvas of San Sebastián, its decoration has been simplified, and its pedestal cropped by the Cuzqueño artist. The image of Saint Sebastian has replaced that of Our

Fig. 1.8. Anon., 1674–80, *Confraternities of Saint Rose and la Linda*. Detail of central portion. Corpus Christi series, Cuzco, Peru (Museo del Arzobispo, Cuzco).

Fig. 1.9. José Caudí, 1663, *Processional Cart of the Tailors' Guild* (Valda 1663; The Hispanic Society of America).

Lady of the Immaculate Conception, and the flying dragon (attached to the Valencian pedestal) has been removed from the Peruvian painted version. Whereas the Valencian engraving shows the carriage to be occupied by five saints, these figures do not appear on the carriage of San Sebastián. Interestingly, while the Cuzqueño artist simplified his prototype by eliminating much of the detail, he added the child who attempts to hitch a ride on the rear of the carriage. Apparently, this pictorial amendment was understood to enhance the meaning of the canvas as a whole, perhaps rendering this fictive carriage more relevant and believable to a parochial audience that would never have actually seen such a contraption.[7]

The significance of the children deliberately misbehaving in the Corpus Christi series is amplified by a brief examination of festive behavior in late-seventeenth-century Cuzco. While no mention is found in available records of unruly children, there is considerable concern expressed over adult, and especially Andean, "misbehavior." As in European art, it would seem that the Corpus Christi children address adult concerns. That the canvases ultimately focus on adult behavior during public festivals is logical, considering that this was an overwhelming concern of Cuzqueño authorities. Religious and state celebrations were particularly important occasions for teaching "rational" European behaviors to Andeans. Ideally, such processions would demonstrate not only who was in charge but also ways of showing respect to that authority (hat doffed, head bowed, voice hushed, knees bent). In these ephemeral events, Andeans were encouraged to act according to European expectations and were punished for behaviors that were deemed as disrespectful (particularly fighting and other disorderly conduct).

From seventeenth-century civil records, we know that unruly behavior during public festivals preoccupied Cuzco's civic and religious authorities. The municipal council, ecclesiastical council, and parish authorities all took steps to discourage public drunkenness, violence, and other manifestations of disrespect on the part of Andeans and the lower classes in general. Indigenous leaders were charged with controlling the putative drunken and unruly behavior of their constituents. The boisterous behavior shown in the Corpus Christi series is mild compared with the actual brawls that often broke out in the midst of festivities. In fact, the artists of the Corpus Christi series restricted violent behavior to the annoying but harmless children armed with peashooters. By showing only mildly unruly behavior and linking it to the irrational behavior of children, implications of serious social discord have been elided, and disrespectful actions appear as isolated manifestations of childish minds. Further, featuring misbehaving children allowed the artists of this series of canvases to acknowledge the existence of rambunctious activity, a hallmark of most celebratory occasions, without sanctioning it. In fact, by linking the misbehaving children to disrespectful commoners, the parishioner, or viewer of the paintings, is encouraged to behave reverentially on future festive occasions. While festivals—opportunities to observe Andean behavior and punish misbehavior—were brief in duration and took place only occasionally, the paintings of the Corpus Christi procession, visible year-round on the parish church walls, sanctified by the Christian God, were a permanent reminder of how to show respect to authority.

The above "reading" of the painted children pivots on the European paradigm of the irrational child. The images of children in the Corpus Christi series could only have served to encourage good behavior if the same conception of the nature of childhood was held by both colonist and colonized. This is so because "child" is an ideational construct not firmly tied to physiology; "children" and thus "childishness" are, to a great extent, created by culture. The equation of naturally irrational children with improperly irrational adults depends upon the recognition of childhood as a separate state of both mental and physical being. Because the notion of what is "childish" is culturally specific, we may well wonder how the images of misbehaving youngsters—and the colonialist discourse about the childlike nature of the colonized in general—were interpreted by the fairly unacculturated indigenous parishioners of the church of Santa Ana in Cuzco.

Andean Conceptions of Childhood

In contrast to the European model of irrationality, evidence indicates that the pre-Hispanic Andean child was distinguished by physiological rather than mental capabilities. Felipe Guaman Poma de Ayala (1988 [c. 1615]: 179–89, 201–9), a native Andean author and artist working at the beginning of the seventeenth century, drew pictures of Andean children and described their function in pre-Hispanic Inka (Inca) society (e.g., figures 1.10 and 1.11).[8] He tells us that native children of

OTABA CALLE
PVCLLACOCVAMRA

Fig. 1.10. Felipe Guaman Poma de Ayala, 1613–15, folio 229 [231], *Andean Female, Five Years Old* (Guaman Poma 1988, 204).

Fig. 1.11. Felipe Guaman Poma de Ayala, 1613–15, folio 208 [210], *Andean Male, Five Years Old* (Guaman Poma 1988: 184).

less than one year of age, still in the cradle, had to be cared for by others, as did those under five years of age who could crawl but who were as yet unweaned. Small children of both sexes were, according to Guaman Poma, without purpose or usefulness in that they served no one and, in fact, had to be served by others. Inka children of ages five through nine, in contrast, were assigned certain tasks. Boys of this age aided their parents and community by watching over younger siblings, performing various domestic chores, and helping to raise orphans. Guaman Poma contrasts the pre-Conquest usefulness of this age group to domestic organization with the post-Conquest practice of removing these boys from their homes to educate them. Girls from ages five to nine served as pages for important females; they also helped their parents by collecting firewood and straw as well as spinning, gathering edible wild plants, minding younger children, fetching water, cooking, and cleaning.

According to Guaman Poma, young males from ages nine to twelve served both their parents and the *cacique* by hunting small birds, herding, fetching firewood, spinning wool, and twisting rope. Girls of this same age served the community by collecting flowers, herbs, and leaves for dying cloth and cooking, as shown in figure 1.12. They could also serve the government and the state religion as human sacrifices. Male youths from ages twelve to eighteen guarded the herds and hunted birds. Females of this age group served their elders by spinning and weaving, shepherding, sowing, tending crops, and making *chicha* (an alcoholic beverage made from maize). They also helped around the house, performing a number of tasks.

Females over eighteen were marriageable and therefore considered adults; in contrast, young males from ages eighteen to twenty served in a special capacity as messengers of the community and lackeys to warriors and great lords. Guaman Poma calls them Indians of half-tribute, noting their status as "not-quite-adults." Each stage of life was thus characterized by what it could do for society, in contrast to the European concept of the excusable irresponsibility of children.

The individual's physical abilities and corresponding duties were the basis of the categories used by Inka census takers. John H. Rowe's (1958) seminal study of the Inka census reveals that Andean age-grades were defined primarily by the individual's ability to contribute to the state economy. In addition to those described by Guaman Poma, named age-grades are recorded by the Mercedarian friar Martín de Murúa

Fig. 1.12. Felipe Guaman Poma de Ayala, 1613–15, folio 227 [229], *Andean Female, Nine Years Old* (Guaman Poma 1988: 202).

(1946 [c. 1611]: 322–27; 1986 [c. 1611]: 396–400), the *licenciado* (lawyer) Fernando de Santillán (1927 [1559]), Father Cristóbal de Castro (1934 [1558]), and a group of Andean record-keepers ("los Señores" 1904 [1542–1575]) who served under Inka lords in pre-Hispanic times. Murúa's list is so similar to that of Guaman Poma that Rowe (1958: 514) suspects that the friar used Guaman Poma as a source.[9] While differing from those recorded by Guaman Poma and Murúa, the categories provided by Santillán, Castro, and "los Señores" are close enough to each other that a common source is indicated. Rowe (1958) concludes that Father Castro was responsible for recording the testimony of "los Señores" and that Santillán used Castro as his source. These three then will be designated as the Castro group in the discussion that follows.

All sources list similar categories for adults, but differ in their divisions of the preadult years, or the years before the individual bore full responsibility for producing tribute. In all lists, over half of the categories describe the preadult years. Once adulthood was achieved (ages twenty to twenty-five), the Andean was not removed from this category until incapable of fulfilling the occupational and tributary functions associated with adulthood. While Guaman Poma describes ten categories for males (six of which designate preadults) and ten for females (five of which designate preadults), the chronicles of the Castro group tell us that there were twelve age groupings, without differentiating male and female.[10] In the Castro group, the teen years are divided into two categories that define the type of service expected. According to Santillán, ages sixteen to twenty were collectively called *cocapalla* (*coca* harvester); he tells us that youth of this category were expected to reap the state-owned *coca* crop. Castro similarly terms ages twelve to sixteen *cocapalla*, and "los Señores" assign ages twelve to twenty to the category *cocapallac*. Santillán terms ages twenty to twenty-five *imanguayna*, which he translates as *casi mozo* ("almost a young adult"), and says these youths contribute to the work of their brothers and relatives. According to Castro, ages sixteen to twenty were called *michoguayna;* "los Señores" term ages twenty to twenty-five *michuguaina* and say the category consists of those who aid their parents and relatives.[11]

According to the Castro group, seven of the twelve age-groupings designate the growth stages of the prepuberty years, although, unlike Guaman Poma, none of them lists specific duties assigned these ages.[12]

What is apparent in this categorization of the years in which the individual experiences rapid physical development is that, to the Andean, "age" was not so much the sum of years as an evaluation of physical attributes, abilities, and dexterity. Cobo (1983 [1653]: 194) confirms this, saying that "age was not counted in years, nor did any of them know how many years old they were. [For the census] they were accounted for on the basis of the duty and aptitude of each person." The two major ceremonies for Andean children marked weaning and puberty—the two most important stages of growth that, significantly, commemorated the increasing independence of the young individual. Weaning, celebrated by the haircutting and first naming ceremony, marked the first stage of the child's physical independence. The puberty rites and second naming ceremony celebrated the age at which the child became a significant contributor to the local economy. The giving of a new name signaled an important reclassification of the individual and his or her significance to society.

Garcilaso de la Vega (1961 [1609]: 245), a *mestizo,* or person of mixed European and Amerindian ancestry, writing at the turn of the seventeenth century, tells us that native children were expected to work from age six onward, but provides few details. He describes harsh treatment aimed at encouraging responsible behavior from a very early age. Apparently, in stark contrast to the Catholic notion of infant depravity, neither young age nor ignorance excused native Andean children from contributing to the community. Indeed, children in pre-Conquest times were themselves often treated as products. We know that they were given to the state as a form of tax payment. In addition, they were highly valued as the most propitious of sacrifices offered at critical junctures such as epidemics, war, and the coronation of new heads-of-state (Acosta 1880 [1558]: 344; Molina 1873 [c. 1584]: 54–58). It would appear that children were perceived, at least from the perspective of the state, as natural resources produced by the community and therefore expected to benefit that community. The phrasing of Guaman Poma, which emphasizes the usefulness of the child from the time of weaning, underscores this interpretation. Evidence thus indicates that any equation of "adult" to one of the stages of "child" would make sense to the pre-Conquest Andean only in terms of physical prowess and productivity rather than the rational/irrational dichotomy of the European paradigm.

An Interpretive Chasm

Because the pre-Hispanic pattern of child rearing continued into the viceregal period, it is likely that the common Andean did not quickly adopt the European concept of childhood irrationality. While most Spanish chroniclers paid little attention to how the Andean adults they were documenting treated native children, a few helpful references can be found. Pedro de Cieza de León (1959 [1553]: 169, 176), writing between 1541 and 1550, commented on the early age at which language instruction began, while the child was still in infancy and as yet unweaned; he also expressed surprise at the ability of "little boys" to fashion fine metalcraft. Arriaga (1968 [1621]: 23, 47) was impressed that indigenous children were expected to behave as adults in native religious ceremonies. Cobo (1983 [1653]: 35–38), on the other hand, did not admire the character of native youth. He decried their lack of manners, virtue, orderliness, and praiseworthy habits. His statement that native children of the seventeenth century "do not know what proper respect and courtesy are," suggests, however, that he judged Andean behavior by European standards, interpreting *different* training as *no* training. Cobo (1983 [1653]: 22) did note that age groups were valued according to their ability to work, saying that "as soon as the poor parents begin to grow weak with age, their ungrateful children forget the natural debt which they have to serve and respect them with even greater care, love, and compassion." Such comments indicate that the pre-Hispanic emphasis on work performance was maintained far into the colonial era.

During the colonial period, while the official transition to adulthood was set at twenty-one according to European custom, children of lower classes assumed adult roles and responsibilities at much earlier ages. Fifteen or sixteen years seems to have been the age at which working youth were able to undertake professions. While little mention of children is made in documentary sources, there are records of arranged apprenticeships. According to these sources, boys were apprenticed at around eight to twelve years of age, with the understanding that they would be fully trained and able to pursue their intended professions by age fifteen or sixteen.[13] Thus, although male youths were considered "minors" until age twenty-one, they functioned as adults prior to that time. The work patterns of the lower Spanish classes during the colonial period then would not have conflicted with the native pattern of child-rearing. Indeed, there is no evidence to suggest that the paradigmatic progression from irrational child to rational adult worked out by European intellectuals ever gained currency among indigenous commoners. The pre-Hispanic emphasis on the introduction to useful occupations early in life has persisted until today among the less acculturated. In the Andean highlands, native children of ages five to ten are put to work herding—quite a responsibility considering that livestock is the family's major economic investment.[14]

In contrast, elite youth in colonial Peru were educated for longer periods and took up adult occupations only later in life. Like offspring of European elites, children of the native nobility were often accorded differential treatment. They were taught Christianity, Latin, and the classical humanities—the same course of instruction received by noble youth in Spain. The emphasis on educating sons of the indigenous nobility is common in the writings of the religious. For example, Arriaga (1968 [1621]: 99) states: "The only way to make the *curacas* and *caciques*[15] behave (and the fact that they do not is, as I have said, an important cause of idolatry) is to begin at the beginning and instruct their children so that from childhood they may learn the Christian discipline and doctrine."

Special schooling increased the acculturation of the native elite, already more Hispanicized than natives of lower status by closer contact with Europeans. To the Andean noble who had himself been singled out as a child and whose male offspring were accorded special educational emphasis, the notion that children were legitimately ignorant of proper behavior was probably a familiar and accepted notion. The images of misbehaving children in the Corpus Christi series as well as the pervasive verbal and textual analogies of Indians to children would have performed as intelligible signifiers, encouraging him to watch out for his constituents' "childish" (mis)behavior. Such comparisons would have underscored the sociopolitical position of the indigenous elites as responsible for the behavior of their constituency.

However, to the common Andean—the primary audience of both paintings and sermons—the equation of a child's irrationality to an adult's misbehavior is of doubtful significance. Considerable evidence indicates that the common Andean did not share the European concept of childhood. The significance of the exceptional images of misbehaving children within the behaviorally segregated world of the Corpus Christi canvases, for example, falters—unless "childish" misbehavior is thought to be a reflection of an irrational mind. While images of "good" and "bad" children undoubtedly evoked special meaning to the Europeanized audience, which included both artists and patrons, we must at least question their ability to bridge the cultural gap that divided Cuzco's colonial society.

The Andean evaluation of youngsters according to physical development, rather than mental state, surely muddied the pictorial analogy. Thus although both visual and verbal analogies of unschooled commoners to children were surely meant to encourage festive decorum in Andeans by equating unruly adult behavior with childish misbehavior, evidence suggests that this message would have been confounded by the fact that the European conception of children differed from that held by the native Andean. It is likely that these differing notions of childhood created an interpretive chasm between Europeans and Europeanized Cuzqueños, on the one hand, and the culturally marginalized indigenous lower class majority, on the other, a chasm that severely limited the ability of Hispanic and Hispanicized authorities to communicate with and, perhaps more significantly, control their charges.

Notes

1. "Andean" will be used here to designate indigenous peoples of colonial Peru, while "European" refers to people of European descent, whether born in Europe or the New World.

2. Ariès (1965 [1960]), who wrote the seminal work on the history of European childhood, claimed that prior to the seventeenth century Europeans had no concept of childhood as a separate state of being. While recent research has taken issue with this particular conclusion, Linda A. Pollock (1983: 113–16) agrees that because Europeans of the sixteenth and seventeenth centuries perceived children to be naturally sinful, education was seen to be of the utmost importance. Similarly, C. John Sommerville (1982: 83–84, 97) dates the increase in concern for a proper education to the Renaissance, especially the sixteenth century; he concludes that, owing to the religious turmoil that characterized that century, education was recognized as a primary weapon in the war for the minds of European youth.

3. Twelve canvases of the Corpus Christi series are housed in the Archbishop's Museum of Religious Art in Cuzco, Peru. Three additional canvases recognized as belonging to the series by Ricardo Mariátegui (1954) are in a private collection in Santiago, Chile. A sixteenth canvas, also in a private collection in Santiago, was identified three decades later by Mariátegui (1983). The identification of the remaining two canvases of the series is more problematic; for a

discussion of this issue as well as the dating of the canvases and possible artists, see Dean (1999: 64–78).

4. Three of the five remaining canvases lack one or two of these planes: two lack the lower sector and two lack the upper sector, while the fifth canvas, which features the culmination of the procession, consists only of festival participants.

5. It was the practice of the Jesuits to establish sodalities dedicated to the cult of the child Jesus in the communities they served. By singling out the special nature of childhood, they were emphasizing their role in educating youth.

6. Teresa Gisbert and José de Mesa (1985: 234, 242–43) first identified Valda's festivity book as the pictorial source for two of the Corpus Christi carriages. Valda's work was, in fact, the source of all of the carriages depicted in the series; see Dean (1996).

7. For a consideration of how these fictive carriages both confound and supplement the documentary mode of these canvases, see Dean (1996).

8. Recently, pre-Columbianist Laura Laurencich Minelli has brought to light a Jesuit manuscript entitled *Historia et rudimenta linguae piruanorum*, found in the family papers of Neapolitan historian Clara Miccinelli. In it is the claim that Guaman Poma merely lent his name to a work that was actually written by the *mestizo* Jesuit and Indian advocate Blas Valera. The portion of the manuscript containing this allegation was likely written by Jesuit Juan Antonio (or Anello) Oliva, who was involved in a legal battle with Guaman Poma. His allegation, motivated by personal antagonisms, may well be false. Certainly, given the very self-referential nature of the *Nueva corónica y buen gobierno*, it is hard to doubt that Guaman Poma was primarily, if not solely, responsible for its production. While the identity of the actual author of the *Nueva corónica* is of crucial import to Andean history—and I believe at least a good portion of the work is by Guaman Poma—for the argument presented in this paper, it matters only that Andean notions of childhood are understood to conflict with those held by Europeans. Blas Valera, as a student of Andean culture, could very well have taken up this theme. Because the thorny issue of authorship has yet to be resolved, I will assume, for this argument, that Guaman Poma is the sole author of the *Nueva corónica y buen gobierno*. For a brief discussion of the Miccinelli manuscript, see Viviano Domenici and Davide Domenici (1996).

9. Guaman Poma and Murúa were contemporaries. Guaman Poma (1988 [c. 1615]: 480, 580, 611–13) refers to Murúa five times, defaming both his deeds and character. Rowe (1958: 514) discusses aspects of their problematic relationship, as do Juan M. Ossio (1982; 1985: iii–ix) and John V. Murra (1992).

10. Santillán's (1927 [1559]) list actually includes only eleven designations, as he skips number nine.

11. "Los Señores" (1904 [1542–1575]) says *michuguaina* means "almost a young man" (*ya casi mozo*). Neither their *michuguaina* nor Santillán's *imangu-*

ayna literally means "almost a young man" in Quechua, however (Rowe 1958: 507).

12. Rowe (1958: 517) doubts that the Inka census employed all seven of the categories listed in the Castro group, noting the fact that prepubescent children had little impact on the state economy. What concerns us here is not the identification of official Inka census age-grades, however, but how pre-Hispanic Andeans perceived and defined childhood.

13. Published contracts are found in Jorge Cornejo Bouroncle (1960).

14. This is not the case in contemporary urban Cuzco, where child-rearing is admittedly permissive. Interestingly, in twentieth-century Corpus Christi celebrations, Cuzqueño children are given considerable behavioral latitude, to the point that petty theft at prescribed processional junctures is sanctioned (Fiedler 1985: 62, 215).

15. *Curacas* is what Quechua-speakers called lords. Spaniards called them *caciques*.

References

Acosta, José de. 1880 [1558]. *The natural and moral history of the Indies*. Translated by E. Grimston and edited by C. R. Markham. London: Hakluyt Society.

———. 1985 [1558]. *Historia natural y moral de las Indias*, 2d ed. Edited by Edmundo O'Gorman. México City: Fondo de Cultura Económica.

Ariès, Philippe. 1965 [1960]. *Centuries of childhood: A social history of family life*, 2d ed. Translated by R. Baldick. New York: Vintage Books.

Arriaga, Pablo Joseph de. 1968 [1621]. *The extirpation of idolatry in Peru*. Translated and edited by L. C. Keating. Lexington: University Press of Kentucky.

Castro, Cristóbal de. 1934 [1558]. *Relación y declaración del modo que este valle de Chincha y sus comarcanos se gobernaban ántes que hobiese ingas y después que los hobo hasta que los cristianos entraron en esta tierra*. Colección de libros y documentos referentes a la historia del Perú, annotated by H. H. Urteaga, 2d ser., vol. 10, 136–37. Lima: Imprenta y Librería Sanmartí.

Cieza de León, Pedro de. 1959 [1553]. *The Incas*. Edited by V. Wolfgang von Hagen and translated by H. de Onis. Norman: University of Oklahoma Press.

Cobo, Bernabé. 1983 [1653]. *History of the Inca empire*. Translated and edited by R. Hamilton. Austin: University of Texas Press.

Cornejo Bouroncle, Jorge. 1960. *Derroteros de arte cuzqueño, datos para una historia del arte en el Perú*. Cuzco: Ediciones Inca.

Dean, Carolyn. 1996. Copied carts: Spanish prints and colonial Peruvian paintings. *Art Bulletin* 78(1): 98–110.

Dean, Carolyn. 1999. *Inka bodies and the body of Christ: Corpus Christi in colonial Cuzco, Peru.* Durham, N.C.: Duke University Press.

Domenici, Viviano, and Davide Domenici. 1996. Talking knots of the Inka: A curious manuscript may hold the key to Andean writing. *Archaeology* 49(6): 50–56.

Durantini, Mary Frances. 1979. *The child in seventeenth-century Dutch painting.* Ann Arbor, Mich.: UMI Research Press.

Fiedler, Carol Ann. 1985. Corpus Christi in Cuzco: Festival and ethnic identity in the Peruvian Andes. Ph.D. diss., Tulane University.

Garcilaso de la Vega, "El Inca." 1961 [1609]. *The Incas: The royal commentaries.* Edited by A. Gheerbrant and translated by M. Jolas. New York: Avon Books.

Gisbert, Teresa, and José de Mesa. 1985. *Arquitectura andina: 1530–1830, historia y análisis.* La Paz: Embajada de España en Bolivia.

Guaman Poma de Ayala, Felipe. 1988 [c. 1615]. *El primer nueva corónica y buen gobierno,* 2d ed. Edited by J. V. Murra and R. Adorno. Quechua portions translated by J. L. Urioste. Mexico City: Siglo Veintiuno.

Mariátegui Oliva, Ricardo. 1954. *Pintura cuzqueña del siglo XVII en Chile.* Lima: Alma Mater.

———. 1983. *Nuevo lienzo auténtico del Corpus Cuzqueño.* Lima: Casa del autor.

Molina, Cristóbal de. 1873 [c. 1584]. The fables and rites of the Yncas. In *Narratives of the rites and laws of the Yncas.* Translated and edited by C. R. Markham. New York: Burt Franklin.

Murra, John V. 1992. Guaman Poma's sources. In *Guaman Poma de Ayala: The colonial art of an Andean author.* New York: Americas Society.

Murúa, Martín de. 1946 [c. 1611]. *Historia del origen y genealogía real de los reyes incas del Perú.* Edited by C. Bayle. Madrid: Consejo Superior de Investigaciones Científicas, Instituto Santo Toribio de Mogrovejo.

———. 1986 [c. 1611]. *Historia general del Perú.* Edited by M. Ballesteros. Madrid: Historia 16.

Ossio, Juan M. 1982. Una nueva versión de la crónica de Fray Martín de Murúa. *Revista de Museo Nacional* [Lima] 46: 567–75.

———. 1985. *Los retratos de los Incas en la crónica de Fray Martín de Murúa.* Lima: Oficina de Asuntos Culturales de la Corporación Financiera de Desarrollo.

Pollock, Linda A. 1983. *Forgotten children: Parent–child relations from 1500 to 1900.* New York: Cambridge University Press.

Rowe, John H. 1958. The age grades of the Inca census. In *Miscelánea Paul Rivet Octogenario Dicata,* XXXI Congreso Internacional de Americanistas, 1st ser., no. 50, vol. 2. Mexico City: Universidad Nacional Autónoma de México.

Santillán, Fernando de. 1927 [1559]. Relación. In *Historia de los Incas y relación de su gobierno por Juan Santa Cruz Pachacuti y el Lic. Fernando de*

Santillán. Colección de libros y documentos referentes a la historia del Perú, annotated by H. Urteaga, 2d ser., vol. 9, 18–19. Lima: Imprenta y Librería Sanmartí.

"Los Señores." 1904 [1542–1575]. Relación del origen é gobierno que los ingas tuvieron y del que había antes que ellos señoreasen a los indios deste reino, y de que tiempo, y de otras cosas que al gobierno convenía, declaradas por señores que sirvieron al inga Yupangui y á Topainga Yupangui y á Guainacapac y á Huascar Inga. In *La imprenta en Lima (1584–1824)*, edited by J. Toribio Medina, vol. 1, 200–215. Santiago: Casa del Autor.

Sommerville, C. John. 1982. *The rise and fall of childhood.* Sage Library of Social Research 140. Beverly Hills, Calif.: Sage Publications.

Valda, Juan Bautista. 1663. Solemnes fiestas que celebró Valencia a la Inmaculada Concepción de la Virgen María por el supremo decreto de N. S. Pontífice Alexandro VII. Valencia.

2

Model Children and Models for Children in Early Mexico

Sonya Lipsett-Rivera

Troubled over her son's conduct, María Gertrudis Gonzáles decided to apply some tough love. In 1800 she appealed to the city of Puebla's municipal officials, who, at her request, jailed her son José Luciano. José Luciano's father protested the imprisonment but suggested the alternative of forced conscription into the army. How did the behavior of a fifteen-year-old boy provoke his parents into taking such drastic actions?

Instead of buckling down to serve as a weaver's apprentice, José Luciano had escaped his house to attend the theater and bullfights. He had also refused to treat his parents and other social superiors with the respect and courtesy demanded by colonial Mexican society (AJP).[1] His pastimes were not so extraordinary for the era, but he clearly challenged his parents' and his master's authority and, as such, defied colonial Mexican conceptions of proper children.

José Luciano's story was a worst-case scenario, evidencing the consequences for children of failing to conform to the models of behavior expected of them. José Luciano rebelled in ways specific to the society in which he grew up; his personal situation (working as an apprentice) and his pastimes were not unusual for youths in colonial Mexico. Yet he pushed the limits of what in colonial society was deemed permissible conduct. It is always difficult to adhere to all the rules of what, at a given time, is deemed proper behavior. What is more, in myriad and subtle ways many people chose not to follow such dictates. Even if they had wanted to, many Mexicans lacked the financial means to conform to a prototype elaborated by elites, and could not expect their children to comply with such norms either. And yet, because these ideas were so strongly ingrained in the mindset of colonial Mexicans, they remained a very strong influence, affecting the daily lives of Mexican children. In this chapter, the ideal set out by various moral authorities in both the colonial and precolonial times will be contrasted to information that can be gleaned from the documents that inform us about the actual lives of the vast majority of Mexican children. Outside of the elite classes, children were very much part of the household economy, performing chores such as running errands, herding sheep, and collecting plants (AGN).[2] All of these activities brought them into contact with a larger world in which they had to negotiate their place based upon the social expectations laid out for them by the moral authorities of their time.

Throughout the colonial period, Mexicans had developed a complex sense of how children fit into their world and how they were to behave. These notions derived from both Spanish heritage and, in Central Mexico—the focus of this chapter—Aztec ideas about children.[3] Moral authorities in both traditions set out the rules for raising proper children and for how children were to interact with the world around them. Among the ancient Aztecs, these ideas were reiterated in speeches by elders during rites of passage or other important events in the lives of children. Spanish missionaries transcribed these speeches, called *huehuetlatolli*, in the sixteenth century. The *huehuetlatolli* set out how the ideal girl or boy should behave and frequently provided a contrast to that perfect child, allowing us to deduce what constituted a breach of decorum. They are extremely important sources of information about the Aztecs, but they must be used carefully. These documents were undoubtedly strongly influenced by the Spanish friars who supervised their transcription. Also, the *huehuetlatolli* may have been more representative of the Aztec capital than of the countryside, reflecting a peculiarly urban ethos (Clendinnen 1991: 278–80).

Spanish and Mexican moral authorities published many guides on the proper upbringing of children, and religious authorities reiterated these ideas in edicts and pastoral letters. These writings were directed to a literate and wealthy audience but all children were, nevertheless, expected to live up to these standards. The ideas elaborated in these guides reflected many societal norms and also were reproduced in legal sanctions. For example, these moral authorities constantly reiterated paternal rights and the responsibility to discipline one's offspring.

Both of these sources, the Aztec *huehuetlatolli* and the Spanish guides about the proper upbringing of children, provide a picture of ideal children but do not reveal how children really behaved. In fact, it is often difficult to find references to children beyond these idealized portraits, and historians need to be resourceful in order to discover the daily lives of young people. One way of going beyond the portraits of ideal children is to look at court records. Apart from recalcitrant youths, such as José Luciano, children were at times witnesses, victims, or participants in legal cases. Such incidents provide us with a useful counterpoint to the ideal portrait.

During the eighteenth century, social expectations of children underwent important changes as thinkers and policy makers began to conceive of children as future citizens. As such, children had to be molded into productive participants rather than haphazardly raised under the guidance of poorly equipped parents (Amar y Borbón 1790; Rossell 1786). The consequences of this change in attitude and policy are seen in a growing emphasis on schooling as well as in the increased stress upon the role of mothers in Mexican society and a certain intolerance for teenage rebellion. At the same time, authorities began to try to implement programs to protect children;[4] programs that marked the way for a growing state interest in child welfare.

In order to sketch out a child's life itinerary from birth to adolescence, I rely upon texts from Spain and Mexico that outline the proper way to bring up a child. These rules of parenting differed according to gender, but both boys and girls were subject to many of the same rules. The manuals emphasized the preparation of children to operate in a world that privileged rank, but also within a society informed by Catholicism. The children of early Mexico had to reconcile the social expectations laid out in guides and the *huehuetlatolli* with the demands of daily life.

Aztec Children

Although it is not always clear to what extent Aztec mores affected colonial society, there are some striking parallels between indigenous ideas and the Spanish culture that followed. Children were of great value to the Aztecs. Parents' love was often expressed very evocatively in the *huehuetlatolli*. Respected persons pronounced these speeches on solemn occasions such as a birth, arrival at the age of reason, the start of formal schooling or its completion (López Austin 1985: 29). One ruler, for example, described his daughter as "my necklace of precious stones, my plumage" (Florentine Codex, as cited in Carrasco 1998: 18). Before giving birth, Aztec women tried to protect their fetuses. In order to ensure a healthy baby and an easy labor, pregnant women made an effort to avoid looking at red objects or a solar eclipse, for example, or lifting heavy objects or fasting (Anton 1973: 17–18). At the same time, the Aztecs conceived of infants as unformed beings who would be shaped into proper adults through correct guidance and a series of rituals. The *huehuetlatolli* directed to pregnant women referred to their fetuses as vegetation about to sprout—images that evoked fresh but unformed life (Joyce 2000: 473–83). Their understanding of infants and small children evokes parallels to Andean ideas about youngsters as without purpose or usefulness (see chapter 1).

According to the texts left by Spanish missionaries and indigenous informants, the Aztecs had very definite ideas regarding the proper up-bringing of children. Parents, midwives, and the community at large socialized children to become productive members of society who knew their place. The picture presented to us is that everyone received babies warmly, greeting them with valuable presents, but also ceremonially placed them on the paths predicated by their gender (Clendinnen 1991: 155). Attendants to the birth gently rubbed the newborn to demonstrate their love (Clendinnen 1991: 110). Right after birth, the midwife tried to cool down the baby because the process of labor was believed to produce a lot of heat. The cooling down of the newborn prepared the young person for the hardships of life, solidified the child's limbs, and improved his or her complexion (Mendieta, as cited in López Austin 1985: 36). Then the family kindled a small fire that was kept burning for four days to strengthen the newborn's uncertain life force (Clendinnen 1991: 58).

But even at birth the divergent paths for boys and girls were made apparent in the normal ceremonial. Midwives greeted a baby boy with war cries, separated him immediately from his mother to indicate his future as a warrior, and gave his umbilical cord to an experienced soldier for burial far from home. In the first weeks of a boy's life, priests pierced his lower lip to prepare him for the warrior's lip plug (Clendinnen 1991:

112). Girls, on the other hand, were destined for domestic tasks. The midwife would bury a baby girl's umbilical cord in a corner of the house because domestic enclosure was her destiny. Gifts presented to new-borns at their naming ceremony had symbolic importance: for girls, a broom and a spindle, for boys, weapons (Anton 1973: 18; Clendinnen 1991: 153).

The parents would then consult a soothsayer who, in accordance with the sacred calendar, could determine the signs associated with the baby's day of birth. Each day of the ritual calendar was associated with either good luck or bad luck. If the child happened to be born on an ill-fated day, the parents delayed the next ritual and chose another day from within the thirteen-day cycle of the child's birth (Stein 1992: 29; Marcus 1992: 111). Four days after birth, both female and male babies underwent a ritual bathing when a priest explained the significance of their birth date according to the Aztec calendar. At this event, boys and girls were dressed in miniature versions of adult clothes rather than the "everyday garments of infants" (Joyce 2000: 476; Carrasco 1999: 13). Mothers breast-fed their children for several years, although noble children had wet nurses (Hellbom 1982: 59).

Although gender marked very different destinies for boys and girls, the first few years of infants' lives were relatively similar. Until their final weaning, at two or three or even four years of age, they stayed close to their mother's side. At two or three years of age, a boy would then leave the female domestic enclosure to learn his father's trade. Boys also went to the temple at five years of age, to learn about religious doctrine and to begin to serve the gods. Girls began to be initiated into the work of an Aztec household. Boys had more freedom to roam about but young girls went to the temples to make offerings and religious observances (Clendinnen 1991: 155–56; Hellbom 1982: 59; López Austin 1985: 24, 49). Parents often made toy versions of their work implements for their children. For example, the Spanish missionary Gerónimo de Mendieta recounts how Aztec parents made miniature *melcapalejos*, or carrying packs, for their children (López Austin 1985: 37).

Every four years, in the month of Izalli, both boys and girls participated in a special feast and ceremony. This rite of passage marked the transition into more structured training. This event was supposed to occur at the age of four but, because it was held only once every four years, the children who participated varied greatly in age. It began at midnight at a local temple when all children had their ears pierced. From this stage the children would begin to expand the hole in their ear lobe so that in adulthood they could wear ear ornaments. People also grabbed them by the neck and pulled them so that they would grow tall. At dawn, the children and their sponsors went home for a feast, singing, and dancing and the next day they returned to the temple to drink *pulque*, an alcoholic beverage made from the maguey cactus, in special miniature cups (Joyce 2000: 477). The Incas also had fairly precise ideas about the way different ages marked the beginning of new life stages and responsibilities. In addition, they also had ceremonies that marked weaning and puberty.

The *huehuetlatolli* that many missionaries documented provide some clues as to Aztec ideas regarding the educational process. These speeches record the forms of discipline that Aztec parents used with disobedient children, but not how frequently such measures were employed. Parents threatened to prick the hands of their naughty eight-year-old children with maguey spines. At nine, physical violence in the form of a slap was acceptable. At ten years of age, recalcitrant children could expect a beating and finally, at eleven, the ultimate punishment was to be forced to breathe in the fumes from smoking chiles (Hellbom 1982: 59; Clendinnen 1991: 192). Such harsh treatment may have been an ideal presented to the outside world by indigenous informants eager to seem rigorous in their handling of children. Nevertheless, in the Aztec world, the disciplining of children could clearly be harsh.

In Aztec society all children attended school, and the state took charge of the education of orphans. At age twelve, boys went to the *telpochcalli*, or House of Youth, where their instructors taught them civic responsibilities and how to soldier. Girls went to a separate school where they were taught womanly arts such as weaving and how to do the complex featherwork so valued in ancient Mexico. Both boys and girls also learned their history, traditions, and religious practices. Boys and girls of the nobility could also enter a separate school, the *calmecac*, which destined them for the priesthood. Their curriculum included reading and writing the pictographic language of the region, prophecy, and the intricacies of the ritual calendars. They were also initiated into the art of poetry and oratory (Anton 1973: 21–22).

The Beginning of a Spanish Tradition

With the defeat of the Aztec Empire in 1521, a new era of Spanish colonialism began and the life of indigenous communities in what became New Spain was forever altered. The transformation of traditional lifestyles was inevitable under colonialism but not accomplished overnight. Indigenous society was gradually brought into a colonial culture that reflected sixteenth-century Spanish-imposed values but that also maintained some of its own beliefs and customs. Similar processes occurred in the Andes, where Spanish and Incan ideas about children were often quite different (see chapter 1). Over the course of the colonial period, the way that parents and the larger community dealt with children—be they paragons of virtue or rebels like José Luciano—was part of an ethos that emerged from both cultures. The influence of indigenous thought and traditions was stronger in small rural communities where the indigenous population predominated. But even in such places, a larger culture imparted through the Catholic religion and the example of the elite altered the notions of how children fit into society.

Like the Aztecs, the Spanish believed that people were part of a system of hot and cold. The Spanish derived their ideas from Aristotle and the classical Greek tradition, and their ideas of hot and cold were also connected to notions of gender. The Spanish moralist, Martín de Córdoba (1542: chapter 9), for example, stated that more boys were born in winter because of the cold, whereas girls tended to be born in the warmth of summer. In his view, cold was a masculine virtue and therefore virtuous parents had boys.

When a woman went into labor, devout communities rang the church bells nine times so that all would know that a new Christian was being born. To support the woman, people were supposed to say nine Ave Marías and think of the holy birth of Jesus in order to invoke the Virgin's assistance (Osuna 1531: 109). In the household where the birth took place only devout people were to be in attendance, and the midwife was supposed to show her piety (Osuna 1531: 110). Among elite families, the newborn would be baptized as quickly as possible but within the enclosure of the house (Torales Pacheco 1996: 426). Among poorer Mexicans, babies, even if weak and dying, were taken to the church for a speedy baptism (AGN).[5] Early on, the Spanish authorities prohibited the use of indigenous names at the time of baptism (Gonzalbo Aizpuru 1998: 46).

These efforts show a concern with bringing the newborn into an atmosphere of religiosity so that the new child could take his or her place in this community of Christians. Like the Aztecs before them, colonial Mexicans had precise ideas about where children fit into their society and what norms would govern their lives. Rituals such as baptism and the naming of children within the Christian tradition placed all newborns within this fellowship. The children's paths were largely mapped out for them at birth, according to their race, social class, or filiation— that is, their birth status as legitimate or illegitimate (see chapter 3).

For a newborn, the decision that a mother made either to breast-feed or hire a wet nurse was probably one of the more crucial in the infant's young life. Contemporary authors continually reiterated the importance of breast milk and urged mothers not to delegate this task (Cerda 1599: 1). Mothers had the obligation to feed their infants for the first three years of life (after this period, fathers took over the responsibility of providing sustenance), and those who did not breast-feed their children sinned (Galindo 1680: 156). The moralists' message seems to have remained unheeded among the elite, however, to whom these books were primarily addressed. Many authors, therefore, included recommendations regarding wet nurses. Breast milk, it was believed, imparted the qualities of the one providing it. A baby lamb that was nursed by a goat, it was said, would be less docile, and its wool less soft (Arrom 1985: 57; Sánchez 1786: 188). When nursing a child, therefore, it was important to avoid being angry or hot (Cerda 1599: 7). Rather, while breast-feeding, the nurse should repeat the names of Jesus, the Virgin Mary, and Saint Michael "so that with the milk [the baby] drinks devotion" (Córdoba 1542: part 2, chapter 3). In wet nurses it was preferable to hire a dark-complexioned woman (because blondes were believed to have sour milk), and one that had sweet breath, white teeth, and, above all, good morals (Amar y Borbón 1790: 23, 31–33; Cerda 1599: 5v).

Stages of Childhood

The first three years of a child's life were defined as *la infancia,* or infancy. Ideally these were years of great intimacy within the family circle, with the mother taking full responsibility not only for feeding and care but also for early socialization (Twinam 1999: 160). After this first stage, children fell under the nominal care of their fathers; this was a legal responsibility that not all fathers took seriously. In any case, children were supposed to become a part of the larger society and to begin to be educated to take their place in this wider world. It was at this point that children were taken to mass—because their infancy was over (Sánchez 1786: 176–77).

The next major step seems to have been at the age of seven. By their seventh birthday, girls were supposed to have developed a sense of modesty that was to carry them through to maturity (Gómez de Terán 1735: 310–11). For both girls and boys, seven marked the beginning of their inclusion in some of the rituals of Catholicism. Until then, they were not required to fulfill the weekly Friday fast of foregoing meat (Sánchez 1786: 176–77). By age seven, colonial law allowed that children had *uso de razón* (judgment) and could marry (Gonzalbo Aizpuru 1998: 81), although the Church only recognized a capacity to marry at twelve years for girls and fourteen for boys (Arrom 1985: 57).

Until they reached ten years of age, children could not legally be punished for any crimes they committed (see chapter 5). Their families had to assume any penalty for laws broken by children under that age. Children aged ten to seventeen began to be held responsible for any criminal acts, but the judicial authorities tended to punish these young offenders less harshly (Haslip-Viera 1999: 98). In the eighteenth century, Archbishop Lorenzana decreed that, after the age of ten, boys and girls had to sleep separately—signaling a concern over their nascent sexuality. Lorenzana noted that many Mexicans lived in very cramped quarters that did not allow for separate rooms but he advised the use of reed mats or other dividers (Lorenzana y Buitron 1770: 45).

Despite these markers toward adulthood, men and women did not reach full legal maturity until the age of twenty-five, although, unless emancipated (by marriage for example), they remained subject to their father's authority indefinitely (Arrom 1985: 57).

Basic Needs

Parents had a moral obligation to provide for their children. They owed them four things: subsistence, education, the means to secure a proper lifestyle, and a good example. Subsistence was defined as the provision of food and drink, clothing, some form of housing and medical care, and finally (in the absence of great wealth) the means to take up a suitable occupation (Sánchez 1786: 25–26). It was a mortal sin to fail to provide for children materially or spiritually (Galindo 1680: 154–55).

Many Mexican parents could not fulfill all these requirements either because of their poverty or a lack of commitment to their offspring or a combination of both factors. Many mothers complained that their husbands failed to provide materially for the family (AGN; AJP).[6] It then became the mother's obligation to feed her children (Sánchez 1786: 174–76), a responsibility that some mothers could sometimes carry out but that often was difficult for them. When Bernardino Antonio came home from work and found his young ones crying, he chided his wife for not feeding them (AGN).[7] More often than not, however, a mother could not provide food for her children because her husband did not give her money. As a result, mothers worked when they could but very frequently relied on the charity of their extended family.

Moral authorities believed that the way children ate as well as what they consumed would influence their development as moral beings. The key principle in the food given to children, especially girls, was moderation. Overindulgence, said these authors, led to breaches in chastity and impiety (Gómez de Terán 1735: 16, 309–10; Escoiquiz 1803: 34–35). Girls were subject to the same rules as boys but, in addition, they had to be instructed in the habit of moderation (Amar y Borbón 1790: 95; Cerda 1599: 15), in food as in all other possible appetites. Father Gaspar de Astete, for example, recommended that girls should eat a few leaves and a bit of fish, but most particularly, that girls should always remain hungry so that they could remain in the proper frame of mind for spiritual exercises (Astete 1603: 152–53). Parents were advised not to give children wine because they would become drunks, but this precaution applied especially to girls (Sánchez 1786: 120–22). Manners were also an important part of education. Boys had to learn table manners. They were to eat cleanly, without using more than three fingers. They had to use the tablecloth or a napkin to wipe stains off their clothes. They had to chew slowly but not too slowly. They were not to chew on bones, strike the bread with bones, or use a napkin to soak up the bone marrow (Gómez de Terán 1735: 450). Beliefs about hot and cold also applied to the food given to children. The young, like women, were classified as warm, so it was best that they eat food that was by its nature cold rather than hot (Vives 1948: 47).

These rules regarding etiquette and food appropriateness had, of course, no bearing on most of the poor, whose principal goal was to secure enough food of any sort. Yet they reflect part of the larger concern with children so prevalent at this time: that they learn their proper place in society and conduct themselves accordingly. These preoccupations with notions of hot and cold and with moderating appetites found echoes in Aztec culture.

Education was defined partly as Christian doctrine although, by the eighteenth century, the emphasis on schooling was changing this notion to mean such things as reading and writing and other subjects. The other part of education concerned proper manners (Sánchez 1786: 25–26). Mothers were expected to provide the children's education in their first years (Rossell 1786: 52–53). In the early colonial period, there was a prejudice against sending girls to school because they could talk to boys and be corrupted (Astete 1603: 164–65). Despite this prejudice, in the sixteenth century, Spanish clerics insisted that indigenous girls and boys of the nobility receive an education outside of the home, in a convent or monastery (Gonzalbo Aizpuru 1998: 46–47). The daughters of the wealthy might be educated at home, but many girls either received no education or studied with the *amigas* (friends)—schoolteachers who ran a type of nursery. The *amigas* accepted children from the age of three and taught them some basic skills.

In the late eighteenth century, changing ideas about women and education provided the impetus for founding many schools for girls (Arrom 1985: 16–18). The Spanish crown also tried to ensure that every child, even in the far-flung villages of the colony, had a local school to attend and that these new schools taught indigenous children the Spanish language. Dorothy Tanck de Estrada (1999: 444) notes that although only 37 percent of indigenous villages within the viceroyalty had the new schools, 77 percent of the children of indigenous villages were taught in them. Teachers reported, however, that children ceased to attend at planting and harvest time (Tanck de Estrada 1999: 398). In fact, for most plebeian children, school took second place to work, as they were, from a young age, an integral part of the domestic economy.

Some women accused their husbands of refusing to provide an education for their children. Women used the term *"educación"* in both of its meanings—schooling and proper upbringing. These mothers reflected what, toward the end of the eighteenth century, was a relatively new preoccupation with the formation of young citizens. They argued that they would take care to instill the right values and conducts in their children. Dolores Gil de Arévalo, for example, stated that her husband showed an "absolute disregard for the proper upbringing of his children; far from inspiring them with the wisdom of proper morality, he induced them to join into his vices by beating, insulting, and mistreating them." Later she stated that he taught them to speak like sailors (AGN; AJP).[8] In 1785, Doña Micaela Posada's lawyer contrasted mother to father by describing her as "honorable and of good disposition." He portrayed her as a good mother whose "children behave properly and know their religious doctrine, they are dutiful and obedient to their stepfather who gives them nothing" (AGN).[9] Luisa López described her husband as an "unnatural father" because he objected to sending his children to school. She asserted that she took charge of both upbringing and schooling over her husband's objections (AGN).[10] Doña María Vargas protested that her husband took the money from her son's *capellanía* (lay chantry) so that she had nothing left to pay for his schooling (AGN).[11]

These women and their lawyers were responding to the increased emphasis on the place of children within the larger society. As policy makers and intellectuals publicly discussed how children should be educated in order to become good citizens, mothers began to assert their role in this process.

Parental Authority

Mothers and fathers did not have the same type of authority over their children. Although the importance of providing food—especially breast milk—in the first few years of infancy was delegated to mothers, subsequently fathers were supposed to direct the upbringing of their children, at least in theory. They were the supreme authority in the lives of their offspring. Pedro Galindo (1680: 164), a Spanish moralist, warned mothers that they sinned if they did not respect their husband's orders in the matter of raising children. By law, fathers governed their children until the age of twenty-five, unless either the child or the father broke this implicit legal dominance. This juridical authority, known as *patria potestad*, could be broken by the children's marriage or taking of religious vows, the father's death or civil death, the father's imprisonment or heresy, and finally, if the father married incestuously (Sánchez 1786: 36–38).

Spanish and Mexican moral authorities recommended a great deal of firmness with children. They warned that natural love could blind parents to their children's need for discipline. Domínguez (1807: 14) cautioned against "a disorderly love," especially for daughters. Doña Josefa Amar y Borbón (1790: 117), another proponent of proper discipline, stated that the main defect that afflicted parents was "to love their children to the extreme." These authors, among others, recommended that parents should not hesitate to hit and punish their offspring if pleasant words or a serious tone of voice did not suffice (Amar y Borbón 1790: 119).

But those authors who treated the question of confession make clear that many parents had reservations about their harshness. In his manual on a proper confession, Pedro Galindo (1680: 398–400) reassured parents that they should not worry about reasonable punishments for their children; it was their duty. He makes clear that many of his parishioners came to him to confess their disciplining actions as parents as sinful. This same author soothed the concerns of mothers who reported having cursed their children with such expressions as "may you choke from the croup and die before tomorrow" (garrotillo te ahogue, no llegues a mañana) (Galindo 1680: 203). Whereas Galindo assured these mothers that they had not sinned, Sánchez (1786: 194) warned that such cursing gave children a bad example.

The prevailing view among authors was that harsh words and blows were standard and even desirable in the process of raising a child. Father Astete (1603: 192) did, however, warn to avoid such extreme severity that might compel the child to rebel. These sources do not provide any information about the actual prevalence of physical violence as a method of discipline in Mexican families, only some widespread attitudes.

Parents and children did not always accept that beatings were justified. One night in 1795, in the town of Xochimilco, outside Mexico City, José Bernardino's father came home at four in the morning and threatened to beat him. When recounting the events, José Bernardino emphasized that his father had no reason to punish him and, consequently, José Bernardino left the house and slept at the bottom of the hill (AGN).[12] The only reason that officials recorded this incident is because José Bernardino's father then killed his mother.

Despite the fact that society endorsed the legal and moral rights of parents to beat their offspring, a child might not always accept his father's right to discipline him. Was José Bernardino a rebellious child, or was he simply unwilling to recognize the authority of a father who failed to live up to societal expectations? The flip side of authority was responsibility,[13] and perhaps José Bernardino rejected his father's right to punish him not only because of his father's drunkenness but also because his father did not fulfill his duties as parent.

In a number of instances mothers also objected to senseless beatings carried out by their husbands. Judicial officials interviewed nine-year-old Francisca Placida after her father murdered her mother in Mexico City in 1805. Initially her mother had hit her for breaking a kitchen implement. But when her father came home and began beating the girl, her mother got angry and defended Francisca Placida. The conflict between the parents centered on the question of whether the father had the right to beat his child when the mother believed such punishment to be unreasonable (AGN).[14] Clearly, the mother believed that she had the authority to discipline and to decide the appropriateness of such actions, but she was assuming a degree of authority over her children that was not recognized in the law.

In another incident, in the village of Actopan in 1808, Bernardino Antonio came home to find his children crying. His reaction was to begin to beat them. His wife defended the children, saying that he should not hit them (AGN).[15] Just as Pedro Galindo, the moralist, makes clear, despite a clear mandate to beat and discipline children, neither parents nor their offspring necessarily agreed that such actions were justified. These examples came to light because of much greater violence—the murder of women—but they allow a glimpse into some dissent on the prevailing model of parental discipline.

In the late eighteenth century, thinkers and government officials started to conceive of children as future citizens. As a result they began to be concerned with their formation and education (see chapter 5). Some Mexican mothers, because their role in this process gave them added importance, began to assert themselves as their children's protectors. Women started to complain about their husbands' treatment of their children, although they did not always provide details.

At the end of the colonial period and especially into the nineteenth century, mothers began to argue for custody (something that the law did not really allow them) and forced fathers to justify their actions as parents. They complained not only that their husbands treated them with excessive cruelty but also that the men were bad examples for their children and abused them (AGN; AJP).[16] Bad fathers were excessively cruel toward their children. Such accusations were quite rare, probably because the right of a father to discipline his children was sanctioned by law and socially accepted. Doña Victoriana de Espíritu Santo, for example, accused her husband of demonstrating a profound hatred of his offspring by beating them frequently and alludes to many other instances of cruelty (AGN).[17]

The question of who could punish children was raised in another case. Pedro Pablo and Sebastiana María Mariso, Indians of the village of San Miguel Totolsingo, complained that Don Blas de Olvera beat their fourteen-year-old daughter Albina Josefa. Don Blas had whipped her so cruelly on her chest, arms, and face that she seemed "painted with blood." Initially it seemed that Don Blas did so because the young girl was collecting seed left from the harvest. However, when Don Blas answered the charge, he gave a very different explanation. Albina Josefa had been rude and abusive to a shepherd boy on the estate. According to Don Blas, his beating was justified by the young girl's rudeness, and faced with this alternative version, her parents agreed (AGN).[18] It is possible that the parents agreed because of pressure to do so, but the documents are silent on this matter. Albina's parents were outraged at the violence perpetrated against their daughter and challenged a powerful man's right to beat her. But faced with her admitted breach of social decorum, they concurred that she was at fault. Albina, like José Luciano, whose story began this chapter, challenged the norms of proper conduct and also paid a heavy price.

Parents or guardians must have used forms of discipline other than beatings, of course, but such methods are not often documented. One custom, almost certainly a holdover from pre-Hispanic practices, was forcing a child to breathe the fumes of a burning chile pepper—a premodern equivalent of pepper spray. In 1791, in the village of Tenancingo, a twelve-year-old girl called Marcela died when her stepparents punished her in this way. She seems to have choked. The officials involved reported that people believed that such a penalty could cure children of wandering and the desire to escape to other houses (AGN).[19] Alfredo López Austin (1988, 1: 128–29) attributes this form of punishment to ancient Nahua beliefs and those of the contemporary Tzotiles (an indigenous group of southern Mexico). The Tzotiles still use forced breathing of chile fumes to cure a child's excess of rage or petulance.

By doing so, they force the child to salivate and with the saliva the child's anger is expelled. The ancient Nahuas believed that excess saliva represented a sign of the body's discomfort and also ire. It should be noted that the Tzotiles recognize the danger of such punishments and would not use the method on children younger than four years of age because it could prove fatal. The report of Marcela's death is very brief and does not say why she lived with stepparents but, in all likelihood, she was an orphan whose remaining parent remarried and then died.

This tragic incident reveals the continuation of some Aztec child rearing practices well into the late colonial period, at least in a small village with a predominantly indigenous population. But it also reveals one of the ways that indigenous and Hispanic ideas converged. Marcela had challenged her stepparents' authority by stepping off the narrow path set out for girls by the *huehuetlatolli*. Yet people of Spanish heritage would have understood the objections to her behavior just as easily. Women, even as young girls, had to live within certain parameters, though the form of punishment may have varied according to cultural background. Marcela's stepparents probably believed that their use of chile fumes would prevent the girl from becoming the kind of wayward teenager that José Luciano, at the beginning of this chapter, had become.

Children in colonial Mexico were probably also witness to considerable violence. Apart from the rowdy streets where people exchanged blows, many children regularly saw their parents fight. Take the experience of Manuela, a girl of eight or nine years of age, who, in 1803, in the small town of Teotihuacan, watched the beating that led to her mother's death. When officials asked her about her parents' relationship, she told them that "many times he [her father] argued with her [her mother]; and he hit her. When that happened she [Manuela] went to tell the neighbors so that they would come and calm them down" (AGN).[20]

Conclusion

Children in early Mexico were born into a world in which their paths largely were laid out for them already. The circumstances of their birth (being of legitimate birth or not, having parents of wealth or not, and their race) demarcated certain limitations. The picture presented of childhood in this essay is conditioned by the available information, and therefore, although race was central to so many social relations, I have been able to discover only little about how it affected the lives of children. We can infer many experiences in children's lives, however. The documentation shows clearly that fathers who felt little obligation toward their offspring existed at all class levels. Children suffered, as a result, from hunger and deprivation, but also from limits on their access to schooling.

Many of the rules regarding the ages of children, such as the way they were supposed to eat and behave, may have been addressed to a general audience but were more relevant to the elite. It was only those parents with some means who could implement these ideals or perhaps were even aware of the precepts. Yet how did society deal with children who fell through the cracks? On the one hand, we have the example of José Luciano, who was jailed and then sent into the army because of his rebellious nature. He was not the only one to suffer such a fate. On the other hand, parents regularly showed their devotion to their children and grandchildren. Those children whose fathers rarely had the wherewithal to feed them were frequently rescued by their grandparents who intervened financially and morally to shore up a household at risk. The obligations of parents set out by various authors did not always translate into children's rights, but the extended family was a bulwark against hunger and despair.

In the eighteenth century, children were no longer under the sole tutelage of the extended family—grandparents, aunts, and uncles—but also received the attention of the state, which began to exert its influence. Both intellectuals and the government started to envisage orderly families raising children to be useful and productive citizens. In practical terms, this trend translated into greater emphasis on education as well as an appreciation of the role of mothers. Mothers began to assert in legal documents a custodial right over their offspring that previously they had probably maintained informally. Yet this alteration in the positioning of children in terms of the society as a whole signaled the beginning of a state interest in children that would eventually lead to many of the programs intended to protect the youngest.

Notes

1. 1800A, número 7258, Puebla. Other similar cases include: 1779A, número 6597, Chietla; and 1799A, expediente 73, Puebla.

2. Criminal, 1808, tomo 184, expediente 10, fojas 241–79, Huichapan; Criminal, 1816, tomo 184, expediente 17, fojas 408–501v, Actopan; Criminal, 1774, tomo 8, expediente 19, fojas 291–300v, Teotihuacan.

3. The Aztecs, also known as the Mexica, were only one of the many indigenous peoples who lived in Mexico at the time of the Spanish conquest. Because the Spanish took the greatest interest in them, the Aztecs are the most extensively documented group among the indigenous peoples of central Mexico.

4. For example, in 1811 Viceroy Venegas proclaimed a *bando,* or edict, to deal with lost children. He noted that alarming numbers of children were reported lost (possibly at times they were abducted). He ordered that these children be brought to the nearest deputation and that those who held children against their will be severely punished. "Bando dado en México el 14 de diciembre 1811 por el virrey Don Francisco Xavier Venegas."

5. Criminal, 1791–1792, tomo 2, expediente 2, fojas 31–69, Chalco.

6. AGN, Criminal, 1748, tomo 105, expediente 9, fojas 302–6, Ixmiquipan; AGN, Criminal, 1812, tomo 142, expediente 15, fojas 468–77, Chalco; AGN, Criminal, 1789, tomo 641, expediente 16, fojas 104–6v, Mexico City; AGN, Criminal, 1785, tomo 641, expediente 17, fojas 107–11v, Mexico City; AGN, Criminal, 1782, tomo 682, expediente 3, fojas 127–60, San Juan del Rio; AGN, Criminal, 1762, tomo 716, expediente 11, fojas 141–50, Mexico City; AGN, Judicial, 1788, tomo 32, expediente 35, fojas 116–17, Mexico City; AGN, Judicial, Clero Regular y Secular, 1760, tomo 192, expediente 2, fojas 18–27, Mexico City; AGN, Criminal, 1799, tomo 130, expediente 9, fojas 334–482, Temascaltepec; AJP, 1776, número 4360, Puebla; AJP, 1799A, expediente 200, Puebla.

7. Criminal, 1808, tomo 118, expediente 5, fojas 158–83, Actopan.

8. AGN, Bienes Nacionales, 1853, legajo 717, expediente 119; AJP, 1170, expediente 15 (4141), 13 July 1770.

9. Criminal, 1785, tomo 641, expediente 17, fojas 107–11v.

10. Bienes Nacionales, 1856, legajo 76, expediente 11. For another example see AGN, Civil, 1848, legajo 92, parte 2, unnumbered.

11. Criminal, 1785, tomo 641.

12. Criminal, 1795, tomo 29, expediente 6, fojas 59–113.

13. Many wives used this argument with their husbands. Although it was expected that they would obey their spouses, many women argued that if their spouses did not fulfill their obligations, such as providing for their families, they did not owe these men obedience. See Lipsett-Rivera (2001).

14. Criminal, 1805, tomo 712, expediente 1, fojas 2–27, Mexico City.

15. Criminal, 1808, tomo 118, expediente 5, fojas 158–83, Actopan.

16. AGN, Bienes Nacionales, 1854, legajo 76, expediente 21; AGN, Criminal, 1856, tomo 76, expediente 43; AGN, Bienes Nacionales, 1856, legajo 76, expediente 47; AGN, Civil, 1848, legajo 92, parte 2, unnumbered (divorcio de doña Rosa Vásques y don Juan Ruiz de la Mota); AGN, Bienes Nacionales, 1836, legajo 470, expediente 32; AGN, Bienes Nacionales, 1853, legajo 717,

expediente 119; AJP, 1773, expediente 28 (4242); AJP, 1773, expediente 28 (4242).

17. Bienes Nacionales, 1856, legajo 76, expediente 41. For other examples see Judicial, 1809, tomo 32, expediente 52, fojas 465–82v; Bienes Nacionales, 1856, legajo 76, expediente 47; Bienes Nacionales, 1853, legajo 717, expediente 119; Bienes Nacionales, 1807, legajo 854, expediente 4; Criminal, 1780, tomo 48, expediente 13; and Clero Regular y Secular, 1766, tomo 192, expediente 2, fojas 18–27.

18. Criminal, 1774, tomo 8, expediente 19, fojas 19, 291–300v.

19. Criminal, 1791, tomo 191, expediente 6, foja 227.

20. Criminal, 1803, tomo 3, expediente 20, fojas 302–56.

References

AGN (Archivo General de la Nación [Mexico City]).

AJP (Archivo Judicial de Puebla).

Amar y Borbón, Josefa. 1790. *Discurso sobre la educación física y moral de las mugeres.* Madrid.

Anton, Ferdinand. 1973. *Women in pre-Columbian America.* New York: Abner Scribner.

Arrom, Silvia Marina. 1985. *The women of Mexico City, 1790–1857.* Stanford, Calif.: Stanford University Press.

Astete, Padre Gaspar de. 1603. *Tratado del buen govierno de la familia y estado de las viudas y doncellas.* Burgos.

Carrasco, David. 1998. *Daily life of the Aztecs: People of the sun and earth.* Westport, Conn.: Greenwood.

———. 1999. Uttered from the heart: Guilty rhetoric among the Aztecs. *History of Religions* 39 (1): 1–31.

Cerda, Juan de la. 1599. *Libro intitulado vida política de todos los estados de mugeres en el qual dan muy provechosos y Christianos documentos y avisos, para criarse y conservarse debidamente las mugeres en sus estados.* Alcalá de Henares.

Clendinnen, Inga. 1991. *Aztecs: An interpretation.* Cambridge: Cambridge University Press.

Córdoba, Martín de. 1542. *Jardín de las nobles donzellas.*

Domínguez, Licenciado Don Juan Francisco. 1807. *Discursos sobre el amor puro y bien ordenado con que se deve veer a las mugeres.* Mexico City.

Escoiquiz, Don Juan de. 1803. *Tratado de las obligaciones del hombre.* Madrid.

Galindo, Pedro. 1680. *Parte segunda del directorio de penitentes, y práctica de una buena y prudente confesión.* Madrid.

Gómez de Terán, Juan Elías. 1735. *Infancia ilustrada y niñez instruida en todo género de virtudes christianas, morales, y políticas que conducen a la Santa Educación y buena crianza de los niños.* Madrid.

Gonzalbo Aizpuru, Pilar. 1998. *Familia y orden colonial*. Mexico City: El Colegio de Mexico.

Haslip-Viera, Gabriel. 1999. *Crime and punishment in late colonial Mexico City, 1692–1810*. Albuquerque: University of New Mexico Press.

Hellbom, Anna-Britta. 1982. The life and role of women in the Aztec culture. *Cultures* 8 (3): 59.

Joyce, Rosemary A. 2000. Girling the girl and boying the boy: The production of adulthood in ancient Mesoamerica. *World Archaeology* 31 (3): 473–83.

Lipsett-Rivera, Sonya. 2001. Marriage and family relations in Mexico during the transition from colony to nation. In *State and society in Spanish America during the "Age of Revolution": New research on historical continuities and change ca. 1750s-1850s*, edited by V. Uribe. Wilmington, Del.: Scholarly Resources.

López Austin, Alfredo. 1985. *La educación de los antiguos Nahuas*. Mexico City: SEP Cultura.

———. 1988. *The human body and ideology. Concepts of the ancient Nahuas*. 2 vols. Translated by T. Ortiz de Montellano and B. Ortiz de Montellano. Salt Lake City: University of Utah Press.

Lorenzana y Buitron, Francisco Antonio. 1770. *Cartas pastorales y edictos*. Mexico City.

Marcus, Joyce. 1992. *Mesoamerican writing systems: Propaganda, myth and history in four ancient civilizations*. Princeton: Princeton University Press.

Osuna, Fray Francisco de. 1531. *Norte de los estados en que se da regla de bivir a los mancebos: y a los casados; y a todos los continentes; y se tratan muy por estenso los remedios del desastrado casamiento; enseñando que tal a de ser la vida del cristiano casado*. Seville.

Rossell, Manuel. 1786. *La educación conforme a los principios de la religión christiana, leyes, y costumbres, de la nación española en tres libros dirigidos a los padres de familia*. Madrid.

Sánchez, Padre Matías. 1786. *El padre de familias brevemente instruido en sus muchas obligaciones de padre*. Madrid.

Stein, Max. 1992. *The pre-Columbian Child*. Culver City, Calif.: Labyrinthos.

Tanck de Estrada, Dorothy. 1999. *Pueblos de indios y educación en el México colonial, 1750–1812*. Mexico City: El Colegio de México.

Torales Pacheco, María Cristina. 1996. Del nacimiento a la muerte en las familias de la élite Novohispana del siglo XVIII. In *Familia y vida privada en la historia de Iberoamérica*, edited by P. Gonzalbo Aizpuru and C. Rabbell. Mexico City: El Colegio de México/Universidad Nacional Autónoma de México.

Twinam, Ann. 1999. *Public lives, private secrets: Gender, honor, sexuality, and illegitimacy in colonial Spanish America*. Stanford, Calif.: Stanford University Press.

Vives, Juan Luis. 1948. *Instrucción de la mujer cristiana*. 4th ed. Buenos Aires: Espasa-Calpe.

3

Historical Perspectives on Illegitimacy and Illegitimates in Latin America

Nara Milanich

In 1783 a young man named Rodolfo brought a case before a court in the provincial town of San Felipe, Chile. His goal was to prove his birth origin and, in so doing, become eligible for an inheritance. Rodolfo claimed that he was the illegitimate son of the recently deceased Doña María Alzamora, a woman from a family of some social standing, who had given him up shortly after birth. The witnesses who testified in the case provide us with a glimpse of the itinerant path of Rodolfo's first years of life. Alejo, a mulatto slave of Doña María's parents, declared that he had seen María give birth to Rodolfo and could affirm that he was her son. Then, Alejo recounted, Doña María gave him the baby, "ordering him to take him out of the house and to find some woman to raise him; that she would pay for the rearing." Alejo gave the baby to an Indian named Isabel Herrera but did not know what had become of him thereafter.

Another witness, a family member, picked up the story from there, recounting that the newborn had remained in this first adoptive home for just a few days. Rodolfo would spend his next years circulating among a welter of households, across social and racial cleavages, to relatives and nonrelatives alike, in a seemingly endless rotation of caretakers: from Isabel's house, Rodolfo's father gave him to his sister-in-law, who placed him in the house of one Pablo Jiménez ("whose wife cared for him for three months"); next he was given to Doña Rosa Orellana, the wife of the witness, where he spent eight months; then he was taken in by some "mulattos named Escobar," where he remained for a few days; and finally he went to live in "the house of María Regalato, in the valley of Putaendo, where they finished nursing him and maintained him until a little before the death of his mother" (Cavieres 1995: 233–34).

It would be an exaggeration to suggest that the extraordinary saga of Rodolfo's early years was typical of childhood in late-eighteenth-century Chile, or in any other Latin American society of the past. Yet one aspect of the youngster's identity that clearly conditioned his experience—his out-of-wedlock birth—was not at all unusual. For reasons that are rarely straightforward, and with consequences that are just beginning to be explored by historians, illegitimacy rates in Latin American societies have historically been very high. One way to appreciate the magnitude of the statistics is to compare them with those of European societies of the time. European illegitimacy rates ranged from a low of 1 to 2 percent in seventeenth-century England to a high of 5 to 9 percent in nineteenth-century France. Compare these numbers with those of Latin American societies, where out-of-wedlock births accounted for 30, 40, or even 50 percent of all births in some communities at certain times. Rates could be even higher among particular subpopulations, such as slaves.

Not surprisingly, illegitimacy rates fluctuated significantly over time and from place to place. Some historians have postulated a positive relationship between illegitimacy and urbanization (Cavieres 1995: 226; Kuznesof 1986). Others (for example, Pérez Brignoli 1981; and Sánchez Albornoz 1974) suggest the phenomenon is inextricably linked to miscegenation, or racial mixing, a hypothesis that will be explored in this chapter. A third explanation attributes widespread illegitimacy to the ineffectiveness of church- and state-imposed social strictures concerning marriage and morality.

Another significant characteristic of illegitimacy is that different social, racial, and ethnic groups often exhibited strikingly different rates of out-of-wedlock birth. A study of parish records in early-seventeenth-century Guadalajara, Mexico, for example, found an overall illegitimacy rate of about 40 percent. But a closer look at the data reveals considerable variability: whereas about one-fourth of Spaniards were born out of wedlock, two-thirds of *castas,* or peoples of mixed racial descent, were illegitimate, and four-fifths of African slaves were so registered (Calvo 1982: 60). Moreover, Indian communities from Mexico to Chile have historically had lower rates of illegitimacy than their white or *casta* counterparts (Borah and Borah 1966; Morin 1977; Salinas and Salinas 1988). Finally, illegitimacy was also tied to social class. While historians have explored the widespread existence of illegitimacy among elites (Nazzari 1998; O'Phelan Godoy 1998; Twinam 1999), it is likely that illegitimacy rates were higher among the poor. In the late nineteenth century, moreover, the association between poverty and illegitimacy appears to have strengthened (Milanich 2002).

But amid a canvas of social and geographic variation and change over time, at least one general trend is clear. In comparison with Europe—the standard against which Latin American commentators judged their own societies until the twentieth century—and North America, the rates of illegitimate birth in Latin America have been very high. One author has suggested that no single factor—urbanization, miscegenation, or the nature of social control—can explain illegitimacy throughout the region because the phenomenon was not everywhere and at all times the product of a single logic. Rather, it is necessary to examine "the fine and dense social mesh of relations between men and women . . . in each historical moment in order to be able to interpret what meanings [illegitimate birth] had" (Moreno 1997–1998: 65). While this chapter will touch on the "macro causes" of illegitimacy, it is less concerned with the statistical frequency of out-of-wedlock birth than with the cultural significance and social position of illegitimate children. In other words, what did it mean to be born illegitimate? How did societies regard such children? Did children like Rodolfo experience a different life course because of their out-of-wedlock birth status? One pattern that will be given special attention is the circulation of illegitimate children. By circulation, I refer to the fact that, like Rodolfo, many children in Latin American societies were raised outside of their natal homes by people other than their biological parents and that they might be shifted frequently from one household to another. The phenomenon of circulation is a crucial aspect of childhood in Latin America.

Just as it is difficult to generalize about the rates or causes of illegitimacy among diverse societies and social groups, so too is it risky to generalize about the meanings of illegitimacy and the status of illegitimates. There was no single experience shared by all such children; rather, illegitimacy was mediated by class status and racial and ethnic identity as well as by more fortuitous factors such as the parents' attitudes and circumstances and the relationship between a child's progenitors.[1] What becomes apparent in examining these diverse experiences, however, is that in the colonial and republican societies of Latin America, one's birth status as legitimate or illegitimate, a status that in Spanish and Portuguese was often referred to as "filiation" (*filiación*, or *filiação*, respectively), functioned in concert with these other factors as a marker of social hierarchy. As a result, it had important consequences for individual experience and for the structure of society in general.

Illegitimacy in Official Discourse and the Law

In the colonial period, illegitimacy was frequently referred to as an "infamy," a "stain," or an "indecent and shameful mark" (Konetzke 1958–1962: 473–74, 335). Such beliefs were of course shaped by Catholic teachings that condemned sex outside of marriage. They were also tied to notions of honor in societies where a "culture of honor provided a bedrock set of values that organized . . . society and . . . individual lives" (Johnson and Lipsett-Rivera 1998: 3). Because a woman's sexual continence was evidence of her honor—as well as of that of her male relatives—an illegitimate birth implied dishonor for the entire family.

Attitudes toward illegitimacy were also intertwined with beliefs about race and ethnicity. One important component of the early modern Iberian worldview was the notion of *limpieza de sangre,* or purity of blood. To have "pure" blood meant that one's lineage was free of "contamination" by Jews, Moors, people of illegitimate birth, and—in the new-world context—Africans or Indians. Thus, *limpieza de sangre* implied that the members of a lineage possessed certain racial and ethnic attributes, a specific religious heritage, and a particular birth status. And because the honor of one's lineage to a large extent determined the honor of the individual, *limpieza de sangre* was a vital indication of individual status. A knowledge of and ability to prove one's antecedents were thus crucial.

The law reflected such social attitudes, and both civil and canon law in the colonial period discriminated against children born out of wedlock. Illegitimates could not be ordained as priests or assume posts in the royal bureaucracy or municipal government. They had only limited rights to parental inheritance.[2] Without the express permission of their fathers, they could not bear a family's last name or its coat of arms, nor could they receive entailed estates. Regulations also limited the access of illegitimates to Indian workers in a period when the ability to control indigenous labor was a crucial prerequisite for economic success.[3] Illegitimates were also prohibited from entering the liberal professions (for example, they could not be doctors or lawyers) and, until 1784, the crafts and trades.[4]

But if the discriminatory spirit of colonial law was patently clear, filiation was in fact a flexible concept that offered certain mechanisms for an illegitimate person to become legitimate. Children could be legitimated if their parents subsequently married.[5] And in the colonial period, people of high enough social standing with the proper racial status and enough money to pay for the expensive bureaucratic procedure could petition the Council of Indies for a *gracias a sacar,* or a royal dispensation that effectively changed their status to legitimate (Twinam 1989; Twinam 1999). Similarly, although illegitimacy was considered an impediment to ecclesiastical office, aspirants to the cloth could receive a special dispensation for their sullied birth status (Castañeda 1981).

Indeed, illegitimacy was not defined in black and white terms in the first place. The law distinguished between different kinds of illegitimacy, suggesting that filiation may best be envisioned as a continuum of possible birth statuses rather than as a hard and fast dichotomy between legitimate and illegitimate.[6] *Hijos naturales* ("natural children"), the offspring of single parents who were technically able to marry, enjoyed a higher standing than *adulterinos,* the offspring of adulterous unions in which one parent was married to someone else, or *espurios,* the children of priests. The categories shifted somewhat over time (one medieval Spanish code, the Ley de Toro, which was applied in colonial Spanish America, recognized no fewer than seven varieties of illegitimacy, including natural children and those born of priests, prostitutes, concubines, adulterous unions, and two kinds of incestuous unions (Mannarelli 1993: 163–64)), but in general, natural children had significantly more rights than all other illegitimates, who were deemed to be products of "punishable and damaged unions." Perhaps the most telling evidence of the distinctions between these categories is the sliding payment scale for their dispensation: whereas the legitimation of an *hijo natural* cost 5,500 reales de vellón, the *adulterino* of a married father paid 25,000 reales, and the *espurio* of a priest 33,000 reales (Konetzke cited in Martínez-Alier 1989: 167).

The early national period witnessed the expansion of state attempts to regulate family formation. With the emergence of civil registries in the late nineteenth century, the power to define and supervise filiation shifted from church to state. But the expanding power of secular authority vis-à-vis sexual and familial morality did not translate into a more tolerant legal environment for illegitimates; on the contrary, their legal status worsened in certain regards. While many of the traditional regulations unfavorable to illegitimates had been done away with or had become obsolete by the end of colonial rule, the civil codes promulgated in the newly independent nations in the nineteenth century tended to reinforce discrimination against illegitimates. Some codes, such as the one enacted in Chile in 1857 and subsequently adopted in a number of other Latin American countries, made it more difficult to recognize or to legitimate children. Perhaps more important, these codes outlawed paternity investigations, such that illegitimate children and their mothers had no legal recourse if their fathers chose not to recognize and support them.[7]

Another aspect of the nineteenth-century civil codes is that they allowed for recognition, whereby the father or mother could acknowledge paternity or maternity in the child's baptismal entry, through a notarized declaration, or by means of a will. Recognition, which created certain rights and responsibilities between parents and children and improved the social and civil status of illegitimates by entitling them to the support of the recognizing parent, was technically only available to *hijos naturales*. The distinction between recognized and unrecognized children tended to replace older distinctions (such as *adulterinos* versus *espurios*) that were based on the identity of the child's progenitors and the nature of their relationship.[8]

The prescriptions and possibilities of canon and civil law offer a starting point for understanding illegitimacy. Yet legal dictates can tell us only so much about actual practices and about popular attitudes toward filiation. In the socially unequal societies of colonial and republican Latin America, the vast majority of people could never have aspired to prestigious posts in the ecclesiastical or civil bureaucracies. While unrecognized children were not entitled to parental support—a fact that would have affected children of all social classes—most aspects of the legal discrimination against illegitimacy were of little relevance to the majority of families. Matters of inheritance, for example, were effectively moot for the propertyless many. Even more important, the law is by definition prescriptive, reflecting what its authors intend rather than what really is. If we want to understand the significance of illegitimacy in everyday practice, we must move beyond merely reading legal codes to ask how they were applied as well as what informal practices existed beyond the scope of the law.

Thus, we return to our original questions. How did filiation shape experience? Were popular attitudes and practices always as discriminatory as official discourse and the law? Such questions are not easy to answer. Everyday attitudes, practices, and experiences—especially those involving the private life of the family—are notoriously difficult to discern. Family life rarely intersected with the recording functions of church and state. In order to address these questions, it is necessary to draw on a wide range of documentary sources. For example, baptismal records and later civil birth registries—which recorded a child's filiation—provide some notion of the contours of illegitimacy. Another valuable source is wills, which contain the provisions parents made for legitimate and illegitimate offspring. In addition, certain kinds of judicial cases, such as those initiated by illegitimates like Rodolfo who sought to prove their origins, reveal important details. Finally, the records of social institutions oriented toward children—most notably foundling homes, which existed throughout Latin America from the colonial period into the twentieth century—offer insight into the life trajectories of illegitimates. Taken together, documents of this sort provide us with a window onto the lives of illegitimate children and their families.

Illegitimate Children and Their Families

The experience of illegitimacy was powerfully shaped by the nature of the family into which a child was born. But what kinds of family formations gave rise to out-of-wedlock birth? What kinds of relationships between men and women produced illegitimate children? One category of social relationships that was associated with illegitimacy had its roots in the doctrines of *limpieza de sangre* and the culture of honor discussed above: these were unions between men and women considered socially or racially unequal. From the dawn of the colonial enterprise, Iberian men formed relationships with Indian and African women whom they never married.[9] The children born of these unions were both illegitimate and of mixed racial identity. Thus, in the colonial imagination, illegitimacy became inseparably identified with miscegenation— so much so that illegitimates and people of mixed race were often considered two virtually interchangeable categories. As a bishop from Huamanga, Peru, declared, "The most common situation is that . . . *mestizos* [people of mixed Indian-European parentage] are illegitimate" (cited in Castañeda 1981: 235). Similarly, in the late colonial period the *cabildo* (town council and court of first instance) of Caracas, Venezuela, defined the racial category of *pardos* in this way: they "are descended of slaves, their filiation is illegitimate, and they have their origin in the union of white men with negresses" (cited in Martínez-Alier 1989: 167). In other words, racial identity and birth status were understood to be intertwined.

Racially mixed concubinage was perhaps especially common in slave societies. Studies of colonial Brazil and nineteenth-century Cuba, for example, reveal that white men readily established relations with free and slave women of color and had children with them, yet they rarely married such women and indeed were likely to marry and engender legitimate children with a white partner concurrently or afterward (Martínez-Alier 1989; Nazzari 1996). What about the progeny of unequal unions? We can imagine that such children—marked by the stigmas of mixed race and inferior birth status—would have had minimal material or affective claims on their fathers. It follows that the children of such racially or socially unequal unions were among the most vulnerable of illegitimates. The seventeenth-century will of Francisco Arce de la Parra, an unmarried merchant from Madrid who resided in Lima, reveals how race influenced his behavior as a parent. Arce de la Parra recognized four illegitimate children in his will. He clearly maintained close relations with all of them, naming one executor of his will, leaving dowries to his two daughters, and carefully specifying that in addition to a monetary inheritance, his youngest son, who was fourteen and lived with him, should receive "a canopy from the bed in which I sleep and all the linens and four shirts of mine and four white pants"—objects of symbolic value that expressed paternal affection for the youngster. Arce de la Parra identified the three mothers of these four children by name and specified that they were all single. But he then went on to expressly repudiate paternity of two other children. Although a mulata named

Felipa de Montoya attributed paternity of her son Josephe to him, the testator declared, "He is not [my son] nor do I recognize him as such." He also denied paternity of a six- or seven-year-old *mestizo* child, Ugenio, who had briefly lived in his house (Mannarelli 1993: 177–78).

Whether or not Arce de la Parra was telling the truth, the fact that he felt compelled to identify the "inferior" racial status of the mothers and children he refused to recognize, in contrast to his silence about the racial status (presumably white) of the children he did recognize, suggests the significance of racial identity in a parent's relationship to illegitimate offspring (Mannarelli 1993: 178). Indeed, the authorities charged with monitoring morality encouraged just such behavior. While the colonial Brazilian church counseled marriage as a resolution to the sinful state of concubinage, when confronted with the reality of interracial unions, it ignored its own teachings and admonished the sinners to separate immediately, a policy that almost certainly had negative consequences for any children the couple might have. In 1779, an ecclesiastical court accused Miguel Raposo, a lieutenant in Guarulhos, a town in the state of São Paulo, Brazil, of living in concubinage with his slave Quitéria. The couple had been together for over fifteen years and had five children, whom Raposo acknowledged as his own. Nevertheless, the court ordered him to sell Quitéria; what became of her or the couple's children is unknown, but for the court, the need to terminate the sinful affair took precedence over the dictates of paternal responsibility or the well-being of the children (Nazzari 1996: 6). White fathers in colonial Brazil rarely recognized illegitimate children of color, and even when they did, the courts were reluctant to reward such offspring their rightful inheritance (Silva 1993: 194–95). In addition to racial prejudice, this fact may also reflect the stigma attached to mothers' unfree status.

Such patterns of selective recognition and acceptance of illegitimate children by fathers based on the (inferior) status of their mothers endured into the twentieth century and involved class prejudices as well. One well known Chilean doctor who directed the Santiago foundling home in the 1920s deplored the wealthy mistresses who forced their maids to abandon children they had engendered with the sons of the household. He described how, spinning a web of lies about the baby's identity, the typical mistress would recur to the orphanage to dispose of "the grandchild of whom she is ashamed and whom she secretly curses" (Calvo Mackenna 1928: 207). Even as sexual and affective relations between men and women routinely crossed the racial, ethnic, status, and class cleavages that undergirded Latin American societies, social and legal norms of endogamy (the principle that like marry like) endured, swelling the ranks of the illegitimate and contributing to the social marginalization of these individuals.[10]

The Offspring of Consensual Unions

Concubinage by no means always involved socially or racially unequal unions. The consensual union of couples who lived together "as if married," as the documents routinely phrase it, was a widespread and enduring social institution, one that was rooted in medieval Iberian tradition.[11] For example, early Iberian legal codes both recognized and permitted consensual unions, defining them as inferior to marriage but conceding certain rights and obligations to concubines and their children that set the practice apart from more casual unions (Elizarrarás Rendon 1951: chapter 2). Latin American legal codes never went so far, but such unions nevertheless existed at all levels of the social hierarchy, though they were almost certainly more common among nonelites. In Latin America, many couples could not or did not, for any number of economic, social, or personal reasons, formalize their union. Periodic crises that in many places constituted structural aspects of the economy made it difficult to secure the material prerequisites of marriage, such as the dowry. Even the marriage ceremony (whether ecclesiastical or, after the late nineteenth century, civil) involved significant and sometimes prohibitive expenses. The inhabitants of late-eighteenth-century Bogotá could expect to pay more than fourteen pesos to be wed, at a time when three-quarters of the city's households earned between four and fifteen pesos a year (Dueñas Vargas 1997: 165–67). In any case, propertyless people would have relatively little incentive to legitimate their unions for purposes of inheritance. Moreover, the fact that natural children possessed significant inheritance rights, and that legitimated children could enjoy equal inheritance with legitimate siblings, meant that in some cases there might have been a weak incentive to marry, even for the propertied.[12]

In addition, the relative weakness of the Catholic Church and of colonial and republican states, especially in remote rural areas, impeded attempts to impose the dominant morality on a wayward populace

(Potthast-Jutkeit 1991). Evidence indicates the existence of popular moral codes vis-à-vis consensual unions and out-of-wedlock births that were very different from those espoused by church and state. In the colonial period, the Inquisition prosecuted individuals such as Gaspar Fernandes and Belchior Preto, who were brought before authorities in Pernambuco, Brazil, in the 1590s for making statements deemed blasphemous. The two had asserted that "sleeping with a black woman or a single woman is not a mortal sin" (cited in Schwartz 1997: 65).[13] Likewise, one historian (Moreno 1997–1998: 73–74) has found that as illegitimacy became increasingly widespread on the pampas of Buenos Aires Province, Argentina, in the early 1800s, people stopped using condemnatory terms like "illicit relations" or "illicit friendship" to describe extramarital relationships, instead employing phrases like "living together" (vivir juntos) or "we got together" (nos juntamos). The value-neutral language suggests that people had begun to attribute a moral legitimacy to such unions. Again, popular norms in such instances seem strikingly independent of official and elite beliefs about honor, sexuality, and illegitimacy.

If their parents recognized them and remained together, and if they did not go on to engender legitimate children, the children born of stable, consensual unions, while technically illegitimate, probably remained largely unaffected by their birth status. They would grow up with parents, siblings, and other family members, and they were likely to use both their father's and mother's last names (in Iberian naming practice, people use both their mother's and father's last name, but illegitimates, especially those unrecognized by their father, often used only their mother's name). Finally, if their parents had anything to bequeath to them, they would not be in competition with the superior rights of legitimate siblings or half siblings. While their filiation may have exposed them to some measure of social stigma, the examples from the Brazilian Inquisition and the nineteenth-century pampas suggest that such prejudices did not exist everywhere and among all social groups.

We have a portrait of one such family in Santiago, Chile, in 1902. The family of Tránsito X, Rafael X, and their seven children became the subject of Monograph of a Working-Class Family, a sociological study conducted by two university students (Errázuriz Tagle and Eyzaguirre Rouse 1903) interested in the nature of urban poverty. At the time of the study, Tránsito and Rafael had been together for over twenty years and had had twelve children, five of whom had died. When asked why they had never formalized their union, the couple explained that such measures were only "a necessity for people who have wealth, so that they can make out their wills" (16). With no possessions to speak of, Tránsito and Rafael had little incentive to marry, and their children were consequently illegitimate. Yet in this case, it is clearly the grinding poverty in which the couple's children were born and raised and not their filiation that fundamentally shaped their chances for survival, their life course, and their future prospects. It is impossible to determine how common such unions were historically or what proportion of illegitimate children grew up in such families. What is clear is that not all, and perhaps relatively few, consensual unions were as enduring as that of Tránsito and Rafael. For reasons that vary from place to place, relationships between men and women in many Latin American societies, in particular among nonelites, were characterized by pervasive instability. In short, it was difficult to establish and maintain an enduring domestic union. While it is impossible to talk about "typical" cases when we are dealing with such a diverse group of societies over centuries of time, the experience of Narcisa Checa and Juan López, who lived on the pampas of Buenos Aires province, Argentina, in the early nineteenth century, can at least be regarded as illustrative of the patterns of flux that characterized gender relations and family formation in many Latin American societies. While young, Checa had. been widowed and left with children to support on her meager earnings as a seamstress. She had had relationships with several different men but eventually met Juan López, who, in his words, "went to live with her and to establish a friendship [relationship]." The couple agreed that as long as López remained with Checa, he would contribute to the rent of the farm and provide for "her subsistence and that of a spurious child and two natural children who lived with her."[14] The couple lived together for an unspecified period, but at some point López moved on, leaving Checa and her children behind. It seems reasonable to suppose that he would not be her last partner (Moreno 1997–1998: 76).[15] As the couple's story shows, nonelite families were perpetually shedding and gaining members. Men made fleeting appearances in families, only to disappear, as in this case; in other instances, women might dissolve their households to become live-in domestic servants, only to reestablish them when they could; and in a practice that will be discussed below, children were born, sent to other households to be raised, or abandoned at foundling homes, but subsequently reclaimed if circumstances permitted.

Such instability was in many places the result of pervasive migration. In colonial Brazil, for example, male migration to mining areas, the excursions of *bandeirantes* (quasi-military parties that penetrated the backlands in search of Indians and gold), and military impressment all contributed to the mobility of the populace and to the instability of family structures (Silva 1993). Migration could result in notable sexual imbalances in the population. In many cases, women migrated to cities to find work as domestic servants, resulting in a "demographic surplus" of women in urban centers, as in seventeenth-century Guadalajara, Mexico, late colonial Bogotá, Colombia, and São Paulo, Brazil, or nineteenth-century Santiago, Chile, and Asunción, Paraguay. In turn, agricultural and mining areas attracted male labor, such that labor markets kept men and women in perpetually separate orbits. In addition, at some moments, high mortality rates among men, often due to warfare, would have contributed to these tendencies.

Illegitimates and Matrifocal Families

The result of these realities is that many children grew up in matrifocal households, in which women were the enduring authorities and breadwinners. One indication of the secondary importance of fathers is the low rate of paternal recognition of illegitimate offspring. As previously stated, recognition was a legal act that gave illegitimate children much expanded legal and civil rights. But it was also a deeply significant cultural act, for in recognizing their offspring, parents acknowledged material, social, and affective obligations to them. María Mannarelli's (1993) study of seventeenth-century baptismal records from Lima, Peru, reveals that about a third of illegitimate children were recognized by both parents at birth but that an additional 40 percent were recognized only by their mothers; in 16 percent of cases, neither parent recognized the child, and 3 percent of the time fathers alone recognized the child. Meanwhile, an examination of thousands of baptismal records from late-nineteenth-century Chile reveals only one father who recognized his illegitimate child at birth (other illegitimate children might be recognized later in life, of course, and even parents who never legally recognized their offspring might still love and care for them).

Such patterns had important consequences for the social and ethnic identity of illegitimate children. In colonial Bogotá, Colombia, few illegitimate children received formal paternal recognition and most were assimilated into and more closely identified with the community, family, and ethnic or racial group of the mother. Here as elsewhere, illegitimates also acquired the mother's class status, regardless of the father's socioeconomic position (Dueñas Vargas 1997). Female-headed families were similarly widespread in nineteenth-century São Paulo, Brazil. There, although relations between men and women were by definition fleeting, extended matrifocal families of older women and their daughters and grandchildren provided some measure of continuity and stability to domestic organization. It was in this environment that many illegitimate children were raised (Dias 1995: chapter 6).

Elite social commentators tended to associate matrifocal families and the children reared in them with disorder, laziness, and delinquency. "Because of the fact that legitimate children are raised by a father and a mother, they are more educated, deferential, and apply themselves to work," opined Don Manuel Samper Sanzo, a lawyer of the Real Audiencia of Santafé de Bogotá in 1791 (cited in Dueñas Vargas 1997: 155). Such views were strikingly persistent. In a 1929 article on "the deficiencies of the home as a factor in the delinquency of minors," a Chilean jurist and juvenile court justice declared, "The father's authority tends to be indispensable to direct the behavior of the children, and frequently the mother's weakness is impotent to replace it" (Gajardo 1929: 204). Such doubts about mothers were also inscribed in the law. Through the doctrine of *patria potestad,* fathers exercised exclusive control over their legitimate children, controlling their property, education, and legal transactions. They did not, however, enjoy *patria potestad* over illegitimate offspring. But the law did not grant mothers *patria potestad* over illegitimate children either. Thus, according to the law, the mothers who raised illegitimates were essentially guardians, not parents, of their children.[16]

The lack of legal recognition of maternal authority had important consequences for the illegitimate children over whom single mothers exercised de facto custody. In societies that valued the labor of children, such provisions made illegitimates vulnerable to removal from their mothers' control and hence more easily exploited. The report of a nineteenth-century official reflects the claims public authorities could assert over the illegitimate children of single mothers: "I have been ordered . . . to investigate those women vagabonds who live in our district without means of subsistence; principally, those who maintain illicit relations and have many illegitimate children. . . . The local inspector orders that the children of those women . . . be deposited in homes of respectable individuals" (cited in Salazar 1985: 289–90).

Meanwhile, the judicial archives provide evidence that single mothers' custody of illegitimate children was challenged not just by public authorities but also by private individuals. In the provincial town of San Felipe, Chile, in 1898, Secundina Brito placed her fifteen-year-old illegitimate daughter, María del Rosario, as a servant in the home of Paulina Carrasco in order that she learn some domestic skills. Carrasco was to pay her daughter four pesos a month, give her periodic raises, allow the mother to visit when she wanted, and "care for her and watch over her as befits a girl of fifteen who leaves her home for the first time to assume employment." The practice of placing children as servants in other people's homes was common, especially among families whose economic situation made it difficult to support their offspring. But in this case, the arrangement quickly turned sour: Brito declared that Carrasco had not paid the girl the agreed-upon wage, failed to attend to her and keep her out of trouble, and, worst of all, "deprived me of the prestige and authority of a mother" by inciting her to disobedience. Brito sought to regain custody of her daughter, but Carrasco rebuffed her (AJSF).[17] Such disputes were frequent in late-nineteenth- and early-twentieth-century Chile, and it is telling that they consistently involved illegitimate children. Even more explicitly, a defendant opposing a woman's attempt to reclaim her five-year-old son from his care conceded "the boy is son of the complainant," but then challenged her claim by immediately adding "but he is not legitimate" (AJL).[18]

The pattern is echoed elsewhere. In one municipality in nineteenth-century Northeast Brazil, the gradual abolition of slavery made the labor of "orphans," that is, fatherless children, increasingly important. Such children were assigned guardians who were charged with protecting their well-being and in exchange benefited from the children's labor; according to the law, only widows who lived morally upright lives had custody over their fatherless children. Unmarried mothers, whose morality was by definition suspect, could be automatically denied guardianship of their children. In a period of high labor demand, potential guardian-employers had a clear incentive to impugn the morality of single women and thereby gain access to their children (Meznar 1994: 507). Thus, because of the lack of legal or social recognition of maternal authority, illegitimate children made easy targets for those seeking to exploit their labor.

At the same time that single mothers were deemed an immoral influence on their children, there existed a parallel belief that illegitimate children were somehow bad for their mothers. Some charitable societies who worked for the moralization of the poor, for example, even sought to remove the fruits of sinful relations in order to rehabilitate fallen mothers. This could be a rationale for sending illegitimate children to orphanages—sometimes against their mothers' will. "The salvation of the mother depends on the placement of these children," wrote the member of one society to the nuns of the foundling home in Santiago, Chile (Libros Entradas).[19] In even starker terms, another declared, "I am sending you the baby Rejina del Carmen . . . daughter of Rosalia, a very young girl; it has been necessary to take the baby from her mother, since she is the cause of her perdition" (Libros Entradas).[20] In this discourse, illegitimate children were not only the products of sin but by their very existence also fomented it.

"Sending Out to Be Raised": The Circulation of Illegitimates

The separation of illegitimates and their mothers was not always blatantly coercive. Owing to stigma, poverty, or the demands of wage earning, many single mothers were unable or unwilling to keep their children. In this case, they might engage in a cultural practice with roots far back in Western culture, temporarily or permanently relinquishing the child to be raised by someone else. The mother would place the child with a neighbor, friend, kinswoman, or relative or even with a perfect stranger. Sometimes this arrangement would be for a stipulated period (for example, until weaning), other times it would last indefinitely, and often there was an exchange of money. While any child might be reared under such circumstances, evidence suggests the practice was especially common with illegitimate children, who lived disproportionately in poor, female-headed households unable to maintain them and who in some social circles occasioned stigma. When five-year-old Luis

Alberto Acevedo died in 1885 in a rural Chilean community he was being cared for by Paulina Liberona, a tenant farmer's wife who had four grown children and several young grandchildren of her own. She identified the boy as the "illegitimate son of Rozenda Acevedo, who sent [him] to be raised five years ago, leaving one year's anticipated payment, and afterward I never saw her again" (AJR).[21] While Luis Alberto never knew his mother, other parents maintained ties with their children and eventually reclaimed them.

Young children like Luis Alberto were first sent out to be nursed. Slightly older ones were placed in homes to be "educated" or to work as servants (activities that were often synonymous). The status of children reared in such families was ambiguous. In the best of scenarios, the children were adopted into families. Such was the case of Ignacia Naranjo, whom Tránsito Figueroa remembered in her 1851 will: "Given the love and affection I have had and have for the youngster Ignacia Naranjo, a girl I raised since her tender years . . . I order that upon my death my executor give the said Naranjo thirty pesos in silver . . . and an image of the Virgin of Tránsito" (ANS).[22] But they might also be incorporated into these "foster" families as servants—sometimes in a lifelong capacity. Archival documents abound with young people who refer to the people who reared them since infancy not as "mother" and "father" but as "master" and "mistress."[23]

At the other end of the social hierarchy, some elite parents, such as those in seventeenth-century Lima and eighteenth-century Brazil, anonymously "abandoned" their own illegitimate children to relatives or kinspeople in order to conceal out-of-wedlock births and salvage their honor. If they maintained discretion in their comportment, they might even be able to maintain contact with the children, who could grow up unaware of their true origins. The parents of such children might surreptitiously serve as their godparents, and illegitimates might even be "taken in" by their own biological parents who disguised their true identity by calling them foundlings (see chapter 4).[24] Such subterfuges were plausible precisely because it was so common for households to raise abandoned or unrelated children.

The circulation of illegitimate children, then, was a generalized practice and involved the poorest and wealthiest of households. Children "sent to be raised" often crossed class and ethnic boundaries; such was the case with Rodolfo (whose story is recounted at the beginning of this chapter), who was born of a well-to-do family but passed through households of varying social levels and ethnic identities. Children could also circulate upward, as when poor youngsters were taken in by wealthy households who acted out of charity. The extended patriarchal households of Iberian tradition, "inclusive entities" that assimilated a wide array of individuals into their fold, were uniquely suited for such eventualities (Schwartz and Lockart 1995: 7). Perhaps the quintessential patriarchal household was the sugar plantation of Northeast Brazil described by Gilberto Freyre, which absorbed large numbers of dependents, including illegitimates, abandoned children, and adopted ones (categories that often overlapped), poorer relatives, servants, and slaves. On such plantations, abandoned or illegitimate youngsters might grow up to become *agregados,* permanent residents who were integrated into the landowner's paramilitary force or given work not entrusted to slaves (Freyre 1956 [1933]; Mesgravis 1975: 405).

The circulation of illegitimate children was not simply an informal, private custom among households, however. It was also an institutionalized, public practice actively fomented by church and state through the functioning of foundling homes. Vast numbers of children were interned in orphan asylums (for example, one of every ten children born in turn-of-the-century Santiago was sent to the city's largest orphanage). And while legitimate children could also be abandoned, the majority—sometimes the vast majority—of children left at these institutions were born out of wedlock, for the same reasons illegitimates made up a disproportionate share of those "sent out to be raised" (in the Santiago foundling home, over 80 percent of children were illegitimate) (Delgado Valderrama 1986; Salinas Meza 1991).[25] Perhaps the most striking feature of such institutions was their almost unimaginably high mortality rates. To cite figures from late-nineteenth-century Santiago once again, death rates of young infants left at the institution routinely surpassed 80 percent and in one particularly bad year, 1892, reached an astounding 97 percent (Casa de Huérfanos 1892). Thus, abandonment to an asylum and the premature death it often brought about were common fates for illegitimates in many Latin American cities, as discussed in the next chapter of this volume.

Illegitimacy and Social Hierarchy

Adoption by poor foster mothers, rearing in the homes of relatives or neighbors as "anonymous foundlings," incorporation into large, extended households as *agregados,* or abandonment to a foundling home all provided for the assimilation of illegitimate children into networks of social relations and patron-client hierarchies. But while these mechanisms provided a social niche for the extensive population of illegitimates and may have mitigated the potential dangers of a rootless, alienated group of individuals, they were also frequently associated with social marginalization. Indeed, quite apart from the bureaucratic or occupational discrimination illegitimates suffered in colonial society and the legal discrimination they endured in the republican period, the everyday cultural practices societies availed themselves of in providing for illegitimate children were themselves frequently associated with social subordination.

Even an illegitimate ostensibly incorporated as one more member of his or her biological family did not necessarily enjoy a status equal to the household's legitimate children. Parents who bequeathed possessions to natural children sometimes framed the transaction not in terms of love and affection or even in terms of concern for the child's well-being but in recognition of services or labors rendered. When Doña Gerarda Berríos dictated a will in 1775, she described how for more than twenty years she had raised her illegitimate son, Antonio Muñoz, who "has accompanied me and served myself and my husband personally with total obedience and subjection." She then stated, "I declare that for his personal service he be given half of the plot that I leave as my goods . . . charging him not to leave Cayetano Zamora, my legitimate son, and to accompany and assist him as he has done with me as the good and obedient son who until today he has been, since the aforementioned [Cayetano] is infirm and cannot . . . personally support himself" (Cavieres 1995: 238–39).[26] The will leaves starkly clear the inferior status Antonio enjoyed vis-à-vis Cayetano, his legitimate half brother and Doña Gerarda's principal beneficiary. Whether Antonio is more a son or a servant is difficult to say.

Indeed, illegitimacy might be associated not only with subordination in the context of the family but with downward social mobility, a fact nowhere more strikingly illustrated than in cases of illegitimates born to high-status parents like Don Pedro Antonio Ramíres. Don Pedro was a very wealthy and politically powerful landowner in mid-nineteenth-century central Chile. A local official, he owned a number of haciendas (landed estates), on which numerous peons labored, and he held additional properties in the cities of Santiago and La Serena. Although married, Ramíres also fathered four illegitimate children (only two of whom survived) with his wife's niece. Immediately following her clandestine birth, Don Pedro's first illegitimate child, Lucinda, was anonymously abandoned in the middle of the night near the house of two low-level employees on one of his haciendas. The couple's son discovered the baby, and their adult daughter agreed to care for her. Lucinda lived with her foster mother for some nine years. For several years, Don Pedro paid for Lucinda's upbringing, but he explained it was "out of charity" to an "anonymous" foundling that he did so, never admitting his paternity. Surely the adoptive family was not so easily duped. Don Pedro's second illegitimate child, Wenceslao, was born several years later. Don Pedro claimed the boy had been given to him by a stranger in Santiago, and he offered the young Wenceslao to the overseer of one of his haciendas, suggesting that the child "could serve him."

The fate of Don Pedro's illegitimate children is striking: the two who survived infancy were incorporated into the families of their elite father's humble and illiterate employees. Born of elite parents who had engaged in a relationship considered both illicit and execrable (they were not only illegitimates but, worse still, *adulterinos*—born of a married father—and *incestuosos*—children, in this case, of relations between a man and his wife's niece), the high-born Lucinda and Wenceslao were stripped of their natal social rank and inserted into the lowest rungs of the hacienda's social hierarchy (AP).[27]

The association of illegitimacy and subordinate class status is a recurring one. A witness in a case concerning the inheritance of the illegitimate offspring of a wealthy Bahian captain-major defended their rights by noting, "The captain-major never sent nor consented to send his sons or grandchildren to any mechanical trade once he had legitimized them, treating them always according to the law of nobility" (Pinho 1982: 179–80). The comment is a particularly clear articulation of the relationship between illegitimacy and inferior social status: here the act of legitimizing a natural son is tantamount to conferring on him a higher class status. An illegitimate, even one born to a wealthy captain-major, is considered fit for the humble mechanical trades.

But the most vulnerable of all in this regard were children of color in slave societies. While late colonial provisions in Brazil declared all foundlings, regardless of their color, to be automatically free, these mandates were often ignored.[28] Children sent out to wet nurses by foundling homes might disappear forever, becoming integrated into the ranks of the enslaved. In some places a trade in foundlings of color evolved. In 1830, lawmakers in Rio de Janeiro considered the enslavement of abandoned children enough of a problem to pass a decree declaring that "whoever sells or enslaves foundlings will suffer the penalty of 30,000 réis, and eight days in jail, which will also be applicable to those who buy in bad faith, if they are proven to be aware of the fraud" (Marcílio 1998: 275; Venâncio 1999: 131–36).[29] Once again, patterns of circulation intersected with existing hierarchical structures to produce the subordination of illegitimate children.

The Early Twentieth Century: Scientific Compassion and the State

If illegitimacy had always been a legal issue, at the turn of the twentieth century it became a public health one as well. Public officials and a nascent corps of professional physicians began to take an interest in illegitimacy because it was believed that children born out of wedlock suffered unusually high rates of mortality. The conclusions of Ecuadorian doctor Antonio J. Bastidas (1933) in his study "Illegitimacy: A factor in infant mortality" were typical: illegitimate children suffered a mortality rate double that of their legitimate counterparts. An Argentine advocate elaborated: "All the problems of childhood become more acute in the case of the illegitimate child: it is he who swells the statistics of infant mortality . . . it is he who, crowding the asylums . . . , transmits infections that devastate the population" (Nelson 1927: 220). Thus, a traditional moral preoccupation with out-of-wedlock birth was assimilated into a new, positivist world view, and illegitimacy came to be seen as a public health problem and social crisis.

Many commentators questioned the traditional stigma attached to illegitimacy. Whereas once out-of-wedlock birth had been a "stain" or an "infamy," now illegitimates were increasingly regarded as blameless victims of circumstance. Thus, the illegitimate child could be characterized as "the scapegoat of others' vices, of seduction, inexperience, ignorance, superstition, individual and social egoism" and even as a "tender victim . . . a silent social reformer" (Nelson 1927: 221). But illegitimacy continued to be heavily laden with negative associations. In the positivist discourses of the era, it was associated with delinquency, crime, disease, and, above all, infant mortality. Illegitimacy rates were even read as indicators of a country's rank on an imagined scale of civilization: "In the most civilized countries of Europe more than 90 percent of births are legitimate, [which] shows that . . . the legally constituted family is the basis of . . . the progress of peoples," declared a Chilean congressman (Rubio 1928). "On the contrary, where illegitimacy reigns, populations . . . are closer to a primitive state . . . and backwardness prevails."

More helpful in explaining trends in filiation than the congressman's dubious notion of "civilization" is the evolution of state formation in Latin America. Expanding twentieth-century states began providing new benefits to their citizens, including war pensions, civil service jobs, and social welfare programs, but made these benefits contingent on formal marriage and legitimate filiation. As the purview of their action expanded, states were probably more powerful arbiters of family formation than ever before. Still, the history of illegitimacy is by no means one of linear decline. In fact, recorded illegitimacy rates in the late twentieth century were in many places as high as or higher than they had ever been.[30]

Conclusion

It is of course difficult to generalize about social and legal attitudes toward illegitimacy or the experience of illegitimates over the course of five centuries and across the diverse societies of Latin America. But it is possible to draw several general conclusions about the significance of illegitimacy in the region's history. Like the categories of race, ethnicity, and gender, filiation is a socially constructed designation that has been fundamental to the production of social hierarchy since the beginning of the colonial enterprise in Latin America. Illegitimacy has endured as a culturally significant category because, historically, family order has been perceived as essential to social order, and filiation has been perceived as integral to the very existence of the family. As an Argentine commentator put it in the 1920s, "undoubtedly the complete equalization of the illegitimate child with the legitimate one . . . would lead to the beginning of the dissolution of the family as we now know it" (Nelson

1927: 227). His comment sums up a conviction that has endured among many political, religious, and social authorities from the colonial period to the present.

Second, it is clear that while birth status had important consequences that lasted a lifetime, those most immediately affected by the practices and prejudices associated with illegitimacy were children. Illegitimates faced the very real possibilities of subordination, downward mobility, enslavement, and, in the context of the foundling home, premature death. On the other hand, the widespread circulation of children and informal cultural practices at all social levels of taking in unrelated children also meant that illegitimates separated from their families of origin could become sons and daughters, or at least servants and dependants, in other households. Subordinated within the social order, they were not necessarily marginalized from it.

Today, many of the social realities associated with illegitimacy endure. The matrifocal households in which many illegitimates grew up continue to be a prevalent family form in many Latin American societies. Meanwhile, the practices of child circulation that have historically transferred children, especially illegitimate ones, into the homes of kin, neighbors and strangers, are very much alive in poor Brazilian communities (Cardoso 1984; Fonseca 1998) and in some Caribbean societies.[31] One Brazilian author has suggested that international adoption is a contemporary transnational manifestation of the historical pattern (Fonseca 1998).

Commentators continue to debate the causes, meanings, and consequences of illegitimacy. Perhaps the most visible recent debate erupted in Chile in 1998 in the context of the proposed New Filiation Law. The law, one of the most significant reforms of the Chilean Civil Code since its promulgation in 1855, eliminated the legal discrimination against illegitimates and instituted new provisions for paternity investigation. The proposal provoked heated debates, with those against it marshalling traditional arguments about the threat it posed to the integrity of the family and those in favor invoking newer ideas about children's inalienable rights to a mother and a father.

Ultimately, the New Filiation Law was passed, and as of 1999 Chilean newborns no longer have their birth certificates stamped "legitimate" or "illegitimate," categories that have shaped the experience of Latin American children for centuries. While the debate in Chile is not yet over—critics have charged that judges have been slow to apply the law and have unfairly dismissed many rightful paternity claims (Solicitan 2000)—it is nevertheless safe to say that today illegitimates across the continent enjoy more legal rights than ever before. But the debates serve as a reminder that the waning of illegitimacy as a legal category in Latin America does not mean it has ceased to be a deeply significant cultural one.

Notes

1. As Mannarelli (1993: 175) suggests of colonial Lima, "an illegitimate man was different from a woman of the same status; an illegitimate Spaniard was incomparable to a slave born out of wedlock."

2. On the complex provisions governing inheritance among illegitimates in Luso-Brazilian law, see Lewin (1992). Much of her discussion is also relevant to Spanish America.

3. The Spanish crown attempted to control the distribution of Indian labor through a variety of mechanisms. Illegitimates could not inherit the grants of indigenous labor known as *encomiendas* that were routinely given to conquistadors as a reward for their services to the crown (Mannarelli 1993: 164–65), nor could they benefit from Indian labor provided by the system of Indian draft labor known as *repartimientos*.

4. Burkholder (1998: 34–37) provides a summary of the many restrictions placed on illegitimates in the colonial period.

5. According to medieval Iberian law, legitimation upon marriage was automatic in the case of natural children (for a definition, see below). Some nineteenth-century civil codes, such as the Chilean one, established additional bureaucratic requisites that had the effect of making it more difficult to legitimate children by subsequent marriage (Milanich 2002: chapter 1).

6. Lewin (1992) provides an insightful overview of the importance of status distinctions between natural children and other kinds of illegitimates in Luso-Brazilian law and practice. As she argues, it is misleading to talk about "illegitimate children" in one breath since contemporaries were more likely to talk about "natural children," "spurious children," etc., treating them as distinct categories (in fact the term "illegitimate" often referred only to nonnatural children). She makes a compelling case that in late colonial and early imperial Brazil, these legal distinctions had social significance. In contrast, it is clear that in other historical contexts such distinctions were legally significant but were not necessarily recognized in practice. In nineteenth-century Chile, for example, contemporaries tended to use the terms "natural" and "illegitimate" interchangeably. While a special stigma was certainly accorded those born of "damnable unions," illegitimacy as a generic phenomenon referring to birth out of

wedlock nevertheless existed as a clear social category. With this fact in mind, I have chosen to refer to "illegitimates" as a group, specifying which kind of illegitimacy I am referring to only when relevant. Finally, it is interesting to speculate about the significance of these contrasting terminologies in Brazil and Chile. Does the contrast reflect broad differences in Spanish-American and Brazilian legal systems or in social customs? Or can it be attributed to the evolution of discrete colonial/imperial laws and practices in the nineteenth century? Further research is necessary in order to adequately address these questions.

7. I explore the impact of the Chilean Civil Code on illegitimates and illegitimacy in chapter 1 of Milanich (2002). The Brazilian "Law of September 2," promulgated in 1847, had many of the same effects in that country. See Lewin (1992).

8. For example, the Chilean Civil Code defined an *hijo natural* not as one whose parents could marry but as one who had been legally recognized by a parent or parents.

9. Such refusal can be attributed to social and racial prejudice, economic self-interest, and even legal prohibition. In any case, by the end of the colonial period in Spanish America the cultural disapproval of unequal marriages was inscribed into law. The Royal Pragmatic on Marriage, which took effect in 1778, gave parents unprecedented authority to control their children's marriages, precisely in order to stymie legitimate unions between unequal partners.

10. Nazarri (1996) suggests that norms prohibiting exogamy contributed to illegitimacy because biracial couples were unable to marry and simply procreated out of wedlock.

11. The notion of "consensual union" sets concubinage among social equals apart from the unequal unions discussed above; the latter were not necessarily "consensual" at all.

12. In other words, as Lewin (1992) notes, illegitimate unions could produce heirs, so in terms of inheritance law, marriage was not technically obligatory.

13. Obviously, the fact that black women, regardless of their marital status, are placed in the same category as single ones starkly illustrates the role of race in delineating the parameters of these practices. In addition, the reference to single women suggests that engendering natural children with an unmarried woman is more acceptable than engendering *adulterinos* with a married one.

14. That López distinguishes between Checa's natural and spurious children suggests that in this particular context, the distinction was important not only in the law but also in popular attitudes. The spurious child to whom he refers could be the offspring of a priest or, more likely, of an adulterous affair (the term "spurious" in this usage probably included all unions in which the parents were not single and marriageable). The natural children were presumably born once Checa was widowed.

15. The couple's story was recorded in the judicial archives when Checa filed a case against López to receive economic support from him.

16. This situation prevailed in many countries into the twentieth century, when women were only gradually granted equal authority over children. Even when women were granted equal authority over legitimate children, neither parent was necessarily given *patria potestad* over illegitimates. A partial but important exception to this trend was in Mexico, where civil codes in the 1870s and 1880s granted women *patria potestad* over natural children (though not over other kinds of illegitimates), contingent on their good behavior (Arrom 1985). It is unclear how these changes affected such families in practice, however. On *patria potestad* in nineteenth-century Argentina, see Guy (1985).

17. The judicial record is incomplete, and we do not know whether Brito was able to get her daughter back (Secundina Brito contra Paulina Carrasco, 1899, caja 115).

18. Melinda Vásquez con Ropajito Astudillo por entrega de un niño, 1925, legajo 301, expediente 41.

19. 1896, Card, M.M. Larrain, número 11987–88.

20. 1909, Letter, Magdalena Márquez, número 6734.

21.* Indagación sobre la muerte de un niño encontrado en el canal Rafaelino [?] en Codegua, 1885, legajo 911, expediente 490.

22. 1851, tomo 51, foja 53.

23. According to Szuchman (1988), child labor of this kind was also rampant in early-nineteenth-century Buenos Aires.

24. See the fascinating cases from late colonial Brazil discussed in Nazzari (1998). This pattern is also discussed for Brazil by Silva (1993: 185–87) and for colonial Lima by Mannarelli (1993: 273–77). Twinam (1999) gives many examples of creative subterfuge among colonial elites.

25. The proportion of illegitimates in Brazilian institutions was considerably lower (Marcílio 1998).

26. Silva (1993: 197) reproduces a similar statement from a late-eighteenth-century Brazilian will.

27. This course of events may well have been derailed when the children's existence was revealed during a lengthy and ultimately successful divorce suit his wife, Doña Juana Josefa Madariaga, filed against Don Pedro. "Doña Juana Josefa Madariaga con Don Pedro Antonio Ramíres por divorcio perpetuo." 1867/68, rollo 1855307, legajos 813–14.

28. The Alvará of 1775, confirmed in 1823, declared Brazilian foundlings free.

29. In addition, Meznar (1994: 504–5) discusses parents' fears that children of color would be enslaved in the wake of the abolition of the slave trade in Brazil.

30. According to FLACSO (2001), 27 percent of Uruguayan children were illegitimate in 1987; 30 percent of Paraguayan children in 1985; over 33 percent of Chilean children in 1988; 41 percent of Costa Rican children in 1991; and 58 percent of Argentinian children in 1990.

31. In Haiti, illegitimate children abandoned by their parents may be

reared by another household as "restaveks," literally "stay-withs," children impressed into a deeply exploitative form of servitude in their adoptive household. See Cadet (1998) for the poignant autobiography of a restavek as well as chapter 8 in this volume.

References

AJL (Archivo del Juzgado de Letras de Menor Cuantía de Linares [Chile]).

AJR (Archivo Judicial de Rancagua [Chile]).

AJSF (Archivo Judicial de San Felipe [Chile]).

ANS (Archivo Notarial, de Santiago [Chile]).

AP (Archivo del Provisor, Asuntos Matrimoniales, Arzobispado de Santiago [Chile]).

Arrom, Silvia. 1985. Changes in Mexican family law in the nineteenth century: The Civil Codes of 1870 and 1884. *Journal of Family History* 10 (3): 305–17.

Bastidas, Antonio J. 1933. La ilegitimidad, factor de letalidad infantil. *Boletín del Instituto Internacional Americano de Protección a la Infancia* VI (4): 357–85.

Borah, Sherburne Cook, and Woodrow Borah. 1966. Marriage and legitimacy in Mexican culture: Mexico and California. *California Law Review* 54: 946–1008.

Burkholder, Mark. 1998. Honor and honors in colonial Spanish America. In *The faces of honor: Sex, shame, and violence in colonial Latin America*, edited by S. Lipsett-Rivera and L. L. Johnson. Albuquerque: University of New Mexico Press.

Cadet, Jean-Robert. 1998. *Restavec: From Haitian slave child to middle-class American*. Austin: University of Texas Press.

Calvo, Thomas. 1982. Familia y registro parroquial: el caso tapatío en el siglo XVIII. *Relaciones: Estudios de Historia y Sociedad* 3 (10): 53–67.

Calvo Mackenna, Luis. 1928. La profilaxia del abandono del niño y el Servicio Social. *Servicio Social* año II. Vol. 1 (3): 200–214.

Cardoso, Ruth C. L. 1984. Creating kinship: The fostering of children in favela families in Brazil. In *Kinship ideology and practice in Latin America*, edited by R. T. Smith. Chapel Hill: University of North Carolina Press.

Casa de Huérfanos. Various. Memorias de la Casa de Huérfanos. Santiago, Chile.

Castañeda, Paulino. 1981. Facultades de los obispos indianos para dispensar de ilegitimidad. *Missionalia Hispánica* 38 (113): 227–47.

Cavieres, Eduardo. 1995. Consensualidad, familia e hijos naturales: Aconcagua en la segunda mitad del siglo XVIII. *Cuadernos de Historia* 15 (diciembre): 219–39.

Delgado Valderrama, Manuel. 1986. Marginación e integración social en Chile: Los expósitos, 1750–1930. Masters diss., Instituto de Historia, Universidad Católica de Valparaíso, Chile.

Dias, Maria Odila Silva. 1995. *Power and everyday life: The lives of working women in nineteenth-century Brazil.* New Brunswick: Rutgers University Press.

Dueñas Vargas, Guiomar. 1997. *Los hijos del pecado: Ilegitimidad y vida familiar en la Santafé de Bogotá colonial.* Bogotá: Editorial Universidad Nacional.

Elizarrarás Rendon, Delfino. 1951. El problema jurídico del concubinato. Law diss., Universidad Autónoma de México, Mexico City.

Errázuriz Tagle, Jorge and Guillermo Eyzaguirre Rouse. 1903. *Estudio social: Monografía de una familia obrera de Santiago.* Santiago: Imprenta Barcelona.

FLACSO (Facultad Latinoamericana de Ciencias Sociales). 2001. Mujeres latinoamericanas en cifras. www.eurosur.org/FLACSO/mujeres. (Website consulted on 10 December.)

Fonseca, Claudia. 1998. *Caminos de adopción.* Translated by J. C. Radovich. Buenos Aires: Eudeba.

Freyre, Gilberto. 1956 [1933]. *The masters and the slaves: A study in the development of Brazilian civilization.* Translated by S. Putnam. New York: Alfred A. Knopf.

Gajardo, Samuel. 1929. Las deficiencias del hogar como factor de delincuencia de menores. *Servicio Social* II (3).

Guy, Donna. 1985. Lower-class families, women and the law in nineteenth-century Argentina. *Journal of Family History* 10 (3): 305–17.

Johnson, Lyman L. and Sonya Lipsett-Rivera. 1998. Introduction. In *The faces of honor: Sex, shame, and violence in colonial Latin America,* edited by L. Johnson and S. Lipsett-Rivera. Albuquerque: University of New Mexico Press.

Konetzke, Richard, ed. 1958–1962. *Colección de documentos para la historia de la formación social de Hispanoamérica, 1493–1810.* Vol. III. Madrid: Consejo Superior de Investigaciones Científicas.

Kuznesof, Elizabeth. 1986. *Household economy and urban development in São Paulo, 1765–1836.* London: Westview Press.

Lewin, Linda. 1992. Natural and spurious children in Brazilian inheritance law from colony to empire: A methodological essay. *The Americas* 48 (3): 351–96.

Libros Entradas. Libros de Documentos de Entradas de la Casa de Huérfanos. Santiago, Chile.

Mannarelli, María Emma. 1993. *Pecados públicos: La ilegitimidad en Lima, siglo XVII.* Lima: Ediciones Flora Tristán.

Marcílio, Maria Luiza. 1998. *História social da criança abandonada.* São Paulo: Editora HUCITEC.

Martínez-Alier, Verena. 1989. *Marriage, class and colour in nineteenth-century Cuba.* 2d ed. Ann Arbor: University of Michigan Press.

Mesgravis, Laima. 1975. A assistência à infância desamparada e a Santa Casa de São Paulo: A roda dos expostos no século XIX. *Revista de História* 52 (103): 401–23.

Meznar, Joan. 1994. Orphans and the transition to free labor in Northeast Brazil: The case of Campina Grande, 1850–1888. *Journal of Social History* 27 (3): 499–515.

Milanich, Nara. 2002. Culture, class, and family in Chile, 1857–1930. Ph.D. diss., Yale University.

Moreno, José Luis. 1997–1998. Sexo, matrimonio, y familia: La ilegitimidad en la frontera pampeana del Río de la Plata, 1780–1850. *Boletín del Instituto de Historia Argentina y Americana "Dr. Emilio Ravignani"* tercera serie (16/17): 61–84.

Morin, Claude. 1977. Démographie et différences ethniques en Amérique Latine coloniale. *Annales de Démographie Historique:* 301–12.

Nazzari, Muriel. 1996. Concubinage in colonial Brazil: The inequalities of race, class, and gender. *Journal of Family History* 21 (2): 107–24.

———. 1998. An urgent need to conceal. In *The faces of honor: Sex, shame, and violence in colonial Latin America,* edited by L. Johnson and S. Lipsett-Rivera. Albuquerque: University of New Mexico Press.

Nelson, Ernesto. 1927. El problema de la ilegitimidad. *Boletín del Instituto Internacional Americano de Protección a la Infancia* 1 (2): 221–48.

O'Phelan Godoy, Scarlett. 1998. Hijos naturales "sin impedimento alguno." La ilegitimidad en el mineral de Hualgayoc, Cajamarca (1780–1845). In *El norte en la historia regional: siglos XVIII-XIX,* edited by Y. Saint-Geours and S. O'Phelan Godoy. Lima.

Pérez Brignoli, H. 1981. Deux siècles d'illégitimité au Costa Rica, 1770–1974. In *Mariage et remariage dans les populations du passé,* edited by E. H. J. Dupâquier, P. Laslett, M. Livi-Bacci, S. Sogner. London: Academic Press.

Pinho, Wanderley. 1982. *História de um engenho do Recôncavo.* 2d ed. São Paulo: Companhia Editora Nacional.

Potthast-Jutkeit, Barbara. 1991. The ass of a mare and other scandals: Marriage and extramarital relations in nineteenth-century Paraguay. *Journal of Family History* 16 (3): 215–39.

Rubio, Santiago. 1928. Cámara de Diputados [Chile]. 2a Sesión Ordinaria, 28 May 1928.

Salazar, Gabriel. 1985. *Labradores, peones y proletarios.* Santiago: Ediciones Sur.

Salinas, Rolando Mellafe, and René Salinas. 1988. *Sociedad y población rural en la formación de Chile actual: La Ligua 1700–1850.* Santiago: Ediciones de la Universidad de Chile.

Salinas Meza, René. 1991. Orphans and family disintegration in Chile: The mortality of abandoned children, 1750–1930. *Journal of Family History* 16 (3): 315–29.

Sánchez Albornoz, Nicolas. 1974. *The population of Latin America: A history.* Berkeley: University of California Press.

Schwartz, Stuart B. 1997. Pecar en las colonias. Mentalidades populares, Inquisición, y actitudes hacia la fornicación simple en España, Portugal y las colonias americanas. *Cuadernos de Historia Moderna* 18: 51–67.

Schwartz, Stuart B., and James Lockhart. 1995. *Early Latin America. A history of colonial Spanish America and Brazil.* Cambridge: Cambridge University Press.

Silva, Maria Beatriz Nizza da. 1993. *Vida privada e quotidiano no Brasil: na época de D. Maria I e D. João VI.* Lisboa: Editorial Estampa.

Solicitan cambios a ley de filiación. 2000. *El Mercurio* (Santiago), 23 June.

Szuchman, Mark D. 1988. *Order, family, and community in Buenos Aires, 1810–1860.* Stanford: Stanford University Press.

Twinam, Ann. 1989. Honor, sexuality and illegitimacy in colonial Spanish America. In *Sexuality and marriage in colonial Latin America,* edited by A. Lavrin. Lincoln: University of Nebraska Press.

———. 1999. *Public lives, private secrets: Gender, honor, sexuality, and illegitimacy in colonial Spanish America.* Stanford: Stanford University Press.

Venâncio, Renato Pinto. 1999. *Famílias abandonadas: Assistência à criança de camadas populares no Rio de Janeiro e em Salvador, séculos XVIII e XIX.* Rio de Janeiro: Papirus.

4

Down and Out in Havana

Foundlings in Eighteenth-Century Cuba

Ondina E. González

Early on the morning of 29 March 1711 a tiny baby girl, Thomasa María, was left in the *torno,* or foundling wheel, of Casa Joseph, Havana's home for abandoned infants. The "wheel," in fact a small revolving door, was set in the wall near the home's entrance, and anyone abandoning a child would place the infant there and ring a bell. A resident wet nurse would turn the wheel from inside and pick up the child (AGI).[1] Because the *torno* protected the identity of the person leaving the baby, it was thought that it would help to prevent infanticide. Within hours, Thomasa was turned over to the care of an *ama,* or wet nurse, in the employ of Casa Joseph, who took the baby into her own home (AA).[2]

Across the Spanish world, infant abandonment had long been a matter of public concern.[3] In the Roman Catholic context, taking in forsaken children was viewed as an act of charity that would redound to the eternal benefit of the person moved by such piety. In colonial Havana, however, there were too few persons thus motivated: in the early 1700s Philip V received word that in the island capital infants were being tossed into the sea, murdered by their parents, or left in city plazas where they were devoured by wild dogs (AGI).[4] He ordered the church and government in Havana to work together to found Casa Joseph as a means to confront this problem.

Clearly there was a need for Casa Joseph. Even before the home officially opened, the bishop was receiving foundlings. Within four months of beginning the renovations necessary to accommodate a foundling home in a house purchased by the church, the bishop wrote,

"They have already left some five or six foundlings [which] I have cared for in various parts [of the city]" (AGI).[5] The city gathered for the dedication of the foundling home on 19 March 1711, the feast day of Saint Joseph. Mass was celebrated in the newly built chapel of Casa Joseph; in attendance that day were the bishop, the governor, and "many people," perhaps even some of the women who would eventually work as *amas* (AGI).[6] If the congregation and the celebrants had any idea of what lay ahead—the struggle for revenue, overwhelming expenses, and, worse yet, the plight of the children themselves—it must indeed have been a solemn occasion. In 1711 the house opened its doors and was taking in unwanted infants (AGI).[7]

Children left at Casa Joseph had by no means found a safe haven: during the first year of operation more than 53 percent of the infants admitted did not live beyond a month; a further 22 percent did not survive six months.[8] In fact, there is no indication that any of the children left at the home during that first year reached the age of five. The death rate seems to have decreased over time, fortunately, and reached a low of 11 percent in 1729, as table 4.1 indicates.

Of the 176 who did survive between 1711 and 1752, 152 reached five years of age while under the guardianship of Casa Joseph. The other 24 children were those who "were returned to their parents because they came for them" (AGI).[9] At least some of the children taken from Casa Joseph were removed from the home's care with the hope that they would survive to become servants. In such instances, Casa Joseph was immediately relieved of all financial and tutelary responsibilities toward those children.

What we know of the children in the foundling home can be attributed to the fastidiousness with which the house's priests kept records. When children were left at Casa Joseph, information about them was noted in the *libro de partida*, a registry that included the date, time, and location of abandonment. One piece of information that appears only rarely is the age of the child; for those about whom this datum is available, over 90 percent were newborns.[10] These infants, along with a significant number of children perhaps only slightly older, 167 in all, were baptized at Casa Joseph. The high percentage of baptisms in the house's chapel suggests that the births may have been unknown even to the priest of the local parish; abandoning a child unbaptized may have ensured the anonymity of the child's biological parents. Some were

Table 4.1. Annual Death Rates of Children at Casa Joseph, 1711–1733*

Year	Number of children at shelter	Recorded deaths	Death rate
1711	28	22	79%
1712	28	17	61%
1713	25	9	36%
1714	44	16	36%
1715	58	23	40%
1716	56	26	47%
1717	50	27	54%
1718	44	17	39%
1719	51	20	39%
1720	52	22	42%
1721	48	18	38%
1722	54	22	41%
1723	58	22	38%
1724	56	23	41%
1725	47	15	32%
1726	39	9	23%
1727	39	18	46%
1728	34	7	21%
1729	36	4	11%
1730	33	5	15%
1731	33	11	33%
1732	29	9	31%
1733	41	5	12%

* These figures include only those children for whom admittance and death information is available. The death rate is calculated by dividing the total of children who died in a given year by the number of children registered at the shelter in that year, whether admitted that year or previously.

willing to risk the damnation of an infant's immortal soul by leaving him or her prior to the performance of this sacrament, which suggests that being known as the parent of an illegitimate child involved great risk or stigma. However, since biological parents did not have to be present for a child's baptism, secrecy in abandoning unbaptized children alternately suggests that the act of abandonment itself carried significant social costs. Having a child out of wedlock or abandoning a child was clearly not inconsequential for a woman of any social class, rich or poor.

If baptism was required, church doctrine dictated that it be the first order of the day. The infant would often be christened with the name indicated on a scrap of paper left at the point of abandonment. Occasionally, the priest at Casa Joseph would give the child another name altogether. But always the child was given the surname Valdez, guaranteeing that those born of unknown parents still had a last name (Esténger 1948: 103).

After being retrieved from the *torno,* an infant would be in the care of the house *ama* until another wet nurse could be found, usually within a day or two, to take the baby into her home (AGI; AA).[11] Once in the home of an *ama,* a foundling was to be nursed for eighteen months and then remain with the wet nurse for another three and a half years. Upon reaching the age of five, children were no longer under the guardianship of the foundling home or its *amas.* If the wet nurses chose not to keep their charges, the children were abandoned to the streets, left to fend for themselves. It was a rare five-year-old who could survive the rains, the heat, and the diseases that plagued colonial Havana.[12]

But why did these children become foundlings? Why were they abandoned, and by whom? Correspondence between Havana and Spain indicates that the mariners on ships at anchor in the busy port of Havana consorted with "women whose husbands were away as with virtuous young single women," *prima facie* evidence that their scions were illegitimate (AGI).[13] The subsequent pregnancies brought shame to the women and their families and resulted in mothers taking drastic action to "hide their defects" (AGI).[14] There were those who terminated the pregnancies before having to decide what to do with an unwanted infant, but many did not.[15] Some waited until the child was born, at which point many resorted to infanticide. The murder of infants was so frequent that a bishop was forced to comment: mothers "would go to the countryside and leave their children there; others would throw them alive into wells, others into the sea (of which there were many and frequent examples), and still others would put them in the doorway of some house" (AGI).[16] These horrid practices were seen as "having been remedied by the erection of the [foundling] home" (AGI).[17] Indeed, Casa Joseph offered an alternative to infanticide, in part by guaranteeing the anonymity of the person leaving the child. Some historians argue that one unintended consequence of that anonymity may have been a rise in abandonment (Fuchs 1984; Boswell 1988).

Abandonment was not practiced by only one class of society. If the condition in which a child was left at Casa Joseph reflected the economic wherewithal of the parents, then abandonment was undoubtedly an experience affecting children from all strata of society. Some children would be dropped off with shirts and blankets made of silk, others with rosaries, and still others "almost naked," or with an "old rag used as a shirt" (AA).

Abandonment was not always the worst option for illegitimate children whose parents did not resort to infanticide. For religious and secular purposes, such as being allowed to take ecclesiastical vows or to serve as public officials later in life, abandoned children were accepted under Spanish law as legitimate (born of a wife and her husband), albeit with the qualification that their parentage was unknown (AGI).[18] However, state policy provided the foundling with parents. As Joan Sherwood (1988: 4) writes, "By means of the foundling hospital, the king assumed the duties of a surrogate father, provided for the infant a surrogate mother in the wet nurse, and thus preserved the honour of the family" and, one might argue, the legitimate status of foundlings. The fictive family created by the state supported the presumption of legitimacy embedded in policies governing foundling homes. So important was this assumption that when evidence to the contrary twice came to light in Havana in 1711 and the identities of the unwed parents of children left at Casa Joseph were discovered, the little ones were returned to their parents and stripped of their status as legitimate (AA). Yet even though the origins of other foundlings suggested that they, too, had been born to unwed parents, royal and religious leaders granted them the rights bestowed with a legitimate birth (AGI).[19]

In addition, the children abandoned at Casa Joseph, like those in any foundling home within the Spanish empire, were accorded "the privilege of nobility" (AGI).[20] Odd as the idea of noble status for abandoned children may strike a reader today, it was the natural order of things for most of their contemporaries, especially given the king's cultural role as surrogate father. Yet the conferral of the status of nobility on children in Casa Joseph was contingent on one stipulation: that the children be "pure white, and not mestizos, mulattos, black, or Indians, because in those parts there is a large portion of one or the other" (AGI).[21] The bishop of Cuba agreed to the restriction and also confirmed that blacks and mulattos would only be given the opportunity of being raised in the house and learning a trade, which would help them earn a living later in life. They were denied the privileges of nobility and the rights granted by legitimate status—to take holy orders or pursue public office (AGI).[22] It seems that officials in Spain did not want to upset the upper classes anywhere in the empire with the hint that a nonwhite might blemish their ranks.[23]

And what of the women who took care of these children? Most were probably of mixed race or black, in either case free, and all were likely poor.[24] A government official commenting on the practices of Casa Joseph reported that foundlings "were turned over to [an *ama*] without regard to her good or bad habits nor to her middling or lowly sphere, [being] black, mulatto, or of another race" (AGI).[25] These women also lived in the poorest sections of the black parishes within the city walls of Havana (AGI; *Mapa Topográfica de la Ciudad de la Havana* 1744).[26] In spite of concern over the race of the wet nurse, however, it was poor blacks and mulattos who were in the employ of Casa Joseph and who, in exchange for their services, were given an allowance of fifty pesos per year per child. From these monies they were to care for, feed, and dress the child for the year. A contemporary observed that the "income [is] so limited that none of those ends is reasonably attainable" (AGI).[27]

The civil status of wet nurses who raised foundlings on such paltry income varied considerably. Some of the women were widowed or married and likely sought to supplement their incomes. Others were single, probably having borne illegitimate children themselves, and in need of support. Some of these may have been none other than the mothers of the very abandoned children for whom they cared, having devised a most ingenious way both to raise their illegitimate offspring and to retain their honor. More than 77 percent of the *amas* known to be single cared for only one child, suggesting that working for Casa Joseph was not, for these women, a job.

Yet, as table 4.2 makes clear, several women—married, widowed, and single alike—took care of more than one child, with the result that 42 percent of all children left at the foundling home were cared for by

Table 4.2. Children per Wet Nurse, 1711–1752

Children per wet nurse	1	2	3	4	5	6	7	8	9	10	12	14	24
Number of wet nurses°	270	64	23	18	8	5	5	3	1	1	1	1	1

° Two hundred and seventy wet nurses took care of one child each; 64 took care of 2 each, etc.

women who never took on more than one charge, though usually not simultaneously (AA; AGI).[28] One such woman was Thereza Lujan. For twenty-two years she worked as an *ama* for Casa Joseph and over that period cared for twenty-four children. Of those, 80 percent died, a death rate that exceeded the already extraordinarily high level of 66 percent among all of Casa Joseph's children for the same period (AA). It is unclear whether Thereza was negligent, murderous, or unlucky, but the mortality of children in her custody speaks to the uncertainty of life for all children left at Casa Joseph.

While Thereza represented a most extreme case, that of Anna María de Estrada and her charge, Joseph Geronimo, was more typical. Joseph was abandoned at eleven o'clock one July evening in 1712. With him was a note stating that he was named Joseph Geronimo because he had been entrusted to the care of Saint Joseph. The next morning Alonso Joseph Trujillo, a man appointed by Casa Joseph to act as godfather, was holding the baby during the baptism performed by the foundling home's priest. On 20 July 1712, just one day later, Joseph was entrusted to the care of Anna María, a married woman living in Havana who served as his *ama*. The baby boy stayed with Anna and her husband, Francisco Vargues, for the next three years and five months, until his death in 1715 (AA).

Joseph Geronimo and others like him were caught in the middle of the fiercely antagonistic relationship between the two parties charged with ensuring the foundlings' proper care—the church and the government in Havana. In an attempt at mediation, Philip V ordered that the bishop convene a meeting with local government officials to discuss how the home would be funded. The conference was a resounding failure: the city's financial obligations were such, argued the secular authorities, that there were no funds from which to draw support; the bishop, undaunted, suggested that the revenue generated from an excise tax on livestock would provide an adequate source (AGI).[29] Finally, in 1718 King Philip ordered that the colonial government in Cuba make an annual payment of 1,000 pesos for the maintenance of Casa Joseph. As the letters and orders that crossed the Atlantic make clear, the government disbursed funds only sporadically and grudgingly. In order to avoid paying, local officials proffered a variety of excuses and exercised numerous delaying tactics, even claiming at one point that the house had been closed and the doors barred for two years, a report that proved false (AGI).[30]

The Cuban church itself paid scant attention to the foundling home. Despite having resources of their own, ecclesiastical authorities chose to wrangle with government officials for financial support of the institution; and, in time, church leaders simply ignored it altogether. Even when an administrator of Casa Joseph complained to the king and urged the crown to order that the bishop in Cuba "dedicate himself to [the house's] permanence, it being inherent to his pastoral duties" (AGI),[31] there was no relief. In his history of Casa Joseph, a nineteenth-century Cuban scholar noted that the house was "the sepulcher of the foundlings, not so much for lack of funds as for the faults of a depraved administration" which could act without accountability to anyone (Zenea 1838: 27).

By the mid-eighteenth century, after forty years of erratic and meager financial support and little oversight, Casa Joseph was near collapse. So dire was the situation that the administrator closed its doors and placed a note outside stating that, until further notice, no more children would be admitted (AGI).[32] Even more pressing than the financial needs of the house, however, were those of the city's unwanted children. A reported increase in the rates of infanticide quickly forced the administrator to reopen the doors. Clearly, more than forty years after its opening, Casa Joseph was still needed in Havana.

The early history of Casa Joseph reveals much about the place of abandoned children in colonial Havana. The decades-long debate about funding and the lack of interest from secular and religious leaders indicate that these unwanted children were, at best, a passing consideration. For the church, the care of the foundlings was an obligation, but one that easily could be overshadowed by other priorities. For the local government, the children only diverted funds from other tasks deemed more important. The actions—and inaction—of all those charged with the care of foundlings were, in effect, another form of abandonment.

It cannot be said that the children were of no concern to any of those who abandoned them, however. Although the records do not give much information about the circumstances of most of the children's births, or even of their race, they do reveal something of the pain that parents experienced in leaving a child. Often the children were found with messages pinned to their clothing; one such note read, "Her parents ask that to this little child you give all the help you can, for the love of God" (AA). Some parents returned for their children, and some paid for their care. Others may have endeavored to raise their own children from behind the veil of respectability that working for the foundling home afforded. Still others may have believed that the best chance their illegitimate children had for a decent future lay in being classified as foundling-legitimate.

As for the foundling Thomasa María whose story opens this chapter, she was placed in the care of none other than Thereza Lujan. She did not survive to her sixth month. Although the same fate befell hundreds of infants left at the foundling home, the prospects of other unwanted children in colonial Havana suggest that those at Casa Joseph could be considered the lucky ones.

Notes

1. Santo Domingo, 1881. Boswell (1988: 433) writes, "The *tour* [as the turnstile is known in French] may have originated as early as the fourteenth century . . . but it is impossible to trace its origins precisely. Its use and significance evoke, pitifully, the poignant contrast between ancient and modern approaches to the problem of unwanted children." For information on the history of the *torno* in Rome, see Bolton (1994).

2. *Libro en que se asientan las partidas de los niños expósitos que se echan en el torno de la cuna de esta ciudad. . . .* 1711–1756, tomo 1.

3. In fact, as early as the thirteenth century, Alfonso X addressed the issue of unwanted children within his kingdom. His 1265 code of law, Las Siete Partidas, states that "Shame or cruelty or evil moves fathers or mothers at times to abandon their small children, leaving them at the doors of the churches or hospitals or other places. And after they have abandoned them, good men or women who find them are moved by pity, and they take them in and raise them or give them to someone to raise them" (*Las Siete Partidas* 1972 [1265]: 4.20.4). Most Spanish laws pertaining to the abandonment of children and regulating institutions designed to provide succor were not promulgated until the late eighteenth century, however.

4. Santo Domingo, 336. The same story is told of Fray Juan de Roca, a Franciscan, who at the end of the sixteenth century was instrumental in the opening of the House of Our Lady of Atocha, one of Lima's foundling homes (Martín, 1989: 92–93). Likewise, legend tells that the founding of the Santa Casa de Misericórdia of Bahia was prompted by the sight of infants left to the

mercy of wild animals (Russell-Wood, 1968: 301). Father Cristóbal de Rivera of Puebla founded a house for abandoned children in 1604 because "he saw some dogs eating a small child" (Aranda Romero and Grajales Porras 1991: 171).

5. Santo Domingo, 512.

6. Santo Domingo, 384, foja 104.

7. Santo Domingo, 334.

8. Unfortunately, we do not know how these mortality figures compare with those of Havana's population as a whole.

9. Santo Domingo, 380AA.

10. René Salinas Meza (1991: 319) suggests in his work on Chile "that abandonment at a more advanced age was forced, generally by some extreme urgency which impeded the parents from continuing to care for the child. . . . In contrast, the abandonment of an illegitimate son or daughter was decided shortly after birth, if not before." Salinas Meza (1991: 323, table 4) also found that from 1770 until the end of the century, 98 percent of abandoned children were twenty-nine days old or younger.

11. AGI reference in Santo Domingo, 1134.

12. By the 1760s, Charles III responded to this inhumane situation by ordering that boys leaving the foundling home be taken to a local monastery where they were to be educated and learn a trade. Young girls were to be sent to a *beatorio* (a home for pious women) where they would remain until taking religious vows or finding a husband (AGI: Santo Domingo, 1881, foja 70).

13. Santo Domingo, 512.

14. Santo Domingo, 512.

15. We know of the presence of abortifacients, but there is no way to determine just how widespread their use was (Socolow 2000: 66).

16. Santo Domingo, 324.

17. Santo Domingo, 324.

18. Santo Domingo, 324. This assumption was based on a 1591 papal brief and on "principles and fundamentals of canonical law and common law" that held that abandoned children were to be considered legitimate, with all the rights and privileges afforded children born of church-sanctioned marriages. There was one acceptable reason for abandoning a child: that he or she was an orphan (*huérfano de madre y padre*).

19. Santo Domingo, 324.

20. Santo Domingo, 336.

21. Santo Domingo, 336.

22. Santo Domingo, 336. By 1772 the idea that abandoned children were of noble birth was still a legal fiction. That year, officials in Spain wrote that "the rules piously established by laws and authors who favor those abandoned in Spain cannot be commonly and wholly adopted in the Americas, because of the great variety of castes that have been produced by the introduction of blacks and by their mixing with the indigenous peoples of those lands. . . .

[Furthermore] neither in Spain nor in the Indies have [abandoned children] merited nor should they merit all the privileges of the truly legitimate, and it would be to contaminate the Republic to classify them as noble and of pure birth, with equality to those whose real parents are known" (Konetzke 1962: 391–93).

23. As late as 1786, Don Juan Antonio Abad Valdés y Navarrete sought from the Spanish court "the favor of the privileges of nobility, in spite of having been a foundling [from the Casa Joseph]," listing his accomplishments and benevolences as evidence that he lacked only the title, not the attitudes or behavior, of a noble. In the court's discussion surrounding this case it is clear that by 1786 the assumption was that foundlings were legitimate and of pure white, not noble, blood. Don Juan Antonio was denied his petition, not because he was a foundling but because he asked that the noble status be made hereditary (Konetzke 1962: 607–14).

24. Enslaved women were probably not used by Casa Joseph because the house itself could not afford to buy and maintain the number of slaves needed to act as *amas*, nor was it the practice of slave owners in Havana to send their slaves to work for someone else.

25. Santo Domingo, 1134; also 1577, número 4.

26. AGI reference in Santo Domingo, 380.

27. Santo Domingo, 1134. In the year 1735 a pair of children's socks cost between 0.75 pesos and 1.5 pesos. A laborer earned, per day, 0.5 pesos in 1746. And in 1754 twenty-five pounds of flour cost 2 pesos (Marrero 1980: 85, 88, 93).

28. AGI reference in Santo Domingo, 380; also Santo Domingo, 1577.

29. Santo Domingo, 512.

30. Santo Domingo, 380.

31. Santo Domingo, 427, número 4.

32. Santo Domingo, 1577, número 4.

References

AA (Archbishopric Archive [Havana]).

AGI (Archivo General de Indias [Seville]).

Aranda Romero, José Luis, and Agustín Grajales Porras. 1991. Niños expósitos de la parroquia del Sagrario de la ciudad de Puebla, México, a mediados del siglo XVIII. *Anuario del Instituto de Estudios Histórico-Sociales* VI, 171–80.

Bolton, Brenda M. 1994. "Received in his name": Rome's busy baby box. In *The Church and childhood: Papers read at the 1993 summer meeting and the 1994 winter meeting of the Ecclesiastical History Society*, edited by D. Wood. Oxford: Blackwell Publishers.

Boswell, John. 1988. *The kindness of strangers: The abandonment of children in Western Europe from late antiquity to the Renaissance*. New York: Pantheon.

Esténger, Rafael, ed. 1948. *Cien de las mejores poesías cubanas*. Havana: Ediciones Mirador.

Fuchs, Rachel G. 1984. *Abandoned children: Foundlings and child welfare in nineteenth-century France*. Albany: State University of New York Press.

Konetzke, Richard. 1962. *Colección de documentos para la historia de la formación social de Hispanoamérica, 1493–1810*. Vol. 3.1, 1691–1779. Madrid: Consejo Superior de Investigaciones Científicas.

Mapa topográfica de la Ciudad de la Havana. 1744. British Library, Additional Manuscripts 15, 717, folios 44v–45.

Marrero, Leví. 1980. *Cuba: economía y sociedad*. Vol. 8, *Del monopolio hacia la libertad comercial (1701–1763)*. Madrid: Playor.

Martín, Luis. 1989. *Daughters of the conquistadores: Women of the Viceroyalty of Peru*. Dallas: Southern Methodist University Press.

Russell-Wood, A. J. R. 1968. *Fidalgos and philanthropists: The Santa Casa da Misericórdia of Bahia, 1550–1755*. Berkeley: University of California Press.

Salinas Meza, René. 1991. Orphans and family disintegration in Chile: The mortality of abandoned children, 1750–1930. *Journal of Family History* 16 (3): 315–29.

Sherwood, Joan. 1988. *Poverty in eighteenth-century Spain: The women and children of the* Inclusa. Toronto: University of Toronto Press.

Las Siete Partidas del Rey Don Alfonso el Sabio, cotejadas con varios códices antiguos. 1972 [1265]. Madrid: Ediciones Atlas.

Socolow, Susan Migden. 2000. *The women of colonial Latin America*. Cambridge: Cambridge University Press.

Zenea, Evaristo. 1838. *Historia de la Real Casa de Maternidad de esta ciudad, en la cual se comprende la antigua casa cuna, refiriéndose sus fundaciones, deplorable estado y felices progresos que después ha tenido hasta el presente*. Havana.

5

Minor Offenses

Youth, Crime, and Law
in Eighteenth-Century Lima

Bianca Premo

In the *plaza mayor,* the very center of viceregal power in Peru, the institutions of crown, church, and city encircled Lima's inhabitants both physically and metaphorically. One afternoon in 1782, while the sun descended behind the building of the Cabildo, the city's municipal council and court, a *niña española*[1] ambled through the shadows cast by the cathedral and the tribunals of the Real Audiencia, along cobbled streets crowded with vendors. She had ventured out in search of a pair of stockings. Stopping at the market stall of a fourteen-year-old *español,* she exchanged the requisite pleasantries with the young merchant. When she reached into the purse she carried strung around her neck, she discovered she had been robbed of 56 pesos. The culprit, it was discovered, was Josef Tunco, a boy of Spanish origin, aged ten or twelve, who had hidden beneath the stall and furtively emptied the girl's bag while she and the young merchant were chatting. An adult bystander detained Josef and turned him over to nearby *justicia ordinaria,* as the Cabildo's police and judiciary were called. He was deposited in the public jail only steps from where he had committed his crime, and in the interrogation room, the *sala de crimen,* Josef confessed not only to this robbery but also to a series of purse-snatchings perpetrated against other young girls who had found themselves alone in the plaza (AGN).[2]

In one of the few works that directly study children in Lima's history, Stefan Röggenbuck (1996) claims that the pervasiveness of Spanish in-

114

stitutions and cultural practices in the colonial capital impeded the development of a culture of *"niños de la calle"* (street children), a culture that he claims is relatively new to Lima but that dates to the seventeenth and eighteenth centuries in many Latin American cities with more politically and economically marginal colonial histories. This view reflects a common presumption about colonial Lima, namely that the strength of institutions such as orphanages, religious houses, and schools in the viceregal capital functioned to enclose children, sealing them off from the streets without. Yet, strong as they were, colonial institutions were not fortresses, and they could not contain all of the city's youth.

Indeed, the crimes of young Josef Tunco draw our attention to institutions where we may not expect to see colonial children: jails and the criminal courts of the Real Audiencia (a combined executive advisory board and high court) and the Cabildo. Examining what happened when youth, these "natural" social subordinates, directly confront the institutions of the "stock and bar," offers a unique perspective on the colonial state. This chapter considers the interactions between the criminal justice system and youths who were victims and suspected perpetrators of crimes in eighteenth-century Lima. Drawing from Spanish laws concerning criminal legal minority, contemporary commentaries in elite publications, and, chiefly, criminal cases heard before the lower-instance court of the Cabildo and the high court of the Real Audiencia, it shows how legal categories and juridical discourses came to life as youths faced colonial officials in interrogation rooms and prisons.

This exploration will lead from the innate tensions in thirteenth-century Castilian legal codes concerning the punishment of minors of age to the city of Lima in the eighteenth century, where such tensions were exacerbated by competing discourses concerning colonial social disorder and the role of the state in reforming errant youths. Accordingly, the first part of the chapter will review laws concerning crime and legal minority, especially in regard to concepts of criminal responsibility and sentencing. It will show how the law commissioned the courts with the contradictory calling to be both stern disciplinarian and merciful patriarch to the king's young subjects. The second part will consider the laws in the context of the courts of eighteenth-century Lima, with special reference to patterns of criminal accusations and arrests and to which young transgressors and victims appeared before judges in criminal trials. These cases make it clear that age was of critical legal importance to the courts and served as a criterion for awarding young suspects the benefits of state protection, particularly in terms of the provision of legal counsel and leniency in sentences. But these relatively simple laws about age worked themselves out in a more complex colonial reality where the protections afforded youths collided and combined with the legalized inequities of colonial caste and gender hierarchies. Finally, in the third part of the chapter, late-eighteenth-century intellectual shifts in the concept of childhood and the state's role in reforming youths will be evaluated for their impact on arguments and sentences in criminal trials involving minors. Despite such transformations, courts continued to dispense privileges and punishment according to a distinctly colonial logic.

Law and Punishment from the Home to the Throne

A guiding political philosophy of the Spanish Empire was an articulated version of the concept of *patria potestad,* or paternal right. In its codified Spanish form, power was described by using the Spanish equivalent to the Latin *"potestas,"* which referred to the power a man held over his subordinates. According the Spanish Christian organicist theory of political society, which linked the family to the state in a chain of unification between lesser and greater powers, *potestad* was exercised at each of the various levels of society, from the home to the throne (Boyer 1989: 254). The power of a father over his family, of a master over his slave, of a bishop over his priests, and, finally, of the king over his subjects—these were the interrelated hierarchies on which civil order was founded (*Las Siete Partidas:* 2.17.3). Fathers possessed, as an element of their *patria potestad,* the right—even the moral and civic obligation—to punish their children. In the seventeenth century, Juan Machado de Chávez y Mendoza (1646, 2: 621) wrote in a commentary of canonical and secular law, "fathers[3] sin if they see their children with vices and distracted and in need of punishment and they do not reprehend them, and punish them firmly *(con valor)."*

Still, the punishment of subordinates was never to be "excessive" or "unjust." Machado de Chávez noted that *patria potestad* entailed not the violent chastisement of children but "a moderate castigation, within the limits of paternal correction" (1646, 2: 621). The official use of violence against subjects by the king or by his judges was to be based on the same logic of paternal correction. Las Siete Partidas, the thirteenth-century law code used throughout the colonial period, stated that the king would be considered the father of the people, divinely commissioned with raising his children with love and punishing them with mercy (*Las Siete Partidas:* 2.10.2 and 2.10.3). Yet, as Machado de Chávez observed, fathers were in fact more limited than the royal state in the imposition of punishment. A father's discipline should never consist of *castigo atroz,* or extreme corporal penalties or capital punishment, because such public measures "pertain only to the Judge, who enjoys public authority within the Republic" (1646, 2: 621).

Machado de Chávez's commentary brings into relief an essential tension in Spanish colonial law. The punishment imposed by judges, on whom the maintenance of organic, civil order ultimately rested, was to be tempered always with moderation and a spirit of paternal correction, especially in regard to youths. Yet judges, if not fathers, possessed the ability to publicly inflict death or physical suffering on young criminals, for the good of the Republic. The royal state was, in effect, the ultimate patriarch, the final arbiter on matters concerning the infractions of young subjects, and was charged with being both compassionate and castigatory.

Individuals under the age of twenty-five were defined as "minors of age" and were to be the beneficiaries of the law's leniency toward youths. If accused of crimes, minors of age enjoyed special protections in the Spanish legal system, particularly the right to the assistance of a legal protector *(curador ad litem).* This role would be taken up by either a *procurador* (legal expert for hire) or an *abogado* (court-recognized attorney) named by the judge to represent the minor in court proceedings. But Spanish law did not regard all minors of age as equally responsible for their actions or equally in need of legal protection. While legal defense in principle was afforded to all accused individuals under the age of twenty-five, criminal responsibility varied according to age.

Children under the age of ten and a half were not to be tried for criminal actions (*Las Siete Partidas:* 7.31.8). Las Siete Partidas did not offer an explicit rationale for this, but the common belief, based on the Roman concept of *"dolix incapax,"* was that children were incapable of the combination of malice and the recognition of wrongdoing *(dolo)* necessary to be held accountable for their crimes. Such a lack of criminal accountability was attributed to an absence of moral understanding and, hence, malice, rather than to a lack of intellect and reason, as it would be in the nineteenth century (Machado de Chávez 1646, 1: 808). Between the ages of ten and a half and seventeen, individuals were believed to enter a new stage of criminal responsibility. It was thought that during this time, termed by one legal expert (Escriche 1851: 586) "the age of discretion," youth began to discern "good from bad, just from unjust," although they still lacked a perfect understanding of the morality of actions.

This intermediate stage in the development of *dolo* was explicitly recognized in Spanish criminal law. Between the ages of ten and a half and seventeen, youths could be charged with and tried for criminal actions but were not to be sentenced as adults. Again, the Partidas failed to detail the underlying reasons for mitigating the sentences of minors of age, stating only that sentencing should be left to the discretion of the judges and that the punishment should be "lighter than that [given] to older individuals who commit the same infraction" (*Las Siete Partidas:* 7.31.8). Individuals who were over seventeen years of age no longer merited lenient sentencing but continued to receive the advocacy of a court-appointed lawyer until they reached the age of twenty-five.

It was during the "age of discretion" that judges would have to find a delicate equilibrium. Nineteenth-century legal scholar don Joaquín Escriche (1851: 586) explained, "the law takes into account and combines the progress of [the youth's] reason with new influences which affect his conduct and, giving him a certain amount of freedom as it sees fit, it places upon him other restrictions and concedes him certain rights in order to preserve him from the dangers to which inexperience and the fieriness of passions draw him." In the eighteenth century, the state began to feel an urgency not only to protect youths from their own passions, but also to ensure that their sentences did not have the unintended effect of unleashing the latent antisocial tendencies that such "passions" inspired.[4]

The concept of the limited criminal responsibility of minors overlapped with a general body of Spanish law based on the privilege of certain members of society. According to Las Siete Partidas, sentences for crimes should vary according to the social and civil status of the convicted, for a judge "never should indiscriminately punish the slave as he would the free, the lowly man as he would the *hidalgo*, the young man as he would the old man, the servant as he would the *hidalgo* or other honored man" (*Las Siete Partidas:* 7.31.8). Preferential sentencing was consistently upheld in practice in Spanish America, buttressing and, in turn, reinforced by the color and class hierarchy of colonialism.[5]

Yet preferential sentencing would have to compete with the privileges of age in the Spanish criminal justice system. Neither the Spanish laws nor legal commentators prescribed a solution for instances when preferential sentencing based on social status might conflict with or expand the entitlement to leniency in sentencing based on age. These very ambiguities in Spanish law provided each generation of Spanish subjects with the ability to interpret the legal codes according to its own social values and perceived needs. In Lima's courts, young victims and suspects, and their lawyers and parents interpreted the criminal laws on minority through the prism of a colonial order based on the hierarchies of gender, social class, and caste.

The Cases

To be "arrested" in colonial Lima meant first that a warrant would be issued by the *alguacil mayor*, or sheriff, calling for the seizure of the suspect's "person" and goods. Suspects then would be detained and locked into a humid, dark cell in the royal or public prison. There, they would wait, often for months, for an opportunity to deny in a formal interrogation (*confesión*) the charges leveled against them. If it was determined that the suspect was under the age of twenty-five, the interrogation would be suspended and a *curador ad litem* named to the case. That *procurador* then was required to be present in the *sala de crimen* to support his client during questioning and to file subsequent petitions and arguments.

Existing records, which span the years 1714–1814, contain the dossiers of 334 people arrested for crimes committed in the city and brought before the Cabildo, which served, among other functions, as a court of first instance for the majority of the city's population. Ninety-nine of the individuals detained by the Cabildo during the period were minors of age. If the Cabildo records are representative (and there is no reason to believe that the records in the archive survived according to some systematic bias), this indicates that the state was not reluctant to use its authority to formally try minors of age for crimes.

Alternative Forms of Punishment

Still, not all youths who broke the law found themselves awaiting sentencing in the city's insalubrious public and royal jails. Many youths involved in crimes would be spared formal trials either because they were considered too young for prosecution, or because, if the crime was considered minor, the matter was solved extrajudicially (Cutter 1995: 9). Parents and guardians undoubtedly served as judge and jury for many wayward youths. Laws specifically established for the New World, however, demonstrated a preoccupation with controlling those youths who lacked such adult supervision. Royal decrees expressed continued concern that the colonies would attract vagrants and "incorrigibles," namely Spaniards and mulattos, who might live among indigenous populations and exploit them through crimes and deception. Vagabonds were to be forced to learn a trade while "incorrigibles" were to be banished to military outposts in the Americas, the Philippines, or Africa (*Recopilación* 1756 [1683]: 4.2).[6] In the early sixteenth century, a growing concern with *mestizo* orphans in the Americas was also worked into the law, and, over time, the term "orphan" would come to be analogous in many ways to "vagrant."

Throughout the colonial period, laws permitting the detention of orphans and young vagrants increasingly were brought into practice (*Recopilación* 1756 [1683]: 7.4.4; AGN[7]). In late-colonial Mexico City, it was not unusual to find adolescent delinquents placed in artisans' workshops without a formal trial (Scardaville 1994). Officials in Lima had long carried out similar sentences. Acting as agents of the king, who was referred to as the "father of all minors," colonial officials would appear with youths before notaries and sign them into apprenticeship arrangements for several years of labor and learning, during which time the artisan held the right to physically detain the youth. A significant proportion of the city's apprentices were Indian "orphans" or "vagrants," a percentage of whom must have come to colonial officials' attention because of antisocial behavior. During the Bourbon years, Lima's new *alcaldes de barrio* (neighborhood police officials) were ordered to step up a campaign against vagrancy and pauperism by seizing custody of any beggar's child over the age of five and placing the youth with a master artisan (BNP[8]; Sylvestre 1765, 8.3; also see Arrom 2001: 24–25). Thus, over time, the state's unease about vagrant youths extended from the transient and orphaned to include the simply poor and mendicant.

Apprenticeship could serve as an option for parents as well as for local officials. For example, in 1796, the mother of thirteen-year-old

Manuel de la Cruz Veleban submitted her son to the tailor Don Aldolfo Ramiro for six "forced" years of apprenticeship (AGN).[9] Parents also turned their children over to colonial officials for "correction," although the youths had never been formally convicted of crimes. When in 1774 Marcelo Matunano, twenty-two years old, was arrested for the robbery of over a thousand pesos, his accuser revealed that it was public knowledge that, years earlier, Marcelo had been incarcerated in the Chilean *presidio* (military outpost) of Valdivia. His parents had turned him over to officials in order "to rein him in from certain youthful pranks [*mocedades*]" (AGN).[10] Slave minors who gave their owners trouble might find themselves placed in *panaderías*, the infernal bakeries of the city, where they would work side by side with adults who had been sent there by master as well as judge. Bakeries and workshops would be the destiny of youths from the bottom of the colonial social hierarchy; among the children of elites, those who bore the title of "don" since birth, placement into convent schools or monasteries would be the parental preference for youths who were hard to control (AGN).[11]

The Strategic Ambiguity of Age

In spite of such informal solutions for the punishment of youths, young Limeños, or residents of Lima, nevertheless found themselves facing the law through the bars of cells and testifying in the *sala de crimen* before colonial officials. Cases reaching the Cabildo and Real Audiencia offer a wealth of information about legal attitudes and practices concerning minors, subjects who had legal grounds to demand the benevolent patriarchalism of the colonial state. Yet a caveat must be made concerning the statistics derived from the extant criminal cases brought before the Cabildo. The Cabildo criminal series, like much colonial documentation, is incomplete; entire years are missing as well as an unknowable number of individual cases. Furthermore, criminal paperwork often abruptly ends, sometimes just before a sentence was handed down. Therefore, the cases cannot be said to offer us any solid numbers of arrests, and even less to paint an accurate portrait of all crime and punishment in the viceregal capital. Nevertheless, the Cabildo cases do reveal general patterns, and taken together with the cases from the Real Audiencia, provide us with an unparalleled inroad to contemporary understandings of legal minority and crime.

The first general pattern that can be gleaned from the surviving Cabildo cases is that youths could not always avoid formal encounters with the law by relying on informal mechanisms of punishment, such as placement in a workshop or convent school. Among the often petty crimes of the Cabildo's court of first instance, almost a third of the total number of suspects were reported to have been minors of age.

While determining the age of a criminal suspect was a standard part of legal protocol, officials did not always follow prescribed practice (Juan y Colom 1761: 207–11). In 29 percent of arrests recorded—that is, 103 individual cases—the age of the accused was not noted. In cases where ages were registered, almost 42 percent of the suspects were minors of age, indicating that, in large measure, court officials ascertained suspects' ages in order to determine whether they qualified as minors of age and merited the court's protection.

Nevertheless, the Cabildo was not anxious to offer criminal suspects the benefits of the law. In fact, eschewing its role as protector, the courts took advantage of the fact that many colonial individuals did not know their ages. In many cases, the court scribe, in the presence of the *alcalde ordinario* (a *cabildo* official) would assign ages to suspects based on their appearance (*"al parecer"* or *"por su aspecto"*). Frequently, ages were given as rough approximations, such as "about nineteen or twenty years old" and, very often, "twenty-five" or "more than twenty-five." It is not difficult to imagine that this process was highly subjective. Such subjectivity was evident in the rounding of numbers, as court officials tended to assign ages at five- and ten-year intervals. And, as chart 5.1 shows, time and again, suspects conveniently "appeared" to be twenty-five years old and thus ineligible for a court-appointed attorney (AGN).[12]

Younger suspects also often reduced their own ages in their testimony, presumably in an effort to garner leniency or the counsel of the *curador ad litem*. For example, in 1772, Bernardo Tagle was arrested for breaking and entering with the intent to burglarize. Bernardo said he was sixteen years old, but his baptismal certificate disclosed that he was over twenty-two. In turn, the *agente fiscal*, the equivalent of a crown's attorney, often challenged the reported age of suspects in order to guarantee the strongest possible sentence (AGN)[13] In Bernardo's case, the agente fiscal not only sought out evidence of the suspect's true age, he attempted to make use of the fact that Bernardo had lied about his age to argue for a stricter sentence (AGN).[14]

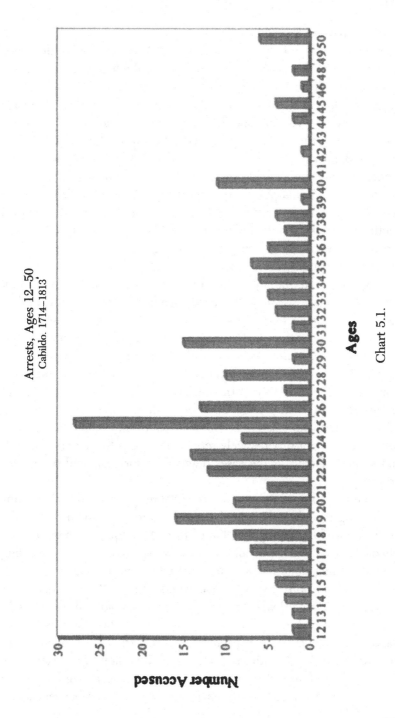

Arrests, Ages 12–50
Cabildo. 1714–1813'

Chart 5.1.

In instances where minors were the victims of crimes, age was also important, although for less technically "legal" reasons. Many of the offenses committed against minors that reached the high court of the Audiencia were instances of rape, generally perpetrated against females. In general, laws concerning rape and seduction focused less on the age of a victim than on a combination of her virginity, prior sexual behavior, and consent in the act (Castañeda 1989: 47; Lipsett-Rivera, 1997: 570; Seed 1988; Lavrin 1988: 70–71; Lavrin 1994: 158–63). While some commentators interpreted the Leyes de Toro, a sixteenth-century law code, as prescribing capital punishment for those who raped girls under the age of twelve, there existed no law specifically defining the rape of youths separately from that of adults. Yet if laws were not specific about the relevance of age in rape cases, the age of a victim was, in fact, deemed germane by the colonials involved in the cases.

Eight-year-old María Josefa de Liñán had been raped by an *español* boy and his slave as they all played together in the courtyard of an *aposento* (complex of single-room dwellings.) Without explanation, María Josefa's mother introduced her daughter's baptismal certificate as evidence in the case. She likely did so to prove how young her daughter was and thus protect her from the character attacks she knew would soon follow (AGN).[15] In some cases, the parents of victims of crimes often reported younger ages for children than the baptismal certificates would later relate. Parents, such as María Josefa's mother, and lawyers also might progressively report lower ages for minors—victims and suspects alike—as the cases dragged on for years and the youths grew older.

Accused rapists could counter by inflating the ages of their victims or claiming that they thought the victims were older than they really were. A horrifying example is that of Justo Manrique, from the coastal city of Ica, who kidnapped and raped a five-year-old slave girl. Finding the girl bathing alone in a stream, he stole the child away on his horse and carried her north toward Lima. When arrested, Justo claimed that he had heard the girl was seven and a half years old and had thought it appropriate to force sex on her because when he asked her if she wanted to marry him, she consented (AGN).[16] The age of the victim in this case was treated with great attention. Testimony was taken from acquaintances of the girl's mother concerning her age, and her baptismal certificate was presented as evidence. The discrepancies between statements of the ages of victims issued by various parties could be staggering. Rape victim Rosa Sánchez's mother called her a toddler *(una párvula)*. The accused rapist, her mother's *compadre* and erstwhile babysitter to Rosa, countered that Rosa was thirteen. Her baptismal certificate showed her to be six years old (AGN).[17]

Thus it was not only the courts that manipulated the reporting of ages of the suspects in criminal cases; both suspects and parents toyed with the ages of victims in order to influence the outcome of criminal trials. The state's conflicted role as protector and castigator rested at the core of this colonial ambiguity about age. Logically, suspects would try to shroud themselves in the state's benevolence by reporting ages that would place them in legally defined, protected categories. Meanwhile, the courts—through the *agentes fiscales*, the scribes, and the *alcaldes* who oversaw the assigning of ages during interrogation—attempted to establish that suspects were not minors of age and therefore not entitled to minority's privileges. The tension in the court's double mandate thus produced a new tension in the justice system that was exploited by colonial state and subject alike.

The manipulation of the ages of victims exposes other ramifications of age that were not specifically addressed in legal codes or ad hoc bodies of law. When parents of rape victims reported lower ages for their children and when suspects claimed that they believed the girls they raped were older than they were, all were invoking an informal, gendered legal minority of sorts. Parents assumed that the court would consider girls under certain ages—in practice, usually younger than eight, rather than twelve years old, as prescribed by law—as sexual innocents. Girls entering adolescence became vulnerable to accusations against their honor, and thus cases against their accused rapists would be increasingly complicated.

Justo Manrique's belief that the little girl he raped could consent to sex may strike us as abhorrent, and it was certainly considered as such by colonial contemporaries. Yet it revealed a commonplace assumption in the colonial setting. Even the sexual purity of very young girls, particularly nonwhite plebeians, was not free of suspicion. In prosecuting six-year-old Rosa Sánchez's babysitter for rape, the *agente fiscal* pointed out, "no stain can fall on her conduct at such a young age" (AGN).[18] Such a comment would seem to us to go without saying. But, in colonial Lima, it did not.

"Weak Patriarchs": Patterns of Arrests and Accusations

Although the state was reluctant to implement its role as protector for those accused criminals whose ages fell on the cusp of minority, patterns of arrests in the city demonstrate that the court used its punitive mandate against all types of young Limeños. Certain groups, however, faced the Cabildo more frequently than others. Rates of arrests varied according to the sex and socioracial status of individuals, and this was true of cases involving minors and nonminors alike.

Those arrested by municipal officials were preponderantly male, although female minors of age were arrested in slightly greater numbers than their adult counterparts (17 percent of minors arrested versus 23 percent of nonminors). White females *(españolas)* were the group least likely to be arrested in both categories. The only *española* minor who appeared before the Cabildo was a married fifteen-year-old *doña*, and her case was prosecuted as far as it was because the accusations also involved her husband (AGN).[19] We might guess, then, that when they broke the law, women tended to answer to private authority in the home rather than to representatives of the king. Yet forty-five women were arrested from 1714 to 1813, and half of these women (twenty-three, in all) were *castas*, or free mixed-race peoples, many of them minors of age. That *casta* women were arrested more often than women or girls in other socioracial groups suggests that patterns in arrests were not conditioned solely by the sex of suspects but also by their racial or economic standing.

Analyzed in terms of racial categories, the cases involving minors demonstrate certain slight, but telling, divergences from the adult pattern of arrests. Accusations against *español* minors of both sexes constituted 24 percent of the total arrests within the minor group but 32 percent of nonminors detained. The rate of arrests of slave minors of both sexes also was lower than that of nonminors, constituting 17 percent compared with 24 percent. We are left, then, with two groups of minors with greater rates of arrests than their adult counterparts: Indians and *castas*.

Indians detained by ordinary justice were almost always minors of age. Indian youths normally were tried by a *corregidor* (provincial magistrate) rather than by *justicia ordinaria*. In general, Indian minors of age whose cases were heard by the Cabildo were temporary migrants to the city, accused of property crimes such as poaching and the illegal

Table 5.1. Arrests by Socioracial and Gender Categories (in cases where both race and sex are registered; n = 258)

	Total				Minors				Nonminors/ Age Unknown			
	M	F	T	%	M	F	T	%	M	F	T	%
Español	74	2	76	29.5	19	1	20	24.1	55	1	56	32.0
Casta	94	23	117	45.3	30	13	43	51.8	64	10	74	42.3
Slave	39	17	56	21.7	11	3	14	16.9	28	14	42	24.0
Indian	6	3	9	3.5	4	2	6	7.2	2	1	3	1.7
Total	213	45	258	100	64	19	83	100	149	26	175	100

M = Male; F = Female; T = Total.

sale of agricultural products. In general, the Cabildo chose to treat the crimes of these indigenous youths rapidly and, often, leniently (AGN).[20] If we turn for a moment to one sentence handed down against a minor by the *corregidor,* we encounter something of the logic behind the leniency in sentencing of Indians. An indigenous minor who was twenty-two years old confessed to having robbed a store of various items of clothing. His lawyer, significantly the Protector of Natives and not of Minors, argued in his defense, "Who would deny that because of my client's circumstance of double minority, due to both his age . . . and to his Indian condition [*condición Yndica*] that he should not be subject to the full rigor of the law but instead be treated with the greatest possible equity?" The young man was absolved of all charges against him in spite of his admission to the crime (AGN).[21] The minority status of Indian youths was thus a compound minority that in theory would afford them the most benevolent treatment in sentencing by judges.[22]

This leaves us with the *castas.* Why should *casta* youths—male and female alike—face the courts more frequently than other groups, particularly slaves? The answer may reside where private patriarchal authority ended and the public power of the colonial state began, in the state's imagined role as "substitute father" to the city's youths. Just as city officials acted on behalf of the king, "the father of all minors," when placing orphaned and vagrant youths in apprenticeships, the police and courts may have been more disposed to use their patriarchal right to arrest and criminally prosecute *casta* youths, who were less likely to have a private patriarch at home who could control and "correct" them. In seventeenth-century Lima, *castas* had the highest rates of illegitimacy in the city, and thus *casta* children would be the most likely group to be fatherless (Mannarelli 1994: 172).[23] Illegitimacy and the dissolution of families were also high among Indians and slaves. But, unlike Indian youths, *castas* did not enjoy the special privileges of "double minority," which might have secured them extrajudicial or lenient sentencing.

Furthermore, urban slave youths eventually would have to answer to private patriarchal authority in the form of a master rather than a father. The courts may have been hesitant to hear criminal cases against slave minors for fear of treading on the property or patriarchal rights of slave owners. In one case, the *curador ad litem* argued that the Cabildo had overstepped its authority in trying a fourteen-year-old slave for robbing his master. He stated that his client "enjoys the privilege of not being judicially accused . . . because he should be considered as a member of the household [*un familiar*] whose punishment is to be practiced at the discretion of his master" (AGN).[24]

Just as minors under the supervision of strong, white patriarchal figures appeared less often before public authority, a close examination of the families of young victims of rape in the city demonstrates that strong patriarchs were less likely to bring cases to court as accusers. In twenty-eight rape cases committed against Limeño minors in the Real Audiencia and Cabildo series, eighteen—the majority—were brought forward by single or widowed women, mostly but not always mothers, who were raising the children. In the nine cases where male heads of households brought charges, it almost inevitably turned out that they were nonwhite or were married to nonwhite women, had been absent from their homes when the rape occurred, and/or were economically struggling plebeians. Together, these cases create a composite "weak" patriarchal profile of the families of girls who were raped, a profile consistent with what other historians have demonstrated for other parts of colonial Spanish America (Castañeda 1983: 110).

The impossible demands of a society that expected young girls to be enclosed *(recogida)* confronted a colonial plebeian reality in which children were sent out to fetch, to work, and to play. Lower-class parents voiced their frustration at being unable to shelter their children from the streets beyond their homes (AGN).[25] Plebeian girls and boys played together in the patios of large housing complexes, ran errands alone in the streets, and worked outside parental supervision as street sellers and in trades. Furthermore, the crowded living quarters of plebeians often placed young girls in close contact with their rapists (AGN).[26]

When fathers did bring their daughters' cases of rape and seduction forward to be heard by public authority, rapists and seducers commonly alleged that their victims' families were in some way racially or class "deficient" and negligent when it came to protecting their daughters (AGN).[27] Susan Socolow (1980) surmised that in the very act of appearing before magistrates to report acts of violence committed against his wife or lover, a man was "publicly admitting his vulnerability, and the fact that he was too weak to seek his own retribution." Such a claim is borne out among the profiles of accusers in Lima, as the infrequent white father who brought a case forward claimed that he had access to private means of seeking vengeance but chose to defer to public authority (AGN).[28] Instances in which strong patriarchs relied on extrajudicial means of avenging their daughters' loss of honor would have left no traces in the court records. Therefore it was not only that plebeian girls were at greater risk for sexual attack that accounts for their appearance in the record but also that weak patriarchal families were more prone to appeal to the public authority of judges in matters of conflict and crime.

Changing Contexts, Changing Arguments, Static Sentencing

A Spanish traveler arriving in the viceregal capital in 1738 noted that not even one-tenth of the city's population could comprise whites, "the number of black men and women, mulattos, Indians and other such riff-raff [*gentalla*] being excessive" (Lanuzo y Sotelo 1998 [1738]). While the Spaniard's impression was somewhat exaggerated, censuses of the urban population demonstrate that between 1700 and 1790, peninsular and creole Spaniards *(blancos)* diminished in percentage from over half of the city's population (57 percent) to 38 percent. The relative population of black and Indian inhabitants also fell. Who, then, populated the capital? It was the racially mixed group of the *castas*—mulattos, *zambos,* and *chinos,* as well as *mestizos*[29]—that grew in number throughout the century. In the Numeration of 1700, the only category for people of mixed race with some degree of African descent was "mulatto." By the end of the century, there were at least six ("Plan demonstrativo" 1791; Cook 1985; Pérez Cantó 1985: 52). The very pluralization of such racial categories is related to the real increase in the mixed-race population of the city, but it also reflects an effort to control social and racial disorder there. The fracturing of socioracial categories into ever more specific groups also reflects increased efforts on the part of the colonial elite to define and segregate the nonwhite population by means of classification (Mörner 1967; Mörner 1970; Sánchez Albornoz 1974: 130; Flores Galindo 1988).

The image of racial disorder in the city coincided with "enlightened" changes in royal policy, transformations that were made manifest in attempts at "social engineering" in the city. The Bourbon reforms of the late eighteenth century were born in the Spanish metropole, but their implementation in Lima took on a decidedly local character. News of the rebellion of Túpac Amaru in the Peruvian highlands and the Haitian revolution reverberated throughout the capital, raising concerns over local plebeian riots and slave rebellions. Crime in city was thought to have reached epidemic proportions, and as Alberto Flores Galindo (1988: 128) comments, "popular classes and dangerous classes" began to become synonymous. I would add that "dangerous classes" and "youth" also began to become equated, as discourses concerning crime and "plebeians" increasingly began to turn on the question of how and when individuals became criminals.

Enlightenment ideas, emphasizing education and elevating childhood to a stage of life during which social values and practices become imprinted on human beings, began to steer judges toward a philosophy of reform. The idea was to "correct" wayward youths rather than to seek retribution for their misdeeds, and judges were warned that milder sentencing would ensure that the courts were not responsible for turning merely troublesome youths into hardened criminals. One *curador ad litem* summed up these overlapping discourses when, in encouraging leniency toward his young mulatto client, he stated, "men normally fall in the first years of their lives, when they are released from the yoke that is needed to contain them" (AGN).[30] Such ideas too were translated into Bourbon policies that attempted to generate greater economic productivity and order in the colonies by employing youths in "useful" occupations.

Before the last decades of the eighteenth century, attorneys arguing for reduced culpability had underscored their minor clients' lack of malice, limited forethought (*menos advertencia*), and imperfect comprehension. At the end of the century, *procuradores* continued using these arguments, but sprinkled them with references to the "docility" and "greater reliability" (*fidedignidad*) of the young and their greater potential to be "corrected" into proper subjects of the empire. In the midst of the Bourbon fervor to create economically productive subjects, the "correction" of youths took on a decidedly reformist character.

In 1773, a *curador ad litem* argued the case of Simona, a slave of ten or twelve accused of stabbing a youth who had insulted her (AGN).[31] The lawyer informed the *alcalde*, "the Law assumes [she possesses] . . . more docility in order to correct and reform her future actions." In another case, a *curador ad litem* openly warned the judge to "not impose a sentence that will make [my minor client] incorrigible in the future [rather] than moderate him in the present." This *procurador* took his argument so far as to deny the punitive function of justice entirely in cases involving minors, claiming that "the laws [on minors] were not established for vengeance, but to benefit the delinquent himself and to ensure public security" (AGN[32]; Chambers 1999: 195–96.)

In the pages of the elite periodicals *Mercurio Peruano, El Semanario Crítico,* and *El Diario de Lima,* "enlightened" discourses concerning education and child rearing were interlaced with local, urban preoccupations. From 10 to 14 October 1790, *El Diario de Lima* issued a series of articles concerning *"crianza"* (literally, child rearing) which, it was underscored, would be "of use" to judges as well as fathers and masters. And, in vintage Bourbon parlance, the anonymous author asserted that *"crianza"* would create subjects "useful to the homeland."

Such attention to child rearing may have been transplanted from Europe, but in Lima, where the terrain was already fertile with fears of fissures in the generational and racial order of the colony, these ideas became deeply rooted. A letter to the editor published in *El Diario* on 15 November 1790 took for granted that readers would concur that "in Peru youths squander their time, and learn nothing more than ridiculous slang." Others lamented that children had lost all respect for their parents—to the point that the little ones addressed them with the informal *"tú."* "What ideas do they have of filial respect and paternal authority?" begged one author (Filómates 1791); "Why do parents regard as a sign of love a condescension so contrary to the subordination and proper control of the people?" Guides to child rearing counseled parents to impress good customs and civil behavior on even older children, for inconsistent instruction would give rise to "those defects and pernicious evils that are the vices which are beginning to ripen" during adolescence ("Plan de educación" 1813).

Discourses concerning the hazards of juvenile pastimes, from dance to games of chance, smoothly combined with worries of crime and racial disorder (Estenssoro Fuchs 1996). The accusations of abetting a ten-year-old slave to rob his master laid against Blas Changay, an eighteen-year-old *mestizo* from the Cercado, illustrate the emergent discourses in the city. Don Tadeo Sandoval, the master of the young slave, first filed charges against Blas, asking the judge to issue the harshest punishment possible, because, he claimed Blas was a vice-ridden, card-playing vagrant, whose example would incite other slaves to steal from their masters if left unpunished.[33]

Such alarm bells sounded in a context where the real figures of juvenile delinquency do not appear to have increased in any discernible manner.[34] Court-appointed defenders of minors found themselves forced to respond to the coalescing image of derelict youths who lacked respect for private and public authority. Court officials, particularly judges, were positioned at a crossroads, confronting the legal system's old and contradictory mandate toward minors in a new context. At the end of the eighteenth century, they were besieged with the perceived dissolution of social order but also caught up in a current of new ideas about education and childhood that compelled them to use their authority to reform young criminals.

For the youngest of Lima's criminals, age might guarantee leniency. But for those approaching the "age of discretion," their fates in the criminal justice system were less determined by their status as minors than by their position in the colonial hierarchy. As judges decided for whom they would act as clement father and to whom they would mete out stern discipline, they consistently fell back on traditional principles of preferential sentencing. Soft sentencing for *español* minors was the exception proving the rule of preferential sentencing. When the pickpocket Josef Tunco, who, as mentioned, was of Spanish origin, was let free, no mention was made of the fifty-six pesos he robbed in the plaza. A fifteen-year-old *española* who admitted having robbed her neighbor of two hundred pesos was absolved with a gentle warning (AGN).[35] On the other hand, a ten-year-old slave who denied having stolen ten pesos from his owner was sentenced to be sold at one hundred leagues' distance from the city, a punishment that many slaves of the day associated with harsh labor and death on Peru's coastal haciendas (AGN).[36]

These and other cases suggest that the city's rhetoric of disorder and Enlightenment principles of reform were channeled through a court that continued to impose sentences to youths according to traditional laws on preferential sentencing. Bourbon social politics were aimed at restoring each individual to his or her proper place in society in order to maximize the colonies' productive capabilities. Lima's courts would find such productive spaces for *español* youths within the walls of the city, regardless of their prospects of being "corrected." On this the judges would insist, even on one occasion forcing a private subject to take on the role of "substitute father" for a rootless white youth (AGN).[37] Yet *casta* or slave minors often would be banished from Lima, expelled from the court's jurisdiction and distanced from its protective shelter. There was no proper place in the city for them.

Conclusion

The Bourbon search at the end of the eighteenth century for a productive place for young delinquents has guided us through the city's courts and interrogation rooms, leading us, in turn, to the city's formidable brick-and-mortar institutions such as workshops and bakeries. It also has carried us beyond the walls of the city, south toward the Presidio of Valdivia and north to coastal haciendas, to important institutions that functioned as repositories for youths expelled from the urban body politic. The creation of sites of punishment out of *presidios,* convents and workshops invites us to reconsider all such institutions not as *a priori* impediments to youth's activities beyond them, but as attempts to limit the real or perceived dangers youths might encounter or pose in the streets of the city. As such, it is imperative that historians treat institutions for raising youths not as colonial monoliths, but as dynamic reactions to changing realities.

Yet even during moments of historical change in the city, such as during the Bourbon Reforms, Lima's courts held constant to particularly colonial principles regarding minors. While the definition of legal minority was fixed in law, its application exposed the underside of a colonial society where the meanings of age depended on a complex combination of factors, the most important of which was the placement of individuals in the socioracial and gender hierarchies of the city. The variation and subjectivity of official attitudes toward youths are made obvious in the uses and abuses of the ambiguities of age—the concentration of arrests of "twenty-five-year-olds" and the manipulation of the letter and the spirit of the law on ages in criminal trials by colonial official, defendant, and accuser alike. Such divergent constructions of the meanings of legal minority were also obvious in sentences, where an Indian youth may enjoy the benefits of a "double minority," a slave might be turned over to his master for punishment, a *casta* youth sentenced to years of uncompensated labor "for the king" in a military outpost far from the city, and an *español* ragamuffin found a home within it.

Finally, these cases involving minors encourage us to revisit crucial methodological and theoretical questions concerning colonial criminal records. Few documents of the colonial period survive that can provide such rich and detailed evidence about everyday relations between families, *"familiares,"* and foes as those generated by conflict and crime. Evidence that the sons, daughters, servants, and slaves of weak patriarchal households were more prone to appear in the court system to seek formal as opposed to extralegal justice or to be accused of criminal activity may help focus future methodological inquiries more sharply on the question of who sought out the colonial courts and, in turn, whom the courts sought out. Rather than demonstrating "deviancy," patterns of crime among minors in Lima point to patriarchal "debility" (Stern 1995). Such "debility" was in many ways a functional *raison d'être* for the colonial justice system itself, as the courts used their power more frequently and punitively against youths who lacked what the court deemed acceptable private authority. The final irony may be that it was the very parents and guardians of such children who were most likely to seek justice from the colonial state.

Taking into account the colonial state's double mandate to be both clement patriarch and stern disciplinarian, we may begin to understand not only the tension in the rules governing the criminal tribunals of the Cabildo and the Real Audiencia, but also something of the colonial process itself. If we consider that the counsel of a *curador ad litem* was only one of the special protections—"corporate privileges," in a sense— that the state provided to colonial subjects, the colonial justice system appears to have offered some individuals benefits, however limited. These perceived protections were sought by lower-caste and class families time and again, as young subjects and their parents continually searched for small patches of legal shelter in their dealings with the court. Yet the court's willingness to protect minors was not easily swayed when it came to certain errant youth. Despite the accelerated social and political change in Lima during the end of the eighteenth century, judges continued to interpret the colonial prerogatives provided to the young in criminal cases according to their own version of the traditional political philosophy that linked father and king, child and colony—a version in which the visage of paternalism displayed by the court depended on which colonial "child" stood before it.

Notes

1 *"Español"* and *"española"* were terms applied to those considered to be of white European ancestry, whether born in Spain *(peninsulares)* or in the Americas *(criollos)*. The term displays the particularly colonial nature of the racial hierarchy in which those at the top were equated with the inhabitants of the mother country. The term *"niña"* literally meant "girl," but was commonly used for single *españolas* (women), as well.

2. Cabildo, 1782, Causas Criminales, legajo 7, cuaderno 4.

3. The author uses *"los padres,"* a term that in Spanish means both "parents" and "fathers." The term presents a continual problem of translation since it is unclear whether authors refer to both parents or only to fathers. I translate the word as "fathers" here because, in the seventeenth century, secular law tended to regard the father as supreme in matters relating to the family.

4. For treatments of eighteenth-century shifts in notions of passion, sexuality, and romantic love, see Ramón Gutiérrez, (1985) and Patricia Seed (1988).

5. For example, royal mandates repeated the order that the imprisonment of individuals should be in accordance with his or her "quality."

6. The first decree was in 1595. Similar decrees were issued against *españoles, mestizos,* and orphans in 1558 and 1609.

7. For the establishment of an institution for "orphans and beggars" see Fáctica del Cercado, 1770 legajo 1, suelto, "Sobre el Hospital de los Pobres en el antiguo Colegio del Cercado."

8. División de Cuarteles y Barrios e Instrucción para el Establecimiento de Alcaldes de Barrio en la Capital de Lima, 1785.

9. Protocolos Notariales, escribano Lucas de Bonilla, 145, folios 274–75.

10. Cabildo, 1774, Causas Criminales, legajo 5, cuaderno 18. Also see Cabildo, 1782, Causas Criminales, legajo 7, cuaderno 4, folio 6.

11. The accusations against an elite *español* student indicated that parents of "incorrigible" youths might send them to monastery schools. See Cabildo, 1806, Causas Criminales, legajo 11, cuaderno 17.

12. The *agente fiscal* could attempt to exaggerate the ages of very young suspects to guarantee that they would stand trial, as the case Josef Tunco demonstrates. See Cabildo, 1782, Causas Criminales, legajo 7, cuaderno 4, and compare folio 1 with folio 11v. Also see Cabildo, 1773, Causas Criminales, legajo 5, cuaderno 9.

13. Examples abound. For one of many, see Cabildo, 1717, Causas Criminales, legajo 1, cuaderno 5.

14. Cabildo, 1772, Causas Criminales, legajo 5, cuaderno 1, folio 43v. *Procuradores de menores* could be complicit in lowering the ages of their clients. See Cabildo, 1773, Causas Criminales, legajo 5, cuaderno 9; Real Audiencia, 1762, Causas Criminales, legajo 4, cuaderno 269.

15. Real Audiencia, 1756, Causas Criminales, legajo 18, cuaderno 209.

16. Real Audiencia, 1768, Causas Criminales, legajo 28, cuaderno 344 and 345.

17. Real Audiencia, 1809, Causas Criminales, legajo 116, cuaderno 1405, folios 1, 12, and 20.

18. Real Audiencia, 1809, Causas Criminales, legajo 116, cuaderno 1405, folio 54v.

19. Cabildo, 1773, Causas Criminales, legajo 5, cuaderno 14.

20. Cabildo, 1792, Causas Criminales, legajo 9, cuaderno 18.

21. Fáctica, Juzgado del Corregidor del Cercado o Sub-Delegado del Cercado, 1800, legajo 1, cuaderno 16, folio 29.

22. Indians were considered legal minors and were called "minors" in the court records (hence the use of the term "minors of age," in this chapter). In theory, Indians were to be treated with the greatest leniency possible before the law. "Greatest leniency possible" did not, of course, preclude whippings, beatings, and the death penalty and does not mean that *hacendados,* mine owners, *caciques,* and colonial officials did not punish Indians harshly and extrajudicially. But, in theory, Indians were not to receive maximum penalties in formal criminal sentencing and were to be represented in court by a lawyer, free of charge.

23. Certainly illegitimacy did not always imply abandonment by fathers, and a number of Lima's youths were probably children of long-term consensual unions. However, Mannarelli (1994) shows that there was in fact a correlation between illegitimate status and fatherlessness in seventeenth-century Lima.

24. Cabildo, 1789, Causas Criminales, legajo 9, cuaderno 2, folio 106.

25. See, for example, Real Audiencia, 1756, Causas Criminales, legajo 18, cuaderno 206 41v.

26. Real Audiencia, 1775, Causas Criminales, legajo 37, cuaderno 408.

27. Real Audiencia, 1757, Causas Criminales, legajo 19, cuaderno 217; Real Audiencia, 1775, Causas Criminales, legajo 34, cuaderno 410; Real Audiencia, 1797, Causas Criminales, legajo 80, cuaderno 1051; Real Audiencia, 1802, Causas Criminales, legajo 102, cuaderno 1244.

28. See Real Audiencia, 1762, Causas Criminales, legajo 24, cuaderno 272; Real Audiencia, 1752, Causas Criminales, legajo 15, cuaderno 161; Real Audiencia, 1775, Causas Criminales, legajo 34, cuaderno 410.

29. *"Mulato," "zambo,"* and *"chino"* were racial designations for those of various degrees of mixed African descent. *"Mestizo"* refers to those of mixed Spanish and Indian ancestry.

30. Cabildo, 1772, Causas Criminales, legago 5, cuaderno 1, folio 103v.

31. Cabildo, 1773, Causas Criminales, legajo 5, cuaderno 9.

32. Cabildo, 1798, Causas Criminales, legajo 10, cuaderno 19.

33. Cabildo, 1785, Causas Criminales, legajo 8, cuaderno 6, folio 1 and folio 10.

34. Patterns in arrests by "ordinary justice" among minors of age remained relatively constant during the period 1714 to 1813, although the total of individuals of all age groups arrested increased significantly during the 1780s, the decade of the most strident police reforms.

35. Cabildo, 1773, Causas Criminales, legajo 5, cuaderno 14.
36. Cabildo, 1789, Causas Criminales, legajo 9, cuaderno 2.
37. Cabildo, 1813, Causas Criminales, legajo 13, cuaderno 11.

References

AGN (Archivo General de la Nación [Lima, Peru]).

Arrom, Silvia Marina. 2001. *Containing the poor: The Mexico City Poor House, 1774–1871.* Durham, N.C.: Duke University Press.

BNP (Biblioteca Nacional del Peru [Lima]).

Boyer, Richard. 1989. Women, *la mala vida* and the politics of marriage. In *Sexuality and marriage in colonial Latin America*, edited by A. Lavrin. Lincoln: University of Nebraska Press.

Castañeda, Carmen. 1983. La memoria y las niñas violadas. In *La memoria y el olvido: Segundo Simposio de Historia de las Mentalidades.* Mexico: UNAM.

———. 1989. *Violación, estupro y sexualidad: Nueva Galicia 1790–1821.* Guadalajara: Editorial Hexágono.

Chambers, Sarah. 1999. *From subjects to citizens: Honor, gender and politics in Arequipa, Peru, 1780–1854.* University Park: Pennsylvania State University Press.

Cook, Noble David, ed. 1985. *Numeración general de todas las personas de ambos sexos, edades y calidades que se ha echo en esta Ciudad de Lima, año de 1700.* Lima: COFIDE.

Cutter, Charles. 1995. *The legal culture of northern New Spain, 1700–1810.* Albuquerque: University of New Mexico Press.

Escriche, Don Joaquín. 1851. *Diccionario razonado de legislación y jurisprudencia.* Paris.

Estenssoro Fuchs, Juan Carlos. 1996. La plebe ilustrada: El pueblo en las fronteras de la razón. In *Entre la retórica y la insurgencia: las ideas y los movimientos sociales en los Andes, Siglo XVIII*, edited by C. Walker. Cuzco: CERA Bartolomé de las Casas.

Filómates, Eustaquio [Demetrio Guasque?]. 1791. Educación: Carta escrita a la Sociedad sobre el abuso de que los hijos tuteen a sus padres. *Mercurio Peruano*, 27 January.

Flores Galindo, Alberto. 1988. *La ciudad sumergida: Aristocracia y plebe en Lima, 1760–1830.* Lima: Horizonte.

Gutiérrez, Ramón. 1985. Honor, ideology, marriage negotiation, and class–gender domination in New Mexico, 1690–1846. *Latin American Perspectives* 12(1): 81–104.

Juan y Colom, Joseph, 1761. *Instrucción de escribanos, en orden a lo judicial utilíssima también para procuradores, y litigantes, donde sucintamente se explican lo ritual, y forma de proceder en las Causas Civiles, y Criminales, assi en la Theoria, como en la Práctica.* Madrid.

Lanuzo y Sotelo Eugenio. 1998 [1738]. *Viaje ilustrado a los Reinos de Perú.* Lima: PUCP.

Lavrin, Asunción, ed. 1988. *Sexuality and marriage in colonial Latin America.* Lincoln: University of Nebraska Press.

―――. 1994. *Lo femenino:* Women in colonial historical sources. In *Coded encounters: Writing, gender and ethnicity in colonial Latin America,* edited by F.J. Cevallos-Candau, et al. Amherst: University of Massachusetts Press.

Lipsett-Rivera, Sonya. 1997. The intersection of rape and marriage in late-colonial and early-national Mexico. *Colonial Latin American Historical Review* 6(4): 559–90.

Machado de Chávez y Mendoza, Juan, 1646. *El perfeto confesor y cura de almas.* 2 vols. Barcelona.

Mannarelli, María Emma. 1994. *Pecados públicos: La ilegitimidad en Lima, siglo XVII.* Lima: Flora Tristán.

Mörner, Magnus. 1967. *Race mixture in the history of Latin America.* Boston: Little, Brown.

―――. 1970. *Estado, razas y cambio social en la Hispanoamérica colonial.* Mexico City: SepSetentas.

Pérez Cantó, María Pilar. 1985. *Lima en el siglo XVIII: Estudio socioeconómico.* Madrid: Ediciones de la Universidad Autónoma de Madrid.

Plan de educación. 1813. *El Investigador,* 22 August.

Plan demostrativo de la población comprendida en el recinto de la ciudad de Lima. 1791. *Mercurio Peruano,* 3 February.

Recopilación de leyes de los reynos de las Indias, mandada imprimir, y publicar por la magestad Católica del Rey Don Carlos II, Nuestro Señor. 1756 [1683]. Madrid.

Röggenbuck, Stefan. 1996. Historia social de la infancia callejera limeña. *Apuntes* 39: 89–112.

Sánchez Albornoz, Nicolás, 1974. *The population of Latin America: A history.* Berkeley: University of California Press.

Scardaville, Michael C. 1994. (Hapsburg) law and (Bourbon) order: State authority, popular unrest, and the criminal justice system in Bourbon Mexico City. *The Americas* 50(4): 501–26.

Seed, Patricia. 1988. *To love, honor and obey in colonial Mexico: Conflicts over marriage choice, 1574–1821.* Stanford, Calif.: Stanford University Press.

Las siete partidas del sabio rey don Alonso el IX, glosados por el Lic. Gregorio López. 1767 [1265]. Valencia.

Socolow, Susan M. 1980. Women and crime: Buenos Aires, 1757–97. *Journal of Latin American Studies* (May): 39–57.

Stern, Steve J. 1995. *The secret history of gender: Women, men and power in late colonial Mexico.* Chapel Hill: University of North Carolina Press.

Sylvestre, Don Manuel. 1765. *Librería de jueces, ultilísima, y universal para toda clase de personas literarias.* Madrid.

6

The State, the Family, and Marginal Children in Latin America

Donna J. Guy

How important have children been to public officials in Latin America, and how can we trace evolution and change in their treatment? The attitudes of public authorities toward marginal children and the changing legal definition of the child in the nineteenth and twentieth centuries reflect the interactions of private individuals and the state. Whereas it is impossible to recount how people generally viewed the social value of children over the course of this period, the public policies of child welfare do offer certain useful clues. This essay focuses on Spanish America, with primary emphasis on Argentina.

Until recently, most historical studies of Latin American families focused on issues of honor, work, marriage, and divorce. Children, when discussed, were often linked to women's issues, the rise of Latin American feminism, and campaigns for protective labor legislation. In the 1990s, however, a new literature appeared that treats children as the principal subject (see, for example, Kuznesof and Oppenheimer 1985; Lipsett-Rivera 1998; Lavrin 1991; Gonzalbo Aizpuru and Rabell 1994; García Méndez and Carranza 1992; Pilotti and Rizzini 1995; Ciafardo 1992; Pilotti 1994; Barrancos 1994; Guy 2000; Varley 2000; and, for a pioneer in the field, Suriano 1990). The history of the welfare state in Latin America is also limited, but growing (see, for example, Passanante

1987; Gomes 1992; Recalde 1991; Mesa-Lago 1978; Guy 1998; Moreno 2000; and Guy 2001).

The links between the history of childhood and the rise of the welfare state are significant, if insufficiently studied, because, from the 1920s onward, child welfare issues became a measurement of modern programs. Yet the historiography of welfare began as an effort to study the impact of workers' demands for protective legislation and fairer compensation. Recently, policies dealing with mothers have attracted attention. Now it is time to focus on the history of welfare in policies regarding children, whose protection and correction were not the exclusive province of private charities, as has been believed traditionally. Instead they became the targets of a series of state-directed campaigns. Of specific concern, particularly to lawyers, was the campaign to get children off urban streets and out of jail and to get juvenile delinquents into reformatories. To achieve this goal, the state had to construct new institutions.

Beginning with an initial concern for abandoned infants and older orphans, Latin American public policy, particularly in urban areas, soon embraced maternal aid. Infant mortality rates were high, and the number of abandoned infants increased rapidly with the growth of urban areas. It was beyond the financial capacity of most Latin American countries, however, to accommodate all abandoned children in orphanages, particularly in cities experiencing massive European immigration or migration from impoverished rural areas.[1] Programs of education, forced labor, or jail were often the alternatives. In the 1920s the need to expand public education and establish institutions for wayward children became more pressing, and this highlighted the situation of older children.

The plight of older children caught up in the legal system moved lawyers and jurists to redefine the nature of childhood and the culpability of children. Juveniles needed education rather than punishment. Basing their ideas on a mixture of positivism, criminal anthropology, and biotypology, early reformists had great faith in good families, proper education, and sanitary homes rather than punishment as the solution to the perceived delinquency of children on the street. Advances in the United States, particularly the formation of juvenile courts after 1899, proved influential (see chapter 7). By the 1920s, the rise of social workers as well as the incipient welfare state led to new forms of residential institutions for older street children and juvenile delinquents. The extent of the problem, as well as the ability to finance new institutions, often affected the success of the programs. Countries such as Argentina had high rates of literacy, for example, while Brazil's general literacy rate was abysmal, although great progress was made in urban areas.

World economic depression, fears of working-class unrest, and the rise of welfare states in Europe and the United States prompted Latin American states in the 1930s to be more determined than ever to promote the well-being of children. They enacted new codes that covered all children and redefined the relationship not only between the child and the state but also between the family and the state. These more ambitious programs were unfocused and expensive and gave rise to underfunded bureaucracies. Though admirable in tone, their desire to help all children, not just marginal ones, created more problems than it solved Equally important, welfare policies placed great strains on families by challenging traditional patriarchal rights and threatening to remove children from parental custody if the children broke laws. If officials took children away from parents or scooped them up off the streets, then the state had to both house and educate the waifs. These realities foreshadowed the contemporary crisis of street children and draw attention to the long history of child welfare initiatives in the Americas.

Childhood, according to the various nineteenth-century civil codes, was embedded in the patriarchal property rights of legally constituted families. Upon the basis of the principles established in the Napoleonic civil code, fathers had not only the duty to feed, clothe, and educate children to the best of their ability but also the right to discipline them, select their occupations, and, for those who had not reached to age of majority—usually between the ages of twenty-one and twenty-five—sanction their marital plans. In return, children had to obey their parents and work for them without wages.

Prior to the rise of the welfare state, parents, particularly fathers, had the principal legal responsibility for minor children. The patriarchal right was a double-edged sword. It meant that men had to acknowledge paternity in order to have a legal heir, and at the same time such acknowledgment meant that fathers had to support their offspring. Single mothers were left with all the stigma and responsibilities of raising a child unrecognized by the father, and often could not support their offspring (see chapters 3 and 4).

Civil codes emphasized rights and responsibilities on the part of children and parents alike, and some, as in Chile, went so far as to proclaim that children should defer more to their fathers than to their mothers (Chile 1886). The laws said little about love and affection, although that did not mean that such sentiments did not exist, or that childhood and children were simply viewed as economic instruments to perpetuate family names and reputations.

Fathers were not the only relatives who watched out for the legal and social interests of their children. At the same time that laws began to define the patriarchal family, the strong influence of family kinship—that is, the intervention of godparents, grandparents, brothers, and cousins—often determined the fate of children whose parents could not take care of them. And, although laws rarely mentioned it, married and single mothers shouldered the principal responsibilities of child rearing and had little protection, while widows did not automatically get legal control of minors. In Brazil, widows needed court approval to administer the property of children, a reality that continued into the early twentieth century. Elsewhere they often became legal guardians, but the courts were swift to criticize them and take custody away. If such a woman remarried, the new husband assumed custody, leaving her with scant legal protection.

The 1866 Mexican civil code, promulgated during the French occupation of Mexico but soon supplanted by another in 1872, was typical of laws that gave primary legal responsibility to fathers. If the father died or disappeared, it placed the financial burden of protecting orphans (fatherless children, or those with no surviving parents) on other family members, but not on the mother. According to the law, orphaned children were made the responsibility of their ascendant relatives, such as grandparents, who had a legal obligation to feed and educate them. Brothers and sisters were also legally responsible for their younger siblings (Imperio Mexicano 1866: chapter 4, articles 145–46). Code law mirrored common practices. As Ann Blum (1998: 241) points out for late-nineteenth-century Mexico, "uncodified practice remained strongly linked to ritual kinship." While relatives could exploit or abandon children as easily as parents could, there is a rich body of evidence to show that families preferred to rely on kin rather than expose children to the public system of orphanages and homes.

Many families were able to assume the burden of caring for minor relatives, but others could not, or would not. The burden was particularly heavy for the poor, and the stigma of illegitimacy could make children undesirable. Children whose kin could not care for them were thus the foremost concerns of public authorities, church officials, and charities. In the colonial period judges or defenders of minors were named by public authorities to handle the legal affairs of these children. Orphanages, at first run by female religious and later, in certain countries, taken over by the state after independence, housed some of the infants and youngsters found on city streets or whose kin turned them over to public authorities with the hope that they would be fed and sheltered.

Early-nineteenth-century Latin American governments, whether national or local, most often acted to protect the welfare of infants and, when possible, help orphans or street children. Such children, whose ages ranged from newborn to the age of majority, have been found on city streets from the colonial era to the present. According to Mark Szuchman, early-nineteenth-century Buenos Aires was depicted by novelist Esteban Echeverría as a place where "everyone was surrounded by the poorly clad children." Szuchman (1982: 58) attributed this to high rates of infant abandonment: "In the parish of Monserrat, 6.1 percent of white and 2.9 percent of colored children baptized in 1840 had been abandoned; in the parish of Concepción, 19.2 percent of the baptized white children were without parents. In Catedral al Norte, the figure stood at 15.5 percent for whites and 31.3 percent for *pardos* and *morenos,* while in 1846 the parish of Chascomús witnessed 45.9 percent of births—nearly all whites—involving abandoned children." While Szuchman may have attributed the presence of poorly clad children to abandonment, other explanations range from the impact of the wars of independence to the living conditions of the freed and enslaved population forced to leave their children on the streets when they went to work. In any case, the presence of children in the streets was equated with parental abandonment and led to the popularity of the late-nineteenth-century French legal term "moral abandonment," which was often applied to children not at school or at home (Schafer 1997).

Evidence from late-nineteenth- and early-twentieth-century Argentina indicates that few abandoned children were returned to their families. This was true both of infants and of older children. In the twentieth century, according to Alejandro E. Bunge (1984 [1940]: 175), as illegitimacy rates declined in Buenos Aires to between 10 and 12 percent of births, they remained consistently higher in the rest of the country, ranging from more than 38 percent in 1910 to more than 40 percent in 1938. According to a report given at the Second Conference on Abandoned Children, held in Buenos Aires in 1944, no more than one-third of abandoned children usually returned to their families. These realities were confirmed historically. In 1909, for example, 1,286 children were abandoned in Buenos Aires, but only 346 were returned to their families. More than 1,000 children per year were abandoned in Buenos Aires until 1925, when 955 children were found and 236 returned. By 1941, however, 149 children out of 470 were returned to families. At that time there were few orphans and abandoned infants in Buenos Aires, the majority of babies sent to the city's main infant orphanage, the Casa de Expósitos of the Sociedad de Beneficencia (Society of Beneficence), having been born in the countryside or in other provinces (Patronato de la Infancia 1944: 366).

Children not returned to families were initially sent to orphanages. This was particularly true of infants, who constituted the majority of abandoned children until World War I and who, owing to epidemics, general unsanitary conditions, and the lack of appropriate food, suffered the highest mortality rates.

Chilean orphans in Santiago rarely survived to be taken in by families. The principal orphanage, founded in the mid–eighteenth century, the Casa de Huérfanos—like the Casa de Expósitos in Buenos Aires— was secularized in the 1820s and placed under the control of city officials (Salinas Meza 1991; Little 1980; Moreno 2000). Between 1770 and 1929 more than one hundred thousand newborns were left at Chilean orphanages, the great majority illegitimate, and from 70 to 80 percent did not survive the first seven years of life. Based upon these statistics, René Salinas Meza (1991: 320) estimated that one infant in ten was abandoned in Chile, and this did not include older children. In Chile, infant abandonment in the Casa de Huérfanos was a death sentence for many babies.

Street children whose families could not provide for them were dealt with by public and private charities. Differences in infant mortality rates were linked as much to indifference and poor sanitary conditions as to incomplete statistics or occasional epidemics. In Argentina, despite the massive European immigration that caused admissions to the Casa de Expósitos to soar, 13,907 children entered the Casa between 1850 and

1895, and the mortality rate ranged from a high of 54 percent during years of epidemics to a low of 10.5 percent. Carefully maintained records indicate that in Buenos Aires infant mortality rates were indeed much lower than in Santiago (Little 1980: 109–10).

The case of Mexico was somewhat different, with far fewer children sent to the Casa de Cuna, or Foundling Hospital, in Mexico City. Nevertheless, infant mortality rates often reached the proportions of the institution in Chile. Little more than a vestige of eighteenth-century charity, the Casa de Cuna was supposed to care for abandoned infants but it was used for many other purposes. It also operated as "a hospital for children of all classes, a place for parents of congenitally ill or deformed babies to send them to die, [and as] a boarding house for the orphaned wards and illegitimate children of propertied families" (Blum 1998: 244–45). The use of the Casa de Cuna as a dumping ground for unwanted and ill babies led to high mortality rates. This tendency to send infants to the home persisted until the end of the nineteenth century, when the numbers of children sent to the institution began to soar and increased 120 percent by 1910, as compared with figures for the 1870s (Blum 1998: 251).

By then, the rapid population growth of cities such as Mexico City, Santiago, and Buenos Aires was reflected in the population of abandoned or orphaned children. In the Mexican capital more contact was maintained between the interned children and their kin than in the other institutions, because working mothers left their children to be cared for in the Casa de Cuna. The home, in effect, was turned into a day-care facility by parents, but the fact that parents visited the children did not seem to affect mortality rates.

In nineteenth-century Argentina, elite women of the Sociedad de Beneficencia operated the principal infant and children's orphanages. Subsidized by income from the national lottery and private donations, their facilities housed thousands of children. Although survival rates there were much better than in Santiago, leaving a child at the foundling wheel (functioning until 1892), or with the matrons who operated the society, gave that child little assurance of survival. For children whose parents left no record of identity, death was not the only bleak prospect. Indeed, these nameless children were recorded, until the 1940s, the same way as victims of military disappearances in the 1970s and 1980s: stigmatized by the initials N. N., meaning "Ningún Nombre," or "No

Name." Without names they had no social existence. The nuns in charge gave the children first and second names, and their matriculation number served as a last name unless they were allowed to use their foster family's name. Once they reached the age of majority, if they had no surname, they usually took the name Expósito (foundling). Until the 1940s, it was either forbidden or very difficult to incorporate these babies legally into families as legitimate heirs (Little 1980; Guy 1994).

The children in these institutions were different from protected children in a number of ways. First, most had no family to protect or care for them. This meant that they had no social identity that would shape their education and training. The situation was even bleaker for children abandoned at birth and left with no identification. They had no family names, traditions, or relatives. Although Uruguay permitted legal adoption as early as 1893, few other countries allowed full adoption, and this made it difficult for children brought into a family to be afforded the same legal status as biological offspring. Instead, popular practices led to either the falsification of civil registers to circumvent the absence of complete adoption or the use of nonbiological children as servants (República Oriental del Uruguay 1893).

In Argentina and throughout Latin America, reports of high infant mortality rates caused more embarrassment than reports of older children being abandoned. Lack of care for infants remained an index of backwardness and posed problems for the future because each child lost diminished the body politic. Older children, in contrast, could fend for themselves. The overwhelming desire to lower infant mortality rates thus initially generated greater emphasis on public health campaigns directed at the relationship between the state and mothers than on a direct relationship between the state and children. Out of this concern emerged a Latin American feminist movement that argued for mothers to be given even greater legal responsibilities within the family and for more state aid to help poor mothers (Lavrin 1995; Stoner 1991; Besse 1996: chapter 4).

Women, both feminist and conservative, defended their right to share legal custody over their children and insisted on the state's obligation to provide hospitals and clinics for poor women. Argentine feminists helped organize the first child congresses in 1913 and called for a hemispheric meeting of child specialists. Buenos Aires thus hosted the first Pan American Child Congress in 1916, and this became an important venue for pediatricians, child educators, juvenile delinquency experts, and lawyers to examine the situation of abandoned, poor, delinquent, ill, and handicapped children, thus promoting public discussion about how to help children. At the end of each congress, experts made recommendations for legal reforms that would expand governmental interest in, and supervision of, diverse groups of youths.

The Argentine Sociedad de Beneficencia, unlike the self-identified feminists, did not have the luxury of focusing principally on the rights of mothers and infants. For the few older children the society could accommodate, orphanages were often workhouses where children remained until they were sent out for foster care, often as servants. The number of children cared for by such organizations initially was much smaller than the number of infants, and a far greater number of older children ended up on the streets or temporarily housed in jails or various charitable institutions founded by religious and secular groups. Nevertheless, 36,880 noninfants entered the institutions of the Sociedad de Beneficencia between 1852 and 1935 (Sociedad de Beneficencia 1936: 81), 33,577 left, and only 138 died. Most were admitted in the twentieth century, after private donations helped the society open new orphanages, and the children in these facilities did not include the tens of thousands helped by other organizations operating in the capital, including the Patronato de la Infancia (The Children's Trust) and the Casa del Niño (Children's Home), and by immigrant communities (Patronato de la Infancia 1993).[2]

The emphasis on infant abandonment and mother–child relations also did not help municipal authorities in Buenos Aires deal with street children. Thousands of older orphans and street children were cared for by the municipal defenders of minors, although they had no residential or educational facilities. By the mid-1880s the defenders in Buenos Aires found themselves swamped with abandoned children but unable to house them. In 1885 the city defenders received 809 children, and within three years the number had jumped to 1,307. In 1898 a total of 1,878 children entered the care of these defenders, and thereafter the numbers began to taper off (Ministerio de Justicia e Instrucción Pública, 1886–1920: 1886 edition, 1: 69, 72; 1889 edition, 1: 131, 136; 1899 edition, 1: 120, 141). Most of these children were placed in foster care as domestic servants.

After 1888, the situation began to deteriorate for children in the care of city defenders. At that time, only 24 percent of children were returned to relatives, while 74 percent were placed with strangers. Ten years later the situation had deteriorated even more, with 5 percent of children being returned to relatives and only 44 percent finding foster parents. The rest had to remain institutionalized, often in jails. By this time the number of children still under the custody of the defenders began to mount, particularly after the police began rounding up children as vagrants. By the 1890s most children reached the defenders after having been incarcerated, and many spent years in jails along with criminals just for having no place to live (Ministerio de Justicia e Instrucción Pública 1886–1920: 1904 edition, 115).

A glimpse into the record of the number of young girls incarcerated in Buenos Aires jails gives a poignant view of the limited resources of the defenders. Noninfant girls were more frequently abandoned than were boys, but they were easier to place as domestic servants. Nevertheless, defenders never had enough jobs for either group, and the number of young girls spending time in jail for being vagrant began to rise sharply. In 1897, as a result of judicial orders, 767 girls were placed alongside convicted criminals. By 1904 the number had increased to 1,072 and by 1913 to 1,532 (Buenos Aires Municipality 1906; AGN).[3]

In other Latin American countries, as in Argentina, older children left to be cared for in private and public institutions were taken in as household help. Indeed, most civil codes declared that biological children should not be paid for helping their parents, while at the same time they protected foster children from having to render unpaid forced labor by requiring a salary to be paid. This was true in the workshops and in foster homes. In Argentina, contracts drawn up by the women who operated the children's orphanages stipulated that the foster parent, usually a woman, not only pay the child a salary but also offer care, education, and appropriate food and shelter. The number of children who ran away from foster homes was a clear indication that the contracts did little to ensure good treatment of youngsters by their employers or foster families (Guy 1994: 222–23).

Within the confines of state- and church-operated orphanages for older children, youngsters were educated for basic literacy and to prepare for a trade, and they were paid minimal salaries. Even jails, which often served as temporary warehouses for street children, had classes in literacy skills and trades for which inmates were paid a pittance. Girls were usually taught domestic skills that could get them jobs outside as maids, seamstresses, laundresses, and cooks. Boys more often were given vocational classes in printing, electrical work, and farming to prepare them to join the paid labor force outside the home.

Children under the legal authority of the Sociedad de Beneficencia could expect a minimum education and lots of work from age six onward. Since the society operated both a boys' and a girls' orphanage, the gendered nature of child manual labor was evident. In 1877 the Asilo de Huérfanas, or Girls' Orphanage, reported that the girls had earned 16,745 pesos, mostly by washing curtains and making jams (AGN).[4] By the 1880s the training offered at the orphanage had expanded to meet the needs of a modern city. In 1886 the Unión Telefónica requested more girls from the orphanage to be trained as operators. Nevertheless, washing and cooking remained the principal work for orphans, and gradually sewing replaced washing curtains (AGN).[5]

Education for girls consisted of vocational manual training rather than academic skills. By 1900 orphaned girls received six years of schooling, and in each grade they were taught different sewing skills. For example, in the fifth grade they learned how to embroider with white, silk, and gold threads. Fourth-grade girls learned general embroidering and some cooking skills. According to the society's annual report, the youngest schoolgirls learned principles of dressmaking (Sociedad de Beneficencia 1900: 5). What began as education soon functioned as a factory routine. A 1910 letter from the Asilo de Huérfanas indicated that there was little time for traditional schooling. By then there were five workshops: embroidery, dressmaking, laundry, and the preparation of underwear and clothing for the children, and a workshop to prepare jams and pastry. Each operated from 8:00 to 11:30 A.M. and from 1:30 to 4:30 P.M. daily except Wednesdays, when the children cleaned up. All fifth and sixth grade girls (as well as those third graders who "for lack of intellectual capacity" were destined for manual work) labored in the workshops. Younger girls attended a "work" class (*clase de labores*) to learn how to wash laundry and make clothing for other inmates. Within this regimen, students could select what type of work they preferred (AGN).[6]

In addition to the general work performed in the workshops, the Sociedad de Beneficencia constantly sought contracts for work from government or commercial entities. On a number of occasions the ladies approached the military to provide employment for the girls. To make the work of their charges both competitive and enticing, on at least one occasion the society tried to undercut competition from factories by offering the services of orphans at no salary. Despite the desire to obtain low bids, not even the military could accept such conditions (AGN).[7]

Female street children under the protection of the defenders of minors often ended up in the Casa Correccional de Mujeres (Women's Correctional Facility) if they could not be sent into domestic service. Officially, girls' ages ranged from five to twenty, yet there is evidence that babies often accompanied their mothers. There, in accordance with their age and labor performed, they received a minimal salary (Ministerio de Justicia e Instrucción Pública 1886–1920: 1903 edition). By the time the first national prison census was taken in 1906, the facility had the capacity to hold 100 adults and 150 minors at one time, operated first- and second-grade primary school classes for illiterate women and children, and provided training in laundry and sewing workshops (Ministerio de Justicia e Instrucción Pública 1886–1920: 1909 edition, 94–95). Eventually the prison offered classes through the fourth grade and often housed more than 1,000 minors for short periods.

The number of girls entering the jail varied tremendously from year to year. During a short stay in the women's jail, all young girls were expected to work. They labored long hours in shops, sewing and doing laundry. Wages were meager at best, partly because most girls did not stay long, but also because they had to pay for all the materials they used.

Boys, regardless of whether they lived in the Asilo de Huérfanos (Boys' Orphanage) or were fostered out by either the defenders or the Sociedad de Beneficencia, all faced very different work situations. For one thing, they were initially targeted as ideal recruits for military service. Officials reasoned that the boys, lacking fathers, belonged to the fatherland. This policy took effect as early as 1874, when the Sra. Jacinta Castro, an orphanage employee, created the Maipú Batallion to train the boys in military maneuvers (Meyer Arana 1911, 1: 372–73). The orphanage was so committed to military education that its leaders criticized public schools for excluding it and accused them of "feminizing" boys instead of teaching them to defend the nation. If other young men learned how to work to defend the nation, then they, too, would be ideal candidates for military service (Sociedad de Beneficencia 1900: 153–254).[8]

The Sociedad de Beneficencia may have been delighted with this form of vocational training, but neither the army nor the navy was particularly pleased with the recruits. Although military officials occasionally contacted the orphanage for musicians for the military band, they often rejected children who, they claimed, could not accustom themselves to military discipline. The boys were also poorly schooled (AGN).[9] Furthermore, some educators hired by the Asilo de Huérfanos believed that a military career was not necessarily the ideal vocation for orphans. Buenos Aires defenders experienced similar obstacles placing minor boys in the military. In 1894 the defender for the southern part of Buenos Aires complained about the experience of some thirty minors sent to several battalion units. They were supposed to be paid two pesos per month once they reached the age of fifteen. Some were sent as musical apprentices. But the defender saw these placements as appropriate only for the most incorrigible. The vast majority were placed in private homes because businesses did not want to take in unruly juveniles (Ministerio de Justicia e Instrucción Pública 1886–1920: 1894 edition, Report of Defensor, 1: 131–46).[10]

One temporary solution employed by defenders was to ship juvenile boys out to the southern territories to work on sheep and cattle ranches. This was done in the belief that urban areas held greater potential to corrupt young boys than rural areas. Some boys were sent away without their parents' permission. In response to complaints about gangs of street urchins, the Buenos Aires defender who covered the lower-class southern side of Buenos Aires announced in 1907 that during the previous year he had petitioned courts to remove the *patria potestad,* or parental rights, of parents who were "incapacitated, inappropriate, or who had abandoned" their sons. During the next few years there was an intensive campaign to rid the city of these boys by sending them, under court order, to work on ranches or "industries" in the National Territories. Most of them ran away from their caretakers, who used them as sources of cheap labor (Ministerio de Justicia e Instrucción Pública 1886–1920: 1906 edition, 110; 1910 edition, 115–16).

Within the Sociedad de Beneficencia, boys ended up in the workshops of the Asilo de Huérfanos (Boys' Orphanage). There they were given technical education and apprenticeships that would offer them employment in the industrial sector.[11] The orphanage conducted a series of workshops that included tailoring, shoemaking, printing, carpentry, and electrical and mechanical work. In the case of shoemaking, the ladies of the society tried to make the shoes more marketable by pricing them 20 percent lower than similar articles. To their dismay, their offers were rejected. Apparently shoe stores preferred to pay a higher price for their merchandise than risk accusations of exploiting orphan labor (Sociedad de Beneficencia 1900: 185).[12]

In contrast to the situation of the girls, the boys were expected to support themselves. In 1900, the purchase of new machinery for the workshops was financed entirely from the proceeds of child labor (Sociedad de Beneficencia 1900: 5). In its report on income produced by the boys, the society boasted of how well the regime functioned and argued that the "education and apprenticeship" received at the Asilo de Huérfanos could be quantified and that such information augured well for the future of the orphans, since such training would benefit them throughout their lives (Sociedad de Beneficencia 1900: 202).

The following year the annual report of the society expressed great optimism about the prospects of obtaining income from boys' labor, suggesting that they had just begun to tap this resource. At the same time they lauded these prospects, they were careful to assert that the nature of the institution was "not purely commercial, but eminently charitable." For that reason government funds should be utilized to "educate, form, and prepare men for the nation." The fact remains that most of the money was used to furnish the workshops with the latest machinery (Sociedad de Beneficencia 1901: 294).

In 1904 the society provided statistics showing the actual costs of educating and maintaining each child. Clearly the children could not support themselves despite the income derived from their labor. Nevertheless the Asilo de Huérfanas (Girls' Orphanage) was a bargain, mostly because the cost of the girls' industrial training—that is, hand sewing and washing—was so low. In contrast to the boys' industrial training, which cost 74.39 pesos per child, girls only needed 14.35 pesos of training each year. This in turn reduced maintenance costs (AGN).[13]

The defenders continued to believe that young boys should be self-sufficient. In his annual report for 1910, Defender Castellanos stated that at least 60 percent of all the boys he received from the courts as juvenile offenders ranged from ten to sixteen years old, were illiterate, and had no trade. Castellanos believed that they should be schooled so that not only "would the state obtain useful citizens for the nation, it would also save important sums of money spent on feeding so many vagrants and vicious boys." He defined education in terms of apprenticeships that would educate them and permit them to save some money while reducing the costs of feeding them. Unfortunately most of these boys were never apprenticed or learned a trade because there was no place to train them (Ministerio de Justicia e Instrucción Pública 1886–1920: 1911 edition, 95).

In the early twentieth century, children made up a significant portion of the Buenos Aires industrial labor force. According to Juan Suriano, children were often apprenticed in factories, without pay, for up to three months. Between 1904 and 1914, however, the percentage of children in factories declined from 10.4 to 3.2, due to protective labor laws and demands that children stay in school (Suriano 1990: 262, 272).

Apprenticeship patterns in public institutions paralleled those seen among private families who sent older children to serve in other families. Implicit in these agreements in which children were offered to potential employers was the obligation on the part of the host family to feed, clothe, and train these charges. It is quite likely that poor or disintegrating families sent their young out to foster care with great frequency. Public officials found out about these arrangements only when they went awry and the biological families went to court to retrieve their children. María Aguirre, for example, went to court in Buenos Aires in 1899 in order to apply to have her new husband named guardian of her fourteen-year-old daughter Mercedes. Seven years earlier, after her husband died, María had sent her daughter to Buenos Aires with a Captain Vicente Posadas, who placed the girl in apprenticeship in what he believed to be a very reputable home. To María's dismay, the host family refused to acknowledge that María was the biological mother and denied her visitation rights. She was horrified to find out that her daughter had not learned to read or write, despite the fact that the family had promised to prepare her for employment. María, herself illiterate, wanted a better life for her daughter, but Mercedes's foster family had not lived up to María's expectations. The judge ordered the foster family to relinquish the child in accordance with María's wishes (AGN).[14]

There were many Marías in Latin America who placed their children in apprenticeships with wealthier families in the hope that they would be educated and learn a trade. In societies where there were few factories and many home workshops (talleres), children were rarely paid if they worked for their families, but often paid a small amount if they were apprenticed to a nonfamily member. The biological families did not have to feed and clothe the children, and their offspring learned how to fend for themselves.

During this period, governments rarely interfered in the child-rearing practices of legally constituted families. They also let orphanages take care of abandoned and orphaned children as their administrators thought best, often subsidizing some of the institutions, but rarely questioning their mission unless issues of hygiene or safety were involved. Thus heads of institutions and defenders of minors, as well as heads of families, were empowered to make most decisions regarding Latin American children so long as governments chose not to intervene.

A 1938 government report by the League of Nations criticized public entities like the Sociedad de Beneficencia and claimed that foster care was "less satisfactory than in other countries because the Argentine Republic is an immigrant country where working-class families . . . are very large. Owing to their precarious economic situation and the fact that they are obliged to move from place to place in search of work, it is these families that supply the largest number of children who have to be educated at state expense in official institutions" (League of Nations 1938: 208). (Although this was true for Buenos Aires, in the interior most abandoned children were native-born and the offspring of mestizo parents.) Despite the criticism, the accompanying statistics for the Sociedad de Beneficencia proudly indicated that 9,722 children had been placed in homes between 1865 and 1937, twice as many girls as boys and most during the period from 1889 to 1919. The society claimed that less than 10 percent of the children had been returned. All foster parents had paid five pesos per month to the society, which, in turn, placed the money in a bank account until the child reached the age of legal majority. What the children did for this pay was not discussed (League of Nations 1938: 209).

The early efforts of the Uruguayan government to regulate foster care for abandoned children received the praise of the League of Nations, which commended the Uruguayan system of childcare as the best in Latin America. It noted that a Public Relief Law in 1910 had extended state support for infant orphans to minors aged between 8 and 14 housed in the Larrañaga Orphanage. According to the League, "Children are never placed in families without a preliminary observation period in which their physical characteristics and the environmental conditions in which they were living at the time when they were abandoned are carefully studied. The choice of foster-mothers is made under very exacting conditions, and both the children and the foster-mothers are kept directly under the close supervision of the establishment [i.e., the Children's Council] through the medium of district doctors and the appropriate social workers" (League of Nations 1938: 210). Perhaps even more critical was the fact that the Uruguayan state, following the French model, paid parents to care for the children rather than insisting that the children be paid a wage. Families that chose no subsidy were further scrutinized regarding the "motives that led the family to ask for a child, and the family's means and its respectability" (League of Nations 1938: 211). This, in effect, prevented exploitation of children without distinguishing them as paid servants.

While the Sociedad de Beneficencia did its best to care for children, Argentina gradually developed plans for a welfare state that would provide comprehensive aid for all children, including those who had committed crimes. Before the turn of the century, the solution to this problem had been simply to lock them up. In August 1892, President Carlos Pellegrini claimed that street urchins, particularly young males, were all criminals. He therefore suggested that a jail be constructed exclusively for young male offenders. He noted that the overcrowded existing facility held adults and children and that "the growing number of corrupted children sent there daily by *defensores* and judges" could never be contained (República Argentina: 1 August 1892, p. 524).[15] What the president failed to tell the deputies was that many of these children were arrested merely for being homeless. Although legislators were quick to authorize funding for a special facility for delinquent boys, which opened in 1903, they never discussed the need to provide similar facilities for either homeless or delinquent girls.

The early Argentine welfare state finally began to question the usefulness of incarcerating children and to perceive the importance of replacing child labor with education. It still, however, had no idea what to do with street children. In 1916 two child-rights specialists proposed a law to protect working women and children, prohibit unregistered nurses from working, insist on mandatory school attendance, and limit children's admission to theaters and movies. It also envisaged a special court for juvenile offenders and the establishment of a Consejo de Menores (Children's Council) to monitor state-operated institutions for children.

Although this particular proposal proved unacceptable, some elements of a plan to deal with male juveniles had already appeared some years earlier. An executive decree of August 1913 mandated the use of a special holding cell for male abandoned minors and juvenile delinquents until there was room for them at the boys' reformatory. This was initially how juvenile males were separated from the adult jail population (Ministerio de Justicia e Instrucción Pública 1886–1920: 1916 edition, 1: 34–35). Five years later a governmental organization called the Instituto Tutelar de Menores (Supervisory Institute for Minors) took control of the abandoned boys in prison. The staff consisted of child-rights specialists who were authorized to develop new programs for the boys but were given no money with which to do so. Nevertheless, they worked within the prison to promote a less coercive atmosphere for the boys until they could be set free or sent to other institutions. Those placed there by the defenders of minors had the opportunity of a primary school education, just like in the inmates of the women's prison (Ministerio de Justicia e Instrucción Pública 1886–1920: 1920 edition, 1: 267–75).

In 1919 the first comprehensive Argentine law giving government authorities substantial jurisdiction over juveniles was passed. As a result, the institute potentially faced responsibility for many more juveniles because the law gave the state the right to order the placing of juvenile delinquents in institutions until they reached the age of majority (Guy 1998: 284). Although the civil code had always allowed the state to intervene in such matters for short periods of time, the 1919 law signaled a new state willingness to deal with child offenders.

The Argentine congress once again failed to fund these programs until the conservative governments of the 1930s. On 24 January 1931, military dictator General José F. Uriburu authorized the successor of the institute and called it the Patronato Nacional de Menores (National Society for the Protection of Minors). In the decree he expanded the responsibilities of the new group to cover all juvenile delinquents lodged in police jails throughout Buenos Aires and the national territories. With new national taxes, funds would be available to install all kinds of workshops and educational facilities. The organization was also empowered to plan and construct new reformatories (Patronato Nacional de Menores 1936). Its responsibilities expanded during the presidency of General Agustín P. Justo from 1932 to 1938. Ironically, many child-rights supporters found a strong ally in an administration generally deplored for its antidemocratic tendencies.

It took many more years to create functional juvenile courts and rehabilitative facilities, but by 1943, on the eve of the rise of Juan Perón, the number of boys and, by this time, girls under the control of the Patronato Nacional de Menores had increased from just over 1,200 in 1931 to almost 2,900 and included youngsters from the interior of Argentina as well as from Buenos Aires, according to an anonymous, untitled article published in the Patronato's magazine *Infancia y Juventud* (January–June 1943: 25). These numbers were still modest, however, compared with the totals cared for historically by the defenders of minors and the Sociedad de Beneficencia. And, even by the 1940s, there still was no public policy regarding street children.

Despite the limited ability of the Argentine state to care for delinquent children, by the 1920s many Latin American governments were responding even more favorably to the notion of comprehensive state supervision of all children and mothers. In 1923 Argentine President Alvear created the Asistencia a la Infancia (Children's Bureau) within the Department of Hygiene, while in Rio de Janeiro a new juvenile court opened to handle street children (Pan American Union 1924: March edition, 316–17; July edition, 743). The following year the municipality of Buenos Aires created a free maternity clinic for poor women and opened soup kitchens in poor neighborhoods for undernourished children. Bolivia held its first child welfare congress, and the Mello Mattos children's home for abandoned children in Rio celebrated its first anniversary.

Notwithstanding these accomplishments, by the end of that decade a specialist in the Pan American Sanitary Office, Arístides Moll, complained that it was difficult to obtain clear information about infant mortality and other issues associated with childhood and family relations in the hemisphere. Information was often incomplete, and in only twelve countries could data be tracked over time. He noted considerable variation in infant mortality statistics, both within and between countries. Among the twelve Latin American countries for which he had the most information, Mexico had the highest infant mortality rates, followed by Costa Rica, Cuba, Chile, Ecuador, and Panama. Clearly the social value of newborn infants was increasingly important to governments in Latin America, but states often had limited ability to influence demographic rates. Juvenile delinquency and street children were similarly intractable problems (IIN 1967).

In April 1934 the Uruguayan government enacted a children's code (Código del Niño) as part of the development of a welfare state. This established, for the first time, a special government body consisting of the director of the Instituto de Clínica Pediátrica y Puericultura (Institute of Clinical Pediatrics and Puericulture), an attorney, a teacher, a representative of the Consejo de Trabajo (Labor Board), a delegate from the Consejo de Enseñanza Industrial (Industrial Education Board), and a representative of private charities. The Uruguayan president had the right to name the last three members of the Consejo del Niño (Children's Board) and the obligation to make sure that at least one woman served. The goal of the board was to monitor all issues related to the "life and well being of minors from the fetus to the age of majority" (República Oriental del Uruguay 1934: Articles 1–2).

Uruguay was not the first Latin American country to enact such a code, nor was it the last. Brazil began this legislative process in 1927, and other countries followed suit in the 1930s and 1940s, including Costa Rica (1932), Argentina (1932), Chile (1934), Mexico (1934), Ecuador (1938), and Venezuela (1939). The codes and agencies differed in name and scope of responsibilities and funding, but all reflected a hemispheric interest in promoting child welfare through a bureaucratic welfare state (Guy 1998).

Chile's experience demonstrated one of the fundamental problems confronting state policies toward children, namely, the influence of political parties and ideologies on the implementation of programs. Interest waxed and waned in the 1920s, depending upon who was in power, and little was done until Arturo Alessandri returned to government in 1932. By the following year it was clear that a crisis existed, because a study estimated that there were 70,000 children living on the streets of Chile while 220,000 were enrolled in school. Through the efforts of Alessandri's government, and those of the Popular Front, whose Minister of Health in the late 1930s was future president Salvador Allende, a number of programs were developed to aid mothers and their children, as well as the poor children living on the streets. Support for these agencies varied with each election (Morales 1994: 49–51).

Most of the early welfare state laws were passed in the midst of the world depression. Chile's 1934 decree, like the Uruguayan code, named key government officials (the governor of Santiago province, the head of the national children's home, the public health director, the director general of protection for minors and others) to the Consejo de Defensa del Niño (Children's Protective Council), which would, in turn, create regional boards for child protection. Mexico's law established a welfare board for minors that had three missions: welfare, consultation, and implementation. In addition to these laws, in Chile and Costa Rica new legislation permitted adoption (Pan American Union 1924: 913–14).

New laws promulgated under Juan Perón's government (1946–1955) allowed for full adoption and eliminated legal discrimination against illegitimate children. But, at the same time, this system reduced the power of fathers. In 1950, for example, the Argentine congress passed a law to punish fathers who did not provide sufficient food to their minor children, and, three years later, a judge ruled that this provision also applied to fathers of illegitimate children. In the public rhetoric of Peronism, the father was demoted from his position as an authoritarian figure to one more like that of a benevolent teacher, while Eva Perón was elevated in schoolbooks to Alma Tutelar de la Nación (Spiritual Guardian of the Nation). In this new world of the welfare state, fathers clearly lost power over their children relative to mothers and the state (Novellino 1955; Guy 1999).

The principle underlying these reforms seemed simple, but the placement of child safety and supervision under the aegis of government bureaus fundamentally challenged basic power relations within the family. No longer would orphans, abandoned children, and street children be the principal focus of government monitoring. All children were subject to government rules, and parents no longer had the exclusive right to determine the fate of their offspring. Thus the rise of the welfare state weakened fathers' rights and responsibilities and placed the value of children as future citizens above their biological and traditional social value as heirs of their parents. While this was an ambitious proposition, it soon became evident that it was financially and politically unfeasible. By the late twentieth century, it was clear that governments could not afford to replace the family unit with institutions, but they did spend considerable sums to help children without families and invested considerable sums in public education.

Nevertheless, the experiment took place over many years in many countries and had Latin American nation states like Argentina grappling with complex issues over long periods of time. Hampered by a lack of funds as well as a lack of consensus, child-rights advocates often had to approach child welfare in a piecemeal fashion. Curiously, they often as willingly aligned themselves with conservative regimes such as the Argentine governments of the 1930s as with revolutionary governments such as that of Fidel Castro in Cuba. Association with political parties could be both beneficial and detrimental, depending upon the party in power. And, throughout this period, parents and children often thwarted, rather than supported, state plans that interfered with patriarchy or the private will of family members.

By the 1950s, many governments had enacted legislation to deal with abandoned infants and youths as well as with the thorny problem of juvenile delinquency. Yet none had truly solved any of the problems, which tended to wax and wane according to economic and demographic conditions. When things improved in the capital city, they often deteriorated elsewhere. Thus despite the best, and sometimes less-than-best, intentions, social problems related to children have remained challenges to public authorities into the beginning of the twenty-first century.

Notes

1. The number of homeless children in Latin American cities has always been a response to specific economic, geographic, and social conditions, rather than a constant phenomenon.

2. The Patronato de la Infancia was originally established by the municipality of Buenos Aires, but claimed to be an early nongovernmental organization (Melcio Farré 1917).

3. For AGN figures, see Fondo Ministerio de Justicia e Instrucción Pública, Serie Expedientes Generales, letra A, 1914, legajo 1.

4. Sociedad de Beneficencia, legajo 160, foja 348, 16 January 1878. Letter from Nicolasa P. de Serantes to president of the Sociedad de Beneficiencia Emma V. de Napp.

5. Sociedad de Beneficencia, legajo 160, fojas 24–25, 23 January 1993. Letter from Petrona de Cordero to president of the Sociedad de Beneficencia, 1882 *Memoria* of the Casa de Huérfanas. Sociedad de Beneficencia, foja 32,

20 July 1883. Letter from F. W. Jones, Unión Telefónica, to president of the Sociedad de Beneficencia. Sociedad de Beneficencia, fojas 96–98, 13 March 1886. Annual report of Casa de Huérfanas.

6. Sociedad de Beneficencia, Casa de Huérfanas, legajo 162, fojas 265–67, 19 January 1910. Letter from Casa de Huérfanas to president of the Sociedad de Beneficencia.

7. Sociedad de Beneficencia, legajo 163, foja 194, 19 April 1915. Letter from Director General de Arsenales de Guerra to the Sociedad de Beneficencia. Sociedad de Beneficencia, legajo 163, foja 195, 23 April 1915. Letter from Director General de Arsenales de Guerra to the Sociedad de Beneficencia.

8. At that time the Asilo de Huérfanos was the only place in Buenos Aires where minors were instructed in military training.

9. Sociedad de Beneficencia, legajo 45, foja 107, 26 July 1906. Letter from Asilo de Huérfanos to Sociedad de Beneficencia (on request for boys for a military band). Sociedad de Beneficencia, legajo 45, foja 113, 24 September 1906. Letter from Escuela de Aprendices Marineros, Dársena Norte, to president of the Sociedad de Beneficencia (on returning naval recruits). Sociedad de Beneficencia, legajo 45, foja 118, 5 October 1906. Asilo de Huérfanos to Sociedad de Beneficencia (on problems encountered by naval authorities).

10. These problems were further elaborated in AGN by J.M. Terrero, Defensor de Menores, to Osvaldo Magnasco, Ministro de Justicia, Fondo Ministerio de Justicia e Instrucción Pública, legajo 106.

11. In December the Sociedad Nacional del Pantaléfono offered to hire several adolescents (fourteen or fifteen years old) who had been training as apprentices.

12. See the comments of the Sociedad de Beneficencia regarding this matter (Ministerio de Justicia e Instrucción Pública, 1886-1920: 1911 edition).

13. See Sociedad de Beneficencia, legajo 176, foja 40 for estimates of the cost to maintain inmates in Sociedad de Beneficencia institutions.

14. Tribunales Civiles, 1899, legajo 436, letra A.

15. The presence of orphans among these children was recognized in a later discussion on 16 September, although no suggestions were discussed that would ameliorate this situation (República Argentina 1892: 16 September, p. 918).

References

AGN (Archivo General de la Nación [Argentina]).

Barrancos, Dora, ed. 1994. *Mujer y género*. Buenos Aires: Centro Editor.

Besse, Susan K. 1996. *Restructuring patriarchy: The modernization of gender inequality in Brazil, 1914–1940*. Chapel Hill: University of North Carolina Press.

Blum, Ann S. 1998. Public welfare and child circulation: Mexico City 1877 to 1925. *Journal of Family History* 23 (3): 240–71.

Buenos Aires Municipality. 1906. *Statistical annuary of the City of Buenos Aires*. Buenos Aires: Buenos Aires Municipality.

Bunge, Alejandro E. 1984 [1940]. *Una nueva Argentina*. Buenos Aires: Hyspámerica.

Chile. 1886. *Código Civil de la República de Chile*. Valparaíso: Librería del Mercurio.

Ciafardo, Eduardo O. 1992. *Los niños en la ciudad de Buenos Aires (1890/ 1910)*. Biblioteca Política Argentina. Buenos Aires: Centro Editor América Latina.

García Méndez, Emilio, and Elías Carranza. 1992. *Del revés al derecho: la condición jurídica de la infancia en América Latina, bases para una reforma legislativa*. Buenos Aires: Galerna.

Gomes, Angela María de Castro. 1992. *Estado, corporativismo y acción social en Brasil, Argentina y Uruguay*, Colección Cuadernos Simón Rodríguez. Buenos Aires: Biblos/Fundación Simón Rodríguez.

Gonzalbo Aizpuru, Pilar, and Cecilia Rabell, eds. 1994. *La familia en el mundo iberoamericano*. Mexico City: Universidad Nacional Autónoma de México.

Guy, Donna J. 1994. Niños abandonados en Buenos Aires (1880–1914) y el desarrollo del concepto de la madre. In *Mujeres y cultura en la Argentina del siglo XIX*, edited by L. Fletcher. Buenos Aires: Feminaria.

———. 1998. The Pan American child congresses, 1916–1942: Pan Americanism, child reform, and the welfare state in Latin America. *Journal of Family History* 23 (3): 272–91.

———. 1999. Rupturas y continuidades en el papel de la mujer, la infancia y la familia durante la década peronista. Paper read at Asociación de Historiadores de América Latina en Europa, 21–25 September.

———. 2000. Parents before the tribunals: The legal construction of patriarchy in Argentina. In *Hidden histories of gender and the state in Latin America*, edited by E. Dore and M. Molyneux. Durham, N.C.: Duke University Press.

Guy, Donna J., ed. 2001. Special issue on the rise of the welfare state in Latin America. *The Americas* (58) 1.

IIN (Instituto Interamericano del Niño). 1967. *Estadísticas básicas sobre menores*. Montevideo: Instituto Interamericano del Niño.

Imperio Mexicano. 1866. *Código civil del imperio mexicano*. Mexico City: Andrade y Escalante.

Kuznesof, Elizabeth, and Robert Oppenheimer, eds. 1985. Special issue on the Latin American family in the nineteenth century. *Journal of Family History* 10 (3).

Lavrin, Asunción. 1991. Mexico. In *Children in historical and comparative perspective*, edited by J. H. Hawes and R. Hiner. New York: Greenwood.

———. 1995. *Women, feminism, and social change in Argentina, Chile, and Uruguay, 1890–1910*. Lincoln: University of Nebraska Press.

League of Nations, Advisory Committee on Social Questions. 1938. *The lacing of children in families*. Vol. 1, document no. C. 260. M. 155. Geneva: League of Nations.

Lipsett-Rivera, Sonya, ed. 1998. Special issue on children in the history of Latin America. *Journal of Family History* 23 (3).

Little, Cynthia Jeffress. 1980. The Society of Beneficence in Buenos Aires, 1823–1900. Ph.D. diss., Temple University.

Melcio Farré, D. Victor. 1917. *La filantropía contra el delito: La "Casa del Niño" de Buenos Aires*. Buenos Aires: La Semana Médica.

Mesa-Lago, Carmelo. 1978. *Social security in Latin America: Pressure groups, stratification, and inequality*. Pitt Latin American series. Pittsburgh: University of Pittsburgh Press.

Meyer Arana, Alberto. 1911. *La caridad en Buenos Aires*. 2 vols. Buenos Aires: Sopena.

Ministerio de Justicia e Instrucción Pública, República Argentina. 1886–1920. *Memoria*. Buenos Aires: Ministerio de Justicia e Instrucción Pública.

Morales, Eduardo. 1994. Políticas sociales y niñez. In *Infancia en riesgo social y políticas sociales en Chile: Desarrollo y perspectivas del Servicio Nacional de Menores y su relación con las políticas sociales, la sociedad civil y el marco jurídico*, edited by F. Pilotti. Montevideo: Instituto Interamericano del Niño.

Moreno, José Luis, ed. 2000. *La política social antes de la política social: Caridad, beneficencia y política social en Buenos Aires, siglos XVII a XX*. Buenos Aires: Trama/Prometeo.

Novellino, Norberto José. 1955. *Nuevas leyes de familia comentadas y concordadas*. Buenos Aires: Temis Argentina.

Pan American Union. 1924. *Bulletin of the Pan American Union* 68 (Jan.–Dec.).

Passanante, María Inés. 1987. *Pobreza y acción social en la historia argentina: de la beneficencia a la seguridad social*. Colección Guidance. Buenos Aires: Editorial Humanitas.

Patronato de la Infancia. 1944. *Segunda conferencia nacional de la infancia abandonada y delincuente*. Buenos Aires: Peuser.

———. 1993. *Cien años de amor: Centésimo aniversario*. Buenos Aires: Patronato de la Infancia.

Patronato Nacional de Menores. 1936. Decreto de reglamentación de funciones (announced 24 January, 1931). *Infancia y Juventud* 1: 99–102.

Pilotti, Francisco, ed. 1994. *Infancia en riesgo social y políticas sociales en Chile: Desarrollo y perspectivas del Servicio Nacional de Menores y su relación con las políticas sociales, la sociedad civil y el marco jurídico*. Montevideo: Instituto Interamericano del Niño.

Pilotti, Francisco, and Irene Rizzini, eds. 1995. *A arte de governar crianças: A história das políticas sociais, da legislação e da assistência à infância no Brasil*. Rio de Janeiro: Instituto Interamericano del Niño/Editora Universitária Santa Ursula/AMAIS.

Recalde, Héctor. 1991. *Beneficencia, asistencialismo estatal y previsión social.* Biblioteca Política Argentina. Buenos Aires: Centro Editor de América Latina.

República Argentina. 1892. *Diario de Sesiones,* Cámara de Diputados.

República Oriental del Uruguay. 1893. *Código civil de la República Oriental del Uruguay.* Montevideo: Imprenta de la Nación.

———. 1934. *Código del Niño,* Consejo del Niño.

Salinas Meza, René. 1991. Orphans and family disintegration in Chile: The mortality of abandoned children, 1750–1930. *Journal of Family History* 16 (3): 315–29.

Schafer, Sylvia. 1997. *Children in moral danger and the problem of government in Third Republic France.* Princeton Studies in Culture/Power/History. Princeton, N.J.: Princeton University Press.

Sociedad de Beneficencia. 1900. *Memorias.* Buenos Aires: Jacobo Peuser.

———. 1901. *Memorias.* Buenos Aires: Jacobo Peuser.

———. 1936. *Sociedad de Beneficencia de la Capital 1823–1936.* Buenos Aires: Jacobo Peuser.

Stoner, K. Lynn. 1991. *From the house to the streets: The Cuban woman's movement for legal reform, 1898–1940.* Durham, N.C.: Duke University Press.

Suriano, Juan. 1990. Niños trabajadores: Una aproximación al trabajo infantil en la industria porteña de comienzos del siglo. In *Mundo urbano y cultura popular: Estudios de historia social argentina,* edited by D. Armus and D. Barrancos. Buenos Aires: Sudamericana.

Szuchman, Mark D. 1982. Continuity and conflict in Buenos Aires: Comments on the historical city. In *Buenos Aires, 400 years,* edited by S. R. Ross and T. F. McGann. Austin: University of Texas Press.

Varley, Ann. 2000. Women and the home in Mexican family law. In *Hidden histories of gender and the state in Latin America,* edited by E. Dore and M. Molyneux. Durham, N.C.: Duke University Press.

7

The Child-Saving Movement in Brazil

Ideology in the Late Nineteenth and Early Twentieth Centuries

Irene Rizzini

The Idea of Child Saving

In the late nineteenth and early twentieth centuries, the plight of impoverished children came to be of great concern in Brazil. This was the moment when childhood was first seen as a social problem whose solution was fundamental to the larger project of nation building. The country's elite sought to forge a nation that was at once "cultured and modern,"[1] along the lines of important European and North American cities, especially Paris, London, and New York, and the transformation of childhood was part of this larger endeavor.

In several influential circles there was talk of the *"magna causa* of childhood" and "the crusade for childhood." Childhood was seen, not only in Brazil but also elsewhere, as "the key to the future" (Cunningham 1995: 42). In Brazil, this nineteenth-century notion that "to save children was to save the country" implied the concomitant imperative of distancing children from the temptations that might lead them astray from the straight and narrow of discipline and work; society had to be protected from those given to vice, from those who threatened public order. New ideologies concerning the control and protection of children paralleled those in other Western countries, suggesting an extensive exchange of information among the political and philanthropic elite of this era.

With special reference to Brazil, this chapter examines the emergence of the idea that childhood was the key to the future; it also considers the problems that were perceived in and the solutions proposed for the task of "saving" poor children and rendering them useful to the overarching goal of "civilizing" the country. The expression "child saving," current at the time, turned on the notion that investing in children was tantamount to investing in the nation's future. I begin, then, with a discussion of the historical context, moving on to examine the child-saving movement in Brazil, its origins and its repercussions.

An examination of ideologies current at the turn of the century suggests that a heightened interest in poor children can be seen as part of an essentially political project. The "idle" segments of the population could be contended with if they were rendered, from childhood, useful elements for the country's capitalist development. At the same time, protecting children was a means of safeguarding society itself. The discourse was therefore double-edged, with children described in the documents by turns as endangered and dangerous. This latter attribution, that children were dangerous, was reserved for offspring of a specific social class, that of the poor.

Concern over the plight of destitute children gave rise to a complex network of laws and institutions. Yet the aim was not to lessen profound social inequities. The poor were denied full rights of citizenship, continued to suffer discrimination, and were to endure a system of education aimed at submission; wealth and privilege remained, and to this day remain, in the hands of a small minority.

The Historical Context

The final decades of the nineteenth century were marked by events of great importance for Brazil. In 1888 slavery was abolished, and 1889 saw the end of the imperial monarchy and the establishment of a republic. As a result the economic, political, and social life of the country was profoundly altered. Meanwhile, new relations of production and of labor proved necessary for the liberal state to adapt to a less mercantilist and more industrial economy (Sodré 1989).

The rapid growth of cities, fed by the arrival of foreign immigrants and by internal migration from rural areas, transformed urban life. The strict social control exercised in the rural context and in small towns was absent, giving rise to pervasive fear. At its extreme, this fear was about rioting, even insurgency against the established order. In such a context, traditional forms of social control proved ineffectual. The new urban conditions called for new responses.

At the center of this analysis, then, is a recently urbanized world that stood in stark contrast to the backwardness of the rural milieu. The lights of the city—the metropolis, "the cosmopolitan center"—were, in the eyes of the contemporary elite, emblematic of everything "modern," "cultured," and "civilized." I focus in particular on what was then the capital, Rio de Janeiro. Of the older but rapidly developing cities, Rio most closely approximated the European or North American notion of "the civilized city." By the end of the nineteenth century, Rio was unquestionably the center of Brazil's political, cultural, and intellectual life. The city also brought to mind images of disorder, disease, crime, and depravity.

Life in the city, so vulnerable to vice and indolence and so different from that of rural areas, was described in alarming tones. The very architectural forms and the spatial division of the city gave rise to a preoccupation with security and order. The existence of corners, alleys, and narrow passageways, dark at any hour of the day (Chevalier 1973: 2), seemed to bring out the ghosts and unexpected dangers inherent to city life.[2]

Rio de Janeiro brought together an unknown and frightening demographic mixture, a population that "could be compared to the dangerous classes spoken about in Europe in the early part of the nineteenth century" (Carvalho 1991: 18). Amid the ostentatious display of wealth could be found all manner of people loitering about: impoverished workers, vagabonds, beggars, ruffians, prostitutes, and street urchins. The term *pivete,* roughly "knave," is still used pejoratively today to describe these impoverished and potentially dangerous children.

Documents from this era suggest that children and young people figured prominently in discussions of abandonment, poverty, and urban disorder. Indignant over the rounding up and incarceration of children on the streets of the capital, the jurist Evaristo de Moraes wrote, "As a rule, children apprehended in the streets are orphans or have been abandoned by their families. Once made to spend a night behind bars or in the barracks, these poor children, deprived of homes and bread, are turned over to a judge" (Moraes 1898).

The unsettling presence in the streets of children who were "materially and morally abandoned," to use the language of the times, led to appeals for the country to confront this grave social problem. Senator Lopes Trovão, in a speech delivered in 1896, proclaimed, "Whosoever with an observant eye ventures across the streets of the capital of the Republic will be saddened to observe that in this milieu so ruinous for the body and soul a goodly portion of our children are set loose to a life of unrestrained liberty—or abandonment—left to suffer disrespect and learn all nature of vices and ready themselves for the commission of diverse crimes" (cited in Moncorvo Filho 1926: 129–30).

The state's role in behalf of such children was defended as part of a larger "patriotic and civilizing mission of healing" and reform. Indeed, in the first years after the republic was established, this mission was envisioned as part of the larger project of nation building. The threat implicit in the discourse of the time was that the country would be overrun by disorder and immorality if it let down its guard in the face of abandonment, particularly of children.

"Saving children" obeyed a logic that was politically compatible with the thinking of the times. It was understood that in protecting children, it was ultimately the country that was being defended—from crime, from disorder, from anarchy.

The Child-Saving Movement

The child-saving movement was based on the belief that a harmful environment coupled with certain innate proclivities made monsters of children, a situation that could have devastating consequences for society as a whole. Saving children was a mission that went beyond the boundaries of religion and family, taking on a political dimension of control justified by the imperative of defending society and preserving social peace and order.

According to historian Hugh Cunningham (1995), the child-saving movement was particularly strong in the Protestant countries of Europe and North America from 1830 until 1920. During that period there was a fresh surge of activity among individuals and philanthropic organizations working to defend the poor and the needy. Children in particular were the intended beneficiaries for this sort of activity, and there was growing pressure on the state to take responsibility for the situation and implement policies to help children. The demand that the state take on a leading role in addressing the problems of children and in implementing programs for them was the cornerstone of a process that began to take shape across the Western world. From that point forward, the same efforts were undertaken almost simultaneously in Europe and North America, and similar ones can be identified, a short time later, in Latin America.

There was a remarkable exchange of knowledge and experience, especially during international congresses where the. elite of the two continents mapped out possible future policies for their countries. It is evident in the Brazilian literature that discussions held at these international meetings were widely cited and employed to add legitimacy to domestic reform campaigns. The tactic was apparently successful.

In *The Child Savers: The Invention of Delinquency*, Anthony Platt offers a critical reading of the North American philanthropic movement. According to Platt (1977: xx) "the child-saving movement" was not a humanitarian undertaking on behalf of the working classes that challenged the established order. "On the contrary," he writes, "its impetus came primarily from the middle and upper classes who were instrumental in devising new forms of social control to protect their power and privilege." Reforms championed by the movement on behalf of children were part of the larger objective of adapting existing institutions to the demands of an emerging capitalist system. In Platt's view they were a reaction to the instability evident in protest demonstrations by dissatisfied workers struggling to improve their social and economic conditions and in the turbulent economic affairs of the late nineteenth century.

Children, suggested the alarmist discourse of reformers and philanthropists, were linked to notions of disorder. It was well known that children had for centuries swelled the ranks of the poor.[3] What was new at this moment was that poverty could not be contained by laws for the poor, parishes, almshouses, workhouses, orphanages, rural institutions, and the like. Poor children were visible on the streets of the industrializing cities and their presence caused alarm.

Children raised amid vice, it was feared, would reproduce disorder. In congresses held during this period, attention was drawn to the preponderance of children among the hordes of vagabonds and beggars in the streets. Given this threat to public order, something had to be done. Those children with potential were to be "saved" and put to work, and the truly recalcitrant restrained. The children identified as potential criminals had to be separated from the world of crime. In 1880 the criminologist Enoch Wines expressed what was on the minds of many at the time: that these children had to be saved, "as they were born for crime and were raised for criminality" (cited in Platt 1977: 45).

The need for the salvation of the soul comes from the Christian dogma about original sin. A German sermon delivered in 1520, for instance, suggested that "Just as a cat craves mice, a fox chickens, and a wolf cub sheep, so infant humans are inclined in their hearts to adultery, fornication, impure desires, lewdness, idol worship, belief in magic, hostility, quarreling, passion, anger, strife, dissension, factiousness, hatred, murder, drunkenness, gluttony, and more" (cited in Cunningham 1995: 49).

The innate passions and depravations of children had to be reined in, for the sake of salvation and in the interests of social order. Augustinian and Calvinist tenets on original sin were employed to justify various sorts of interventions in family life and child rearing. As Saint Augustine himself asked, "Who can recall to me the sins I committed as a baby? For in your sight no man is free from sin, not even a child who has lived only one day on earth" (cited in Sznaider 1996: 13).

Despite the ideological differences between Catholics and Protestants, many similarities can be found in their understanding of children. The idea of the child as key to the future has had enormous influence on Western societies. This notion, born in the sixteenth century, was invoked in particular during moments of great pressure for reform and was a catalyst for what the French historian Philippe Ariès (1962) has described as the moment when children came to be sharply differentiated from adults. Children were to occupy a new social space, and their upbringing would require considerable attention if they were to be made into the sort of adult considered ideal for the nation.

The idea of children as the key to the future was linked to a new concept of childhood that had considerable impact on the conceptual formulations and practices of the West, namely humanist notions of childhood in Renaissance Europe associated with Erasmus. The virtues of the family, responsible for the upbringing of children, would reflect the virtues of the state.

The notion of children as so much earth to be shaped, for good or for ill, raised new concerns about their upbringing. For childhood to be reshaped, it would be necessary to create institutions capable of challenging the hegemony of the family. In the sixteenth century, schools began to do just that. Other more clearly coercive institutions and measures were created to contend with poor families, whose relationship to the church and the state was one of submission, through dependency or force.

This discussion was not always driven by the concrete social condition of real children. Childhood within the European Christian world was conceptualized in abstract terms, terms that also had enormous influence in the colonies, including Brazil. In the sixteenth century, Jesuits were already present in Brazil, and they established an institutional culture whose imprint is still evident.[4]

Saving Children to Save the Nation

Brazilian children described as being in need of salvation tended to hail from families deemed unworthy or unfit to raise them. Social reformers were particularly concerned about children in a state of "moral abandonment" (Moraes 1900). Ferri and Lombroso, leading figures of the famous Italian school of criminology, championed this idea and others followed their lead. Caring for physically abandoned children was the responsibility of the state. But what of children whose moral well-being had been abandoned? Challenging the family and paternal authority—institutions until then protected by the church and by law—was no simple matter.

A consequence of efforts to protect children from moral abandonment, however, was that many families came to be labeled as delinquent. Accused of leading their own sons and daughters down the wrong path, families could lose custody of their children. The family's upbringing of its children was to be monitored, as a patriotic obligation. A guardian was needed to keep a tight rein on the situation of children, and that guardian would be the state. It was incumbent upon the state to save children—"the children of the fatherland," as they would come to be called[5]—to take them in and to render them useful for the nation. Implicit in the conflation of the ideas of saving children and saving the nation was the hint that the nation, not unlike children themselves, could be shaped.

Like a father who sees his child as an immature being, the concerned Brazilian elite viewed their country's majority as primitive, semibarbaric. This elite included some of the growing number of jurists and doctors whose work brought them face-to-face with poor children. Urban life only heightened the perceived differences between the common man, seen as brutish and ignorant—in a word, infantile—and the elite, the modern industrial capitalist class. Given the putatively backward condition of much of the country and the countless shortcomings of her people, the challenge was not merely to properly educate (in the broadest sense of the word) children, but to educate a childish population, a people still in its infancy. In a speech delivered in 1920, Arthur Moncorvo Filho (1920: 4), a doctor and one of the leaders of the children's defense movement, suggested, "I have always accepted as an unshakable truth what the Englishman William Cheverry said only recently: 'Nothing defines the dignity of a country so much as the way it cares for its children.' And further, 'The progress of a country can be deduced from its childhood.'"

If children embodied hope, the future of the nation, they were also seen as a threat. Their innocence was called into question and elements of cruelty and evil identified in their souls. Children came to be regarded as potentially delinquent and were to be distanced from the "schools for crime," especially the street and jails. In the words of a contemporary jurist, "Let us admit that the myth of the innocent and pure soul of the child is now dead" (Lobo 1907: 28).

In turn-of-the-century Brazilian discourse, this ambivalent view of children as at once endangered and dangerous became something of a leitmotiv. And childhood itself was divided in two. The term "minor" gained currency in everyday usage. Closely associated with aspects of criminality, it came to refer only to those children who were poor and potentially dangerous.

In the interests of maintaining social order and safeguarding the future of the nation, a variety of measures were endorsed. Professionals in the field of health were to identify means (both physical and spiritual) of treatment and rehabilitation; the legal authorities were to oversee the protection of children, and of society, in cooperation with public institutions; and philanthropic agencies were to minister to the poor and downtrodden.[6] These public and private initiatives took shape in the first three decades of the twentieth century and, despite a sometimes disharmonious discourse and practice, shared a common goal—that of saving children in order to save Brazil. As Senator Lopes Trovão was to declare, "We have a homeland to rebuild, a nation to secure, a people to forge . . . and to undertake this task, what more supple and pliant element do we have than childhood? The time has come for us to cultivate through childhood a better youth and a more perfect humanity" (Trovão 1896).

Despite a new rhetoric about Brazil as a country to be remade, power was not exercised in a truly new fashion. The lettered elite that dominated the political arena promoted education, but not to the detriment of their inherited privileges. "Instructing the people"—that is, offering training for work—was seen as a *sine qua non* of progress. The challenge was to do this while keeping the poor in check.

Laws and Services: Child Saving in Brazil

In a 1913 declaration (cited in Moncorvo Filho 1926: 73), Ataulpho de Paiva, the influential Rio jurist, member of the Brazilian Academy of Letters, and advocate of "New Justice" (Nova Justiça) for children, argued that "Simple repression—the fundamental idea of our codes— has always misinterpreted the plight of minors, leaving them unprotected before the law and the justice system. Juvenile delinquency is a crisis of alarming proportions, especially in that it is being compared to adult criminality."

Reformers turned to the fields of sociology, psychology, psychiatry, and anthropology in an attempt to understand what factors led children to commit crimes. In an article published in the *Jornal do Commercio*, Ataulpho de Paiva (1916 [1912]: 70) placed the blame on "the nefarious influence of a deleterious social milieu . . . coupled with lack of education." He also called for reform: "Formerly, the only concern of the criminal judge was to classify the crime and apply the corresponding punishment."

Brazilian advocates for children were also inspired by a larger international movement for legal reform that sought individual regeneration through education, rather than through an exclusive reliance on punishment. But the fear that motivated these reforms was clear. As jurist Hélio Lobo (1907: 23) suggested, "frightened by the alarming increase in juvenile crime, civilized countries have sought to protect themselves from this evil." Elsewhere (as cited in Paiva 1916 [1912]: 27), he argued, "it would be no exaggeration to say that society has never faced a more serious threat to its security and peace."

Leaving children in a state of moral abandonment was said to encourage their becoming delinquents. Reformers argued that Brazil was failing to follow the example of more civilized countries that took juvenile justice seriously. The solution, as they saw it, lay in reorganizing the justice system on a new foundation, taking inspiration from the humanitarian tradition of the nineteenth century but adapting it to modern, twentieth-century civilization. The perceived malleability of children and youths was said to augur well for their chances of recovery.

Through the combination of new legislation and services, the state was to take on, in the early twentieth century, a guardianlike role in relation to children. In the legal sphere, the responsibilities of the state were no longer to be limited to punishment and repression; the state now had social responsibilities. It carried these out with the aid of philanthropic organizations, which had access to the poor and needy. The philanthropists, in turn, saw in the legislators the solution to the increasing dangerousness of the poor. As such, the alliance between philanthropies and legal authorities was built upon the perceived need for change in contending with the poor.

Throughout the 1920s, calls for "New Justice" continued. Municipal and state bodies, particularly those of Rio de Janeiro and São Paulo, debated bills about children. The process eventually led to new regulatory measures, such as the creation of a special juvenile justice system (os juizados de menores) and the implementation of special legislation, the Código de Menores (Minor's Code). By championing the virtues of discipline and work, representatives of the legal sector and philanthropists together sought the moral regeneration of society.

In Defense of Children and Society

The juvenile justice system in Brazil was influenced by an international debate in the late nineteenth century about stemming juvenile delinquency, and Latin America became a sort of willing laboratory for ideas originating in Europe and North America. Juvenile justice, though seemingly wide in scope, was in fact concerned with poor children raised in families deemed not to adhere to contemporary models of morality; children who had come to be known as "minors."

The talk of the times was of the possibility of recovering minors, with the supposed success achieved in the United States offered as an example to follow. Yet these new measures had an old objective, that of forging useful citizens out of individuals who otherwise would be a burden on society. The discourse of protecting children was integrally linked to the aim of defending society from the proliferation of the idle and criminal, who were clearly hazardous to capitalist relations of production, as well as from insubordination and disorder.

In Brazil, from the beginning of the twentieth century until 1927, when the Minor's Code was approved, numerous bills were introduced and debates held on the intertwined challenges of protecting children and protecting society from them. Although the proposed activity went beyond the bounds of legislation, the prime movers were, overwhelmingly, representatives of the legal profession. The jurists worked together with the police, politicians, medical associations, and charitable and philanthropic organizations, encouraging debate, publishing their ideas, and establishing strategic alliances with elected representatives, newspapers, the leaders of philanthropic associations, universities, and international academic associations.

Shortly after the republic was established, bills were introduced in the Chamber of Deputies that identified abandoned and delinquent children as the responsibility of the state. And, through the legislative, judicial, and executive branches of government, the state was granted the power to intervene in family life. The "laws for the protection of and aid to minors" were promulgated, asylums and penal facilities for children reorganized, and a system of probation (*liberdade vigiada*), aimed at keeping an eye on minors outside of institutions, created.

The measures proposed during the early twentieth century concerned, above all, the policing of the streets and dealing with those apprehended, including children and youths. For example, Law 947, which went into effect on 29 December 1902 and was entitled "Reform of Policing in the Federal District," includes the following text: "The executive branch of government is authorized to create one or more correctional facilities for the rehabilitation, by means of work and instruction, of any able-bodied beggars, vagabonds or vagrants, ruffians, and vicious minors as may be found in the Federal District and judged as such." In Brazil the state took on a tutelary role of authority and control of almost monopolistic proportions, a situation not dissimilar to that in many Latin American countries.

The Route of Social Exclusion

Children and youths came to be classified according to their "type of abandonment" or "degree of dangerousness." The law permitted the apprehension of children found to be abandoned or depraved or "in danger of so becoming." A child's physical appearance or style of dress or mere suspicion on the part of the authorities was sufficient grounds for arrest; according to the law, "If a minor is not caught in the very act, but the proper criminal authorities find it expedient to restrict his liberty, they shall proceed according to paragraphs two and three of Article 86" (República Federativa do Brasil, 1927).

The early-twentieth-century judicial and institutional measures regarding children contributed to the social exclusion of the poor. Although the state was concerned with "rehabilitating minors," it did not make universal education a priority. When the idea that children were the future of the nation was invoked, it was understood that what was vital was shaping children in such a way that the great majority of the population would remain submissive, as in earlier times.

Although lip service was paid to education, an element of the republican ideology of "order and progress," education was also seen as a "dangerous weapon." It remained decentralized in the early years of the republic and lacked support from the national government. The result of this laissez-faire attitude was not only complete lack of coordination among the states but considerable disorganization in how education was actually delivered. The outdated schools of the empire were inherited by the republic. According to one contemporary observer (cited in Carvalho 1989: 24), the result was "schoolhouses without light, children without books, books without a methodology, schools without discipline, and teachers treated like pariahs."[7]

The very use of the word "education" *(educação)* in this period did not seem to refer to the enlightenment of the masses or to a means of achieving greater social equality. Education was spoken of as a sort of antidote to idleness and criminality. The Escola Quinze de Novembro (Fifteenth November School) for the "rehabilitation of minors" is an apt example. The bylaws of the school, which took in "minors" rounded up in the streets, stated that "As the institution is meant for social pariahs, the education imparted herein shall not go beyond that which is indispensable to the integration of the internees within society. The vocational training necessary for a trade shall, however, be offered." In 1905 Brazil's president, Rodrigues Alves (cited in Vaz 1905), argued that "A healthy modern city requires a population purged of its worst elements. . . . It is imperative and urgent that vagrancy, criminality, and vice be contained through the creation of correctional facilities and that the young people for whom these are intended be protected by means of education imparted in the appropriate institutions."

The reality of "children's aid and protection" mean a dichotomization of childhood. Just as the majority of the population was denied the full benefits of citizenship (Carvalho 1991), "minors" were given minimal education, just enough to make them useful workers. In highlighting the "minor" as one type of child, a type that represented danger to society, the allied legislative and service provision sectors could easily justify their attempts at rehabilitating this group. After all, the goal was to civilize the country.

The Child-Saving Movement and Its Repercussions

This chapter has examined the political arguments that awakened interest in childhood, arguments found in the late-nineteenth- and early-twentieth-century attempt to make Brazil a "civilized country." Paradoxically, the example of countries that Brazil sought to emulate made it clear that it would not be easy to have a population that was at once educated and docile, hardworking but amenable to the established order, efficient but unaware of the value of its labor, patriotic but uninterested in governance. The challenge was especially daunting given the instances of insubordination in the very "civilized" countries whose example the Brazilian elite wished to follow.

Notwithstanding the magnanimity of many Brazilian reformers, the discourse of child saving was in truth an impediment to the extension of the rights of citizenship in Brazil. Although the future of the country was said to rest on the (re)education of children—that is, poor children—this meant they were to be conditioned for submission. The country focused on the creation of laws and charitable services for children deemed potentially troublesome rather than on a national policy of quality education accessible to all. This history forms a backdrop to the current reality of a country of profound contradictions where discourse and practice about the condition of children are nearly always at odds.

The political choices made in the early years of the republic served the interests of those in power and paved the way for the vast social and economic inequalities the country now suffers. To this day, millions of Brazilian children are kept at the margins of society, and seen, like the poor in general, as a threat to law and order.

Notes

This chapter was translated from the Portuguese by Tobias Hecht.

1. Numerous terms in this chapter, culled from the literature of the period—books, dissertations, speeches, newspaper articles, and laws—appear between quotation marks, not as quotations but as illustrations of a way of thinking. The chapter emerges from extensive archival research, especially on the discourse of the concerned elite who took on the "cause of childhood." This group, made up for the most part of men trained in medicine and law, some of whom worked in charitable organizations, held considerable sway in politics, in the press, and in the universities.

2. For further discussion of these issues, see the works of British historian Gertrude Himmelfarb (1983; 1991).

3. Records suggest that 42 to 53 percent of the poor receiving relief in English parishes in the sixteenth and seventeenth centuries were children, even with an infant mortality rate in excess of 50 percent. According to Cunningham (1995: 111), these figures were similar in other parts of Europe.

4. For a discussion of the "institutional culture" underlying approaches to child welfare in Brazil in the twentieth century, see Rizzini (1992; 1997) and Pilotti and Rizzini (1995).

5. Similar terms were employed in France—les enfants de la patrie (Donzelot 1980: 35)—and in the United States (Peixoto 1933: 148).

6. In contrast to the idea of charity, based on religious—i.e., Christian—precepts, philanthropy is associated, in the modern era, with a spirit of rational-

ity and science. Gertrude Himmelfarb (1983) has argued that the eighteenth century was described as an "era of benevolence," in which philanthropic entities ministering to the poor proliferated. The humanitarianism characteristic of this period is associated with the emergence of a liberal capitalist society. See also Sznaider (1996).

7. The comment was made in 1894 at the inauguration of a schoolhouse.

References

Ariès, Philippe. 1962. *Centuries of childhood: A social history of family life.* Translated by R. Baldick. New York: Random House.

Carvalho, José Murilo de. 1991. *Os bestializados: O Rio de Janeiro e a república que não foi.* São Paulo: Companhia das Letras.

Carvalho, Marta M. Chagas de. 1989. *A escola e a república.* São Paulo: Brasiliense.

Chevalier, Louis. 1973. *Laboring classes and dangerous classes in Paris during the first half of the nineteenth century.* Princeton: Princeton University Press.

Cunningham, Hugh. 1995. *Children and childhood in Western society since 1500.* London: Longman.

Donzelot, Jacques. 1980. *A polícia das famílias.* Rio de Janeiro: Graal.

Himmelfarb, Gertrude. 1983. *The idea of poverty: England in the early industrial age.* New York: Vintage.

———. 1991. *Poverty and compassion: The moral imagination of the late Victorian.* New York: Vintage.

Lobo, Hélio. 1907. Criminalidade infantil e assistência penal. *Revista Forense* 8 (48): 23–28.

Moncorvo Filho, Arthur. 1920. *Pela infancia tudo!* Discurso pronunciado na solenidade da inauguração do Instituto de Protecção e Assistência à Infância de Petropolis.

———. 1926. *Histórico da protecção à infância no Brasil, 1500–1922.* Rio de Janeiro: Empresa Gráfica.

Moraes, Evaristo de. 1898. Criança na detenção. *Gazeta da Tarde,* 11 October.

———. 1900. *Creanças abandonadas e creanças criminosas (notas e observações).* Rio de Janeiro: Guimarães.

Paiva, Ataulpho de. 1916 [1912]. A nova justiça: Os tribunaes para menores. In *Justiça e assistência.* Rio de Janeiro: Jornal do Commercio.

Peixoto, Afrânio. 1933. *Criminologia.* Rio de Janeiro: Guanabara Waissman Koogan.

Pilotti, Francisco, and Irene Rizzini, eds. 1995. *A arte de governar crianças: A história das políticas sociais, da legislação e da assistência à infância no Brasil.* Rio de Janeiro: Instituto Interamericano del Niño/Editora Universitária Santa Úrsula/AMAIS.

Platt, Anthony M. 1977. *The child savers: The invention of delinquency*. Chicago: University of Chicago Press.

República Federativa do Brasil. 1927. *Código de Menores*. Decreto N. 17.943 A, de 12 de outubro.

Rizzini, Irene. 1992. 100 años de evolución hacia una nueva legislación sobre la infancia. In *La infancia en América Latina*, edited by Ministerio de Asuntos Sociales. Madrid.

————. 1997. *O século perdido: Raízes históricas das políticas públicas para a infância no Brasil*. Rio de Janeiro: Editora Universitária Santa Ursula/ AMAIS.

Sodré, Nelson Werneck. 1989. *A república: Uma revisão histórica*. Porto Alegre: Universidade Federal do Rio Grande do Sul.

Sznaider, Nathan. 1996. Compassion and control: Children in civil society. Unpublished paper. The Academic College of Tel Aviv-Yaffo, Behavioral Science Department.

Trovão, Lopes. 1896. *Discurso do Senador Lopes Trovão*. Brasil: Lei 104.

Vaz, Franco. 1905. *A infância abandonada*. Rio de Janeiro: Imprensa Nacional.

8

How Haitian Artists Disclose Childhood of All Ages

LeGrace Benson

Artists of Haiti bring to light the entwined doubled heritages from Africa and Europe, now and then with a thread of the extinguished Taíno, who called their island, alternately, Kiskeya and Ayiti. They carve and weld and paint in a country of twin tradition and sensibility, where the nerve and circulation systems of language and religion are everywhere in duality or even trinity. The artists live in the cities where a daughter of impoverished rural parents is the unpaid *restavek* servant of the talented young woman who will soon be off to study at the Sorbonne, both of them bearing the same French family name. Out in the streets the shadow of the Catholic church spire falls across a *hounfo*, or Vodou place of worship, in early morning and the Pentecostal Holiness chapel in the late afternoon. The woman selling fruit at curbside says in the Kreyol everyone understands, *"M gen bon mango jodi-a"* (I've got good mangoes today). In the bookstall farther up the street a man offers to the few who can read, *"Ici, le texte pour l'étude de l'histoire du Cap Haïtien."* The artists live with this *marasa*[1] condition, making art out of the twined, braided, twilled stuff of everyday myth and exigency.

The artists' images of children are seldom simple, for all the children of Haiti live in extraordinary circumstances. All of them live with the knotted duplicities arising out of their divisions. Scions of unordinarily rich parents ride their imported horses and motorcycles through the woods beyond Kenskoff. Children of the small middle-class sweat over their homework, recognizing even in the lower grades that education is

181

the *sine qua non* of freedom from the terrifying fears of disease, hunger, or oppression. Infants in the storm of poverty, rescued by some benevolent group from overseas, march to school extraordinarily dressed in their donated starched, bright uniforms and shined shoes. The only truly ordinary children are the myriad gaunt poor, surviving despite an extraordinary lack of potable water, substantial shelter, sufficient food, adequate health and safety, or schools.

Photographers from outside produce images of Haitian children for letters, newspapers, and calendars that assistance groups send north to beg. "Here are these pitiable children. Send money. Care. Say prayers." Appealing to affluent donors, they tend to sort out into two groups. Some photographs have backgrounds of luxuriant tropical colors and radiate the charm that pictures of children often exert on adults. Then there are the black and white ones that confront the well-fed and elaborately housed with wistful eyes and distended bellies—starving, unmedicated street dwellers. The alluring exotic. The alluring terrible. They are pictures framed out of the real world of Haitian children. The super rich, the middle class, the *restaveks* all live outside these pictures.

What local photographers frame is in stunning contrast. There is almost a rage for photographs, the favored subjects being baptism, first communion, school graduation for those children so fortunate, engagement, marriage, and obsequies. Even quite poor families will scrape together a little money to commemorate these rites of passage with at least one or two photographs. There is a familial moment; the subject is dressed in as much splendor as can be begged or borrowed for this moment at the periphery of the tempo and texture of ordinary time.

This selective discontinuity of images by photographers native or foreign haunts and obscures. The painters and sculptors frame-out too, but they have ways to incorporate materials from the opulent reality of Haitian psychological, philosophical, and religious sensibilities. Their depictions of children are often covert or explicit emblems of hope and despair, of Eros and Thanatos, of daily tasks and playtime, disguising profound old conversations from Africa or France or the vanished folk of Kiskeya. Coming to the tasks of art from the several social environments of the country, their images hide and disclose divisions of class, race, religion, and wealth. It is the painters and sculptors who bring the complexity of Haitian childhood to light.

All the intersecting worlds of Haitian childhoods, whether lived out in affluence, middle-class struggles, or degrees of destitution, share a pervading environment of fear. A photograph of a police sergeant walking his two infant daughters to school joins disparate sections of a shared city. The father heads off to work to help guard the privileges of wealth, investing a sacrificial portion of his small wages to ensure his children's move out of the world of impoverishment. His walk down the street from the bidonville where they live to the school and then on to his station in affluent Pétionville makes actual the conjunction between the two worlds of his daughters' childhood: their bridge over troubled waters. His duty is to protect those who fear losses and uprisings from the underclasses. Food, clothing, shelter, medical care, education, and uprisings against the government are also the stuff of his fears for himself and his family. The little girls enter into this climate of multiple uncertainties intensified by the tales every poor or rich child hears: the *lougawou* (werewolf) might bite you and drain your blood; some neighbor may send a bad *pwen* (spell) to injure or make you sick; the magic fish will pull you underground if your family offends it. These evade the cameras. Artists must capture them.

The artists disclose another theme of Haitian life not framed by photographers and little remarked upon by economists, sociologists, historians, or even ethnographers: that is, a pervading juvenency. "Juvenency," a nearly obsolete word, refers to a state of youth as a stage of life and avoids the alternatives "juvenile" or "infantile." These more common terms carry negative connotations of developmental inadequacy not intended here. There is a saying heard in Haiti: "You are never an adult in Haitian culture" (Moss and Stephenson 1999–2000).[2] The patron and his clients, the papa of the family and the younger members of families, the *houngan* or *manmbo* (male and female Vodou spiritual leader, respectively) and the initiates of the Vodou *fanmi* ("family" or congregation), the priest or pastor from his flock, the leaders of the numerous Masonic lodges, all share a structural similarity in which the adherents habitually look first to these position-holders before initiating actions on their own. For the schoolchildren it is the same: they sit in orderly rows, memorize their books or lectures and repeat them back to the teacher. The teacher, like the priest, the father of the family, or the patron landowner, is strongly respected even now when many individuals in seats of relative power have been undermined or actually toppled.

An authority position may be eventually achieved by a select few

Fig. 8.1. Policeman takes his daughters to school. Photo by LeGrace Benson, Arts of Haiti Research Project Archives.

from among the children or adults who meanwhile consent to play out their dependent, subordinate roles. Arrival at positions of dominance is most commonly through prescribed stages and degrees, not unlike those of Masonic orders. Far less commonly, an exceptional figure will wrest such a position through charisma or hostile action. It is interesting to note how many such personages will then refer to their followers or constituents as "my children." It is the unspoken theme of Haiti's history from the colonial era to the present. Juvency appears in many works by several artists depicting people who are adults yet curiously childlike in form or demeanor. The images also relate partly to the *marasa* theme, for the *marasa* are understood to be perpetual children, making demands of the sort Sigmund Freud, in his *Interpretation of Dreams,* described as "infantile omnipotence."

Portraits of actual children, or depictions of children as an ordinary part of everyday life in genre paintings, appear in the art of Haiti from the period of independence forward. Nearly all of these come from the studios of artists who are formally trained in art academies and are either members of the affluent classes or attached to them by patronage.[3] This is unsurprising, for it would be the well-off who would commission such works to begin with. The substance and experience of childhood and of parenthood are relatively rare topics for art of any era or place. The influential French Academy considered such subjects unsuitable for "serious" art, and the domestic scenes of many now-honored artists of the nineteenth and twentieth centuries were declared unworthy of "high art." Yet, portraits of the scions of wealth and privilege abound, not so much family pictures as signals of heritage and sometimes as *memento mori*.

It is the artists from the populations living in more rural areas and more strongly attached to traditions of the countryside—the *andeyo*—who produce the images of the more mysterious children, the *marasa* and the juvenate adults. The Haitian works that first came to wider attention outside were those done by these artists who had grown up in the predominantly rural culture. There ordinary life and ordinary environment are laced with a deep awareness of the presence of the *lwas*, complex spiritual beings who guide, protect, demand fealty, insure blessings, and mediate both social discourse and healing. Much of these artists' attention to the world was strongly shaped by the continual show-and-tell of the "Long Conversation" reiterated, adjusted, added to, subtracted from, all the way back to the forebears.[4]

There is a sense in which if a society exists, it thereby has a Long Conversation, and indeed that the Long Conversation is essential infrastructure creating and sustaining any society. "Conversation" is sentences and stories, certainly, but it is also symbols and images, and, importantly, the transfer of technical skills in procedures that depend absolutely upon a subtle ecology of language and action (the "show-and-tell"). It is the medium of children's education. Where a people emphasize or depend entirely upon speech, song, action, and graphic images rather than on the production and exchange of writings, the Long Conversation has characteristics that contrast to one degree or another with the Long Conversation of people who consistently utilize writings to carry on traditions and transfer technologies. They have in common at least one consequential factor: the apparently ineluctable need of human beings to communicate. This seems to entail an elaborate process of actually conveying information about something or some-one to someone else together with expression of a self, experiencing a moment. As an everyday action that ensures the continuity of life, it is not simply "content" but also "style," intensity, and affect. To call this process a "Long Conversation" rather than a "tradition" is to bring atten-tion to the fact that it is the complex acts of people talking with and showing one another that creates, maintains, and transmits the informa-tion that becomes a society's tradition.

The Kreyol artists of Haiti grew up in a world of songs, stories, and show-and-tell recipes for food, making things, healing, finding love, passing the soul from visibility to invisibility—nearly all of it accom-plished face-to-face. The city artists grew up with some of that but also with the Long Conversations from more distant places, conveyed in books or films or radio along with the face-to-face encounters. The latter were often heavily shaped by the conversations from outside their every-day space. For Haitian artists and for Haitian children, the Long Con-versations once again reveal the *marasa* condition: two intertwined but separate continuities.

One of the first of the Kreyol masters to appear on the larger art scene of Haiti, Paris, and New York was Hector Hyppolite. An artist from the hills near the port town of Saint Marc, he was a devout follower of Vodou who had progressed through all but the final degree of becom-ing a Vodou *houngan* at his untimely death in the mid-1950s. Hence, a substantial portion of the Long Conversations that came to him per-sonally had been repeated over and over since the time of the African captives. He also had an ear and an eye for the conversations of Roman Catholic missionaries. His work includes few depictions of children other than *Saint Francis and the Christ Child,* painted, as were many of his works, after a dream in which the image arose. In Roman Catholic iconography Saint Joseph the Carpenter or Saint Anthony of Padua take the fostering role. For example, a *dwapo* (Vodou ceremonial flag) uses a typical Catholic oleograph of Saint Joseph and Christ Child at its cen-ter. But Hyppolite creates a unique image using a saint who is ordinarily shown alone or with animals in his role as Vodou *lwa.* In strictly Catholic imagery, flowers would be white lilies, and if a dove appeared, it would be white or gray, sometimes with an aureole. Hyppolite created a twined image—a "Kreyol Christ Child," as the artist asserted to the director of the art center where he presented it. The director may not have known that Saint Francis is also one of the Vodou *lwa*. Moreover, he may have little noted that the Child wears a robe in the color, rose, associated with the *lwa* Ezuli,[5] the most important in the great families of spirits, patroness of love of every variety. The dove is also bright pink, and on either side the figures are encircled with arabesques of pink hibiscus, the flower of Ezuli and of the Haitian nation. Two sets of birds inhabit the floral surround, avian manifestations of the sacred African twins, *marasa*, while simultaneously serving as the traditional companions of Saint Francis. At the bottom of the painting, on either side of the dove, are a smaller angel and a larger angel, the Kreyol *ti bon anj* (the good, small personal spirit or guardian angel) and *gwo bon anj* (the good, large personal spirit or guardian angel), believed to chaperone each individual Haitian.[6] The mystical infant of Christianity appears, then, in a work suffused with the spiritualism of Vodou, depicting a literal loving relationship and adumbrating a transcendent love in both Christian and Vodou traditions.[7]

The thousands of images of the Infant Jesus, the Son of God come to earth to live in humble and ultimately tortured circumstances, are both gnomon and generator of powerful influence on Western art and intellectual sensibilities, even in their most superficial and sentimental versions. Moreover, countless artists make the concept of a mythicised mother-child bond graphic in both museum and mass-distributed versions of the Virgin Mother Mary and Infant Jesus. The history of Haitian art provides examples of such images from pre-independence forward. Especially in the Catholic churches this image was frequent, often as copies or copies of copies from works of the Italian Renaissance. Printed versions of some of these famous works began to appear in the late nineteenth century, and by the late twentieth century the street vendors in any Haitian city invariably offered rows of Our Lady of Perpetual Help with Christ Child or Our Lady of Czestochowa with Christ Child, along with Our Lady of Carmel, Our Lady of the Immaculate Conception, and Our Lady of the Assumption. Those with Christ Child are the most popular and are the images most frequently copied or modified by Kreyol artists. Hyppolite was unusual in placing the Child in the arms of a male. Certainly such images have little or nothing to do with actual Haitian childhood, and much to do with lingering juvenency and the desire for protective, fostering love.

The Perpetual Help and Czestochowa images became the criterion

Fig. 8.2. Hector Hyppolite, *Saint Francis and the Christ Child* (Milwaukee Art Museum, Gift of Richard and Erna Flagg, M1991.132).

Fig. 8.3. Dwapo (ceremonial flag) for lwa Ogou Balinjo, sewn by Clotaire Bazile and Ana Wexler. Photo by Ana Wexler, Arts of Haiti Research Project Archives.

images for artist Ishmail Saintcilius, who created an uncounted number of small canvases, most of them going to collectors outside Haiti. For Haitians, his works were understood to represent Ezuli Dantor and her daughter Anaïs, Ezuli Dantor's manifestation being associated with parental love. Yet the artist himself insisted, at least some of the time, that these were "Not at all Ezuli. They are the Virgin Mary and Jesus."[8] Many other artists use these two images as well, and in conversations over a period of years with makers of the images as well as with the domestic users, it appears that ordinarily the images are meant to be and are used as mystical and metaphoric, simultaneously bearing meaning from Vodou and from Catholic Christianity. In no wise depictions of Haitian childhood or of Haitian parental domesticity, they are graphic myths, patents of a desired ineffable love between mother and child.

One of the most startling versions of the Mother-Child, Mary-Jesus, Ezuli-Anaïs images appeared in 1991 on the wall of a settlement in one of the poorest districts of Port-au-Prince. The Virgin held on her lap not the Infant Christ, but a small though clearly adult Catholic priest, Jean-Bertrand Aristide, who had just been inaugurated as president of Haiti. Such an image had a previous history (which may or may not have been known to the artist). During the rule of the Emperor Soulouque (1849–1858), banners and placards had appeared in Port-au-Prince, depicting Soulouque in the Virgin's lap.[9]

In contrast to such deifications of political leaders, which give an ironic twist to the motif of juvency, are the sad Nativities that appear with some frequency in Haitian art. One by Bourmond Bryon (now in the Flagg Collection of Milwaukee Art Museum) places the Nativity in a bleak, dark Haitian village, the scene illuminated only by glories emanating from the newborn Christ. As a young artist conflicted between loyalties to the Christian church and to his *lwa* Ezuli, Wilson Bigaud fashioned an exceptionally dark and brooding Nativity with the

Fig. 8.4. Anonymous street mural of President Jean-Bertrand Aristide at the time of his inauguration, 1991. Photo by LeGrace Benson, Arts of Haiti Research Project Archives.

Fig. 8.5. Fritz Ducheine, *The Birth of Jesus*. Photo by Fritz Ducheine, Arts of Haiti Research Project Archives.

Kreyol baby in a manger from Christmas card conventions adored by a standing couple and a peasant farmer. A makeshift palm-frond roof scarcely shelters them from the dark night closing in. A more recent work by Fritz Ducheine continues the tradition, intensifying the bleakness by placing the drama in an arid, leafless environment that could be the stony Savane Désolée in the north of Haiti. These artists set the mythical into the ordinary: *bébé kom bébé nou-menm* (a baby like ours).

There are secular "maternities" that encompass a range from Rose-Marie Desruisseaux's warm realism to the idealist renditions of artists of the *"avancés,"*[10] incorporating the styles and techniques of European impressionism and cubism. One by Dieudonne Cédor uses the style of Picasso's Parisian "blue period" to present a thin mother with her thin baby and thin toddler entreating, *"Ki kote-m ap fê?"*—"Where can I go to?" Unusual are the realistic renditions of, for example, a little girl playing with a top, by Villard Denis, or a pensive adolescent girl by Luce Turnier, or a solemn young boy by Gesner Armand. All of these are works intended for viewers outside the immediate social milieus of the artists, and, in contrast to the canvases of the Kreyol artists that draw upon community sensibility, these are nearly all expressions from an individual artist. They are reflections more upon the condition of childhood as it is understood in the West and as emulated among the elite than upon the distinctive nature or condition of the several other kinds of Haitian childhood.

The few domestic mother-and-child paintings from the hand of Kreyol-speaking artists from the *andeyo,* that is those that do not invoke the iconographies of Madonna and Child or Ezuli and Child, are nonetheless more sacred than secular. Hector Hyppolite created a mother holding her child, her dark shawl pulled up around the twosome. A *djab,* or little devil figure, sits at her knees and in the sky are several ominous flying creatures, more *djab* than bird. The mother protects her child from the encircling fears and terrors. Hyppolite's contemporary, Robert Saint Brice, called into visibility several versions of a protecting figure, sheltering an infant, all done in the dotted style that some Western viewers have mistaken for an attempt at impressionism. The dotting more likely shares an old tradition to be found in Haiti and in sub-Saharan West Africa of signaling the presence of spirits, divinities and ghosts by depicting them with dots or by covering the body or a dancer's costume with dots. Saint Brice's flickering woman and infant do indeed appear evanescent and impalpable. They, like Hyppolite's work or the Nativities of Bourmond, Bigaud, or Duchiene, solemnly emerge out of an afflicting darkness permeated with dangers.

A painter of the next generation after Hyppolite and Saint Brice, Raphael Denis likewise came to art out of a collective, rural sensibility. Beginning his work in the Saint Soliel project in the mountains beyond Port-au-Prince, his style and subject matter are typical of that group of self-taught artists. A four-armed, mothering *lwa* seems to present *marasa twa* (*marasa* triplets), two of whom, laced together with a ribbon, are simply heads of infants, while the third lies swaddled at her waist. There are spirit dots, as in the work of Saint Brice, and other background sections of the painting are decorated with arabesques of flowering vines. The dots, the vines, the *marasa,* and the mother are symbols related to the precarious nature of life around the artist, especially the lives of infants trying to grow up with scant nourishment and plentiful disease.

Notions of all human beings as forever the "children" of a devasta-

Fig. 8.6. Raphael Denis, Untitled (Issa El Saieh Collection, Port-au-Prince). Photo by LeGrace Benson, Arts of Haiti Research Project Archives.

ting creator reach a bitter culmination in such works as Francisco Goya's *Chronos Devouring His Children,* where a monstrous God-of-All-Time feasts on the dismembered and bloody corpses scattered at his knees. Contemplation of such terror can return even a mature adult to the darkest moments of dependent childhood. In Haiti, that "country of hunger," as some name it, voracious death is always on the edge of consciousness, summoning up fearfulness about one's own self, fearfulness for the offspring of one's mortal body. Childbirth, infancy, and early childhood mortality statistics for the country are stark enough without Goya's image. In this country of yearning appetites, artists create some startling veiled images that are alarming once their symbols are learned.

One of these veiled images is that of a Haitian family, painted around 1950 by Castera Bazile, one-time yard boy at the Centre d'Art, who developed high artistic abilities. The imposing main figure is a seated woman, her husband settled on the ground beside her. His agricultural tools lie on the other side of her chair. One of their children clings to the mother's skirts, and the other is suckling at her breast. From their actions, the children should have the features of infants or toddlers, yet in proportion to the parents they are even smaller than real infants and their bodies are those of undernourished adolescents. The unreality of scale relationships suggests a mythic couple upon whom all the people are dependent. The mother wears garments of saturated blue and red, the colors of the Haitian flag. The child at breast is nude, and the one at her knee wears only a little sleeveless undershirt vertically divided between red and white. Such a parti-colored garment is actually used by rural Haitian parents as a protection for the child. It is a type of *chemiset maldjok*—a shirt against the evil eye, put on an especially pretty or healthy child to prevent jealous neighbors from sending it a bad spell. (Some of the universality of such a motivation is signaled by the Kreyol word *malocchio*, the evil eye, which in this case comes from Italy.) This painting then, which presents itself as a bright and charming work depicting family life in Haiti, carries in its colors and in its curious size relationships another story of family life in Haiti. It is the one that cries out to higher forces of the nation and to the armaments of magic for protection and nourishment.

Similarly encoded for a mothering Haiti who will take care of all her yearning children are *Haïti chérie*, by Mécène Brunis, and *Pour cueillir la rose géant*, by Jean-Louis Sénatus (Alexis 2000: plates 82 and 83). *Haïti chérie*, dressed in the blue and red of the national flag, stands in the center of the composition, at the front of a line of stone crosses that transmute into her figure. Above her in the blue sky, six angels trumpet her arrival while a white dove emanates rays of light that fall upon her. Surrounding her feet and no taller than her knees are her children, adult Haitians. When looked at carefully, the rocky outcropping beside her

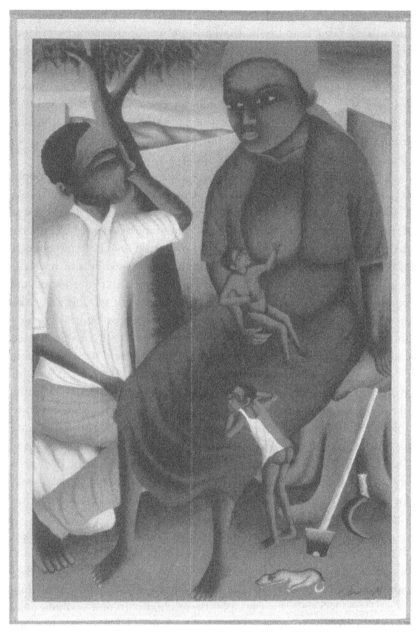

Fig. 8.7. Castera Bazile, *Haitian Family* (Milwaukee Art Museum, Gift of Gabriele Flagg Pfeiffer, M1993.288).

reveals itself as a sad old man. *Pour cueillir la rose géante* is equally metaphoric. This time the matriarch is a towering promontory of land, framed in a pale aureole, with a tree that devolves into a path to her embrace. In the foreground, tiny Haitians process along the road, out of scale not only with the fostering mother but also with the ordinary features of the landscape. In a prominent place below a denuded tree is the giant rose (symbol of both the Virgin Mary and Ezuli), arising from a stony circle. Here again, the adults are reduced to the size of dependent children, a variation of the motif of juvenency.

The apparently cheerful works of Jacques-Richard Chèry are popular purchases by tourists to Haiti and buyers in galleries outside of Haiti. People seem amused by the "little children" carrying enormous baskets of fruits and vegetables on their heads. The impossible scale of the produce serves as a hyperbolic metaphor for desired bounty in the country of the famished. When looked at more closely the "children" have the head-to-body proportions of toddlers under three, but the torsos and breasts of adults. This is a poetry of appetite. In one of Chèry's works, an elaborate presentation for human rights, freedom from oppression and extortions, as well as freedom from hunger, the artist sends these children of Haiti with their offerings of outsized food to serve a table of guests of all colors and nations. It was his wish for Haiti and for everyone. He remarked that we already knew that unless we became like children, we would not enter the kingdom of God (where, presumably, all would be fed). Chèry began painting without instruction until his work came to artist Philomé Obin's attention. Having grown up in the history-rich North, he was prepared for Obin's lessons in history and in the importance of painting as a way of creating a visual "book" for those who could not read. His work is as didactic as it is "colorful" and "exotic."

Alix Roy, educated both in private school and by artists of the Centre d' Art, created cheerful genre scenes in which, as in Chèry's works, the adults all have the body proportions of very young children. Yet they carry out adult activities. In his *Bamboche* (Nadal-Gardère and Bloncourt 1986: 158–59), for example, these child-men and -women celebrate a riotous party, a veritable bacchanal, with smiling, shouting and kissing musicians, dancers, drinkers, and eaters, served by companions who bring in yet more food and liquor under a streamer-decorated pavil-

Fig. 8.8. Jacques-Richard Chèry, *The Misereor Cloth*. Photo by LeGrace Benson, Arts of Haiti Research Project Archives.

ion. This is a Haiti seldom seen, with a population that exists in the imagination.

Lionel Saint-Eloi, in *Maître Grand Bois* (Alexis 2000: plate 206), exemplifies a way of presenting relationships in a Vodou ceremony that can be seen in works by others as well. The *houngan* kneels, his sacred rattle held up in the direction of the *lwa Gran bwa* (an important Vodou forest divinity). He is larger than his encircling devotees—the *hounsis,* who bring offerings to place at the feet of *Gran bwa* seated above all of them in the crotch of a hollow tree, and in turn, larger than the *houngan.* The hierarchy of degrees of juvenance—*hounsis* to *houngan, houngan* to *lwa* are as clearly marked in this work as in Egyptian paintings where the order of dependency is exactly specified by relative size.

If Chèry's and Roy's charming images at first conceal a cry from the gut, and Saint-Eloi's an ambivalent veneration and fear of the spirits, there are others that do not seduce with delights of color and attractive ostensible subjects. These are the works, only recently offered for sale or for viewing to outsiders, that incorporate heads and bodies of baby dolls. In a variation of the motif of conflating child and adult in a single figure, one of the most striking of these places a chubby-cheeked, smiling head of a doll baby atop the dark-gray-clad body of Bawon Lakwa (Baron LaCroix), a member of the Gède family of spirits of death, graveyards, funerals, and sex. Used in a *Bizango*[11] ceremony, the doll baby is attached to a plaque of light wood upon which are a wooden cross surmounted by a wood and metal crucifix on either side of the fully dimensional Baron figure. Baron's two up-reaching hands are baby doll heads. The hats on these heads are like fur-trimmed Santa Claus caps except that they are a funereal gray. Despite the color shift, the cap of Saint Nicholas[12] divulges the connection that the saint, who is also a *lwa,* is believed to have with the sacred children, the *marasa,* the doll-face hands thus almost certainly meant to signify the sacred children. The *marasa* twins (often also triplets) have multiple and complex meanings for Haitians, and in certain ceremonies become ritually projected back onto real twins, triplets, and their sibs (Houlberg 1995).[13] Invariably they have to do with hunger and gluttony, with sapping strength from sibs, and with death.

In the same museum collection with the *Bizango* dolls is a flexible board covered with colored fabric splotched with gray. Children's balls, also splotched, and of a size similar to human skulls, are arranged around two baby dolls, one with up-reaching arms, the other armless and legless. Curiously, the works resemble some of the dismembered doll works of the Surrealist artist Hans Bellmer. While it is unlikely that the Artibonite fashioner of these pieces ever saw Bellmer's work, the violent presence of death unveils a universally present, albeit covert, human awareness. In another district of Haiti, an artist refused to let a similar object be photographed. He had fashioned a doll with a papier-mâché bull's head, seated in a miniature chair. The bull consumes the arms and legs of gory, red-streaked doll body parts: Goya's Chronos at work in the hills above Saint Marc.

Antithetically, the *Bizango* images evoke a startling contrast to Italian and Spanish Madonnas who gently levitate into the empyrean, accompanied by flights of infant angels, which also sometimes lack arms and legs. Are they the other side of the same coin? The altarpiece of the Cathedral of Cap Haïtien Assomption de Notre Dame de Bon Secours,

Fig. 8.9. Anon., *Baron LaCroix* (Bizango Cult Collection; Fondation pour la préservation, la valorization et la production d'oeuvres culturelles haïtiennes). Photo by LeGrace Benson, Arts of Haiti Research Project Archives.

attributed to Thimoleon Déjoie (circa 1825)[14] presents a cloud-seated
Madonna encircled with cherubs, rising above a shoreline. Above her,
the monogram of the Virgin, surmounted with a crown, floats in a bril-
liant sky beneath dark clouds. The models for the Haitian's work may
have been Latin American religious works from nearby countries, in
turn derived from the Spanish Baroque, such as the works of Murillo.

It is helpful to carry the long artists' conversation with the European-
images-come-into-the-Caribbean beyond Murillo and back two or three
more generations. The images of the Virgin Mother with her cohorts
of baby angels appear in Europe some years after the population deci-
mations inflicted by the Black Death. These fecund images came into
Haiti as imports by missionaries as early as the beginning of the eighteenth century, where they remain to the present. They appear in Catholic churches and chapels, in missionary-printed illustrations, and find
their way into most Haitian Vodou *hounfos*. For many Haitians, then,
the images arrive over a twin route, via both of their major religions.
The Madonna and her sweet cherubs well disguise existential fright, but
at the ground-of-being join with the baby doll *marasas* of the cemetery
spirits. The gruesome images of *Bizango* are kith and kin of milder Haitian uses of the commercially produced baby dolls, transformed by
clothing and attachments of objects found in the local environment into
representations of Ezuli and her children. The monogram of the Virgin
in the Cathedral is exactly the one embroidered on the sacred flags for
Vodou ceremonies where Ezuli is called down. In both cases the conflation of child and adult, child and angels and spirits is worth pondering.
On the one hand death lurks either as an immediate threat or as a terror
to be combated with forceful amulets. On the other hand, often simultaneously, there is a vigorous procreative, erotic response and insurance
of life. The baby dolls are serendipitously found objects, coming into
Haiti from North American and Chinese toy factories in the twentieth
century. Yet it would be hard to claim that the use of a childlike image
in ritual circumstances associated with profound desire or mortal danger
is merely happenstance. In the hands of Vodou priests and priestesses
or artists, the dolls (or *putti*) almost immediately transfigure from cute-
ness to the serious manifestations of love, sex, healing, the allaying or
creating of fears, even death. The Kreyol images lay bare some of the
veiled meaning of the postplague Madonnas.

Easier on the spirits, but no less paradoxical in its conflations of child and adult, religious and secular amours, is a painting using one of the popular themes in Haitian art since 1948, Adam and Eve in paradise beside the forbidden tree. In an unsigned, undated work seen in a Haitian gallery in Washington, D.C., a prepubescent Adam and Eve loll beneath an apple tree in a northern latitude, Eve with the red fruit in her hand. The style is highly reminiscent of late-nineteenth-century French erotic picnic scenes, and the figures both have white skin. The Haitian artist uses this favorite Paradise motif, arrived in Haiti via imported books on Italian and French art, relocates the event into the middle Atlantic east of the United States, and uses Greco-Roman and Renaissance *putti* figures to confront viewers with a romantic vision of children about to lose their sexual innocence. This profoundly creole image is Haitian and global in a single stroke of the brush. Paradoxical, yes, but not as disturbing as the *Bizango* melding of child and death.

The use of a child-image to present dimensions of young-adult or mature-adult human experience calls to mind such schemes elsewhere and in other times. For many Africans both in Africa and in diaspora, the Haitian images may strongly recall carved figures from African lands. The resonance for many Europeans and North Americans may be scriptural, literary, and artistic presentations of Christianity, where the faithful are often characterized as children, and indeed encouraged to take on the open and trusting minds and hearts of children in order to assure salvation. Perhaps there is also, even if elusive, the childhood experience English Romantic poet Wordsworth evokes: "Not in entire forgetfulness, / and not in utter nakedness, / But trailing clouds of glory do we come / From God, who is our home: / Heaven lies about us in our infancy."[15]

Christian congregations in Haiti as well as in Europe and North America hear sermons on these matters. Becoming spiritually innocent and receptive like a child to the point of metaphorically being born again is a frequent exhortation from pulpits. Another exhortation is to take good care of actual children, which frequently results in sending assistance of one kind or another to far-away children, the ones on the calendars and newsletters. The children that members of the congregation have in their own homes and neighborhoods are mostly attended to as projects for inducing proper behavior or productive diligence with school lessons. The mysteries of childhood are almost entirely located as an attachment to the Christ Child for a few days in December. The mystery of being "born again" and reentering one's own adulthood with the spiritual transparency of early childhood seldom is fastened to ritual enigmas or to the creation of visual works of art. Quite the opposite: witness the thousands of images of angels transformed into infants which serve to desacralize both childhood and angels.

Educated, "cosmopolitanized" Haitians generally maintain a distance from the "interesting" spirit-dot mothers and babes or the doll-hands of Saint Nicholas. They can be observed to desacralize the ineffable mystery of both personal and collective Haitian childhoods, just as their French and North American friends do. Parents from this population have primarily secular notions concerning their survival and that of their offspring. Food is abundant for the majority of them, professional medical care is expected to do the work of healing and it is rare (though possible) to encounter a parent or child who genuinely fears a *lougawou*, a *maldjok*, or a spell cast at a ceremony. Conversations with "born-again" Christians (who are mostly from less affluent or impoverished populations) likewise seem devoid of complex figures of speech and imagery that include aspects of childhood marvels. Examining the print and interview material over several years of North American and European (particularly French, Belgian, Dutch, and German) discussion about how to protect, educate, and provide for children, one sees a mundane point of view and understanding of children. Television programs aimed at children offer vicarious adventure and amazing feats, phantasms without transcendence. The French poet Stéphane Mallarmé regretted, "The child lives in a secular world. To adapt to this world the child abandons its ecstasy."

He spoke of the Western child. Most children in Haiti live only partly in the secular world. Out in the mountain villages, children live their earthy lives in a pervading spiritual environment. Some Haitian artists, speak of growing up aware of such spiritual presences. In contrast, most contemporary, academically trained adults have so well adapted to the secular world that they will usually fail to view Haitian childhood and Haitian images of childhood with the kind of comprehension a Wordsworth or a Mallarmé or another Haitian might discover there. Play and joy are exceptional Haitian images; tenderness and nurturing of an other-than-sacred child infrequent, as they seem to be in most art most times and places. A catalogue of a posthumous retrospective exhibition of the two artists, Bernard Séjourné and Jean-René Jérôme illustrates exceptions. Among the works were two mother and child idealizations. Séjourné depicted a gently smiling young woman holding her happy infant. The two live in an elegant swirl of white voile surrounded by a lavender ambience scattered with white and lavender flowers. Jérôme's mother and infant, their features more "African" than Séjourné's pair, are enveloped in an earth-colored, womblike structure made up of semitransparent folds, carrying a design of sunflowers and small, organic zygotelike shapes. Burnt umber forms lurking in the transparencies may be other people or spirits. The mother and child smile contentedly. Beyond their protective folds the canvas is dark as night. Both painters' works exhibit a background in art studies, and a thorough acquaintance with art history of the west and contemporary, international art. The mother and child images are ideal, romantic and secular.

Out of the Long Conversation in Kreyol comes the hammered sheet steel *Gwo Fanm Ak Ti Bebe* (Grand woman with little baby) of Fontenel Pointjour. From a distance, the woman could be a domestic servant with the babe seated on her large apron. They exchange a kiss that attenuates both faces into a taut little iron bridge. Despite the household worker's "apron," jewelry encircles Gwo Fanm's ears, neck, arms, wrists, fingers, and ankles. Two large fish form her ballooning skirt. From the gills of one hangs a bell, and from the other a tiny head. No domestic, she, but the *lwa*, La Siren, Ezuli's oceanic manifestation. The "Ti Bebe" likewise yields a second image on closer look, his torso readable as an old man weeping. This old man, we have seen before with Mother Haiti. He is Atibon Legba, the oldest of all the *lwa:* he who opens up the path between the sacred spirits and the ordinary people. The motif of mother and child bears a freight of danger and petition.

Some important images of the world of children in Haiti show aspects of the reality in part stripped of symbols, magic, or eroticism. A painting by Émil Similcar of around 1990 moves out of the world of spirits into that of medical reality. In "Mother with Sick Child," a woman with a stricken, imploring face holds out the sagging body of a child against a background geometry of dense blacks and browns. The artist, creating this image out of his own life and the lives around him, compels attention to the intertwined suffering of parent and endangered off-

Fig. 8.10. Fontanel Pointjour, *Gwo Famn ak Ti Bebe* (Big woman with tiny baby). Photo by Fontanel Pointjour, Arts of Haiti Research Project Archives.

Fig. 8.11. Emil Similcar, *Woman with Sick Child* (Musée de l'Art Haïtien, College Saint-Pierre, Port-au-Prince). Photo by LeGrace Benson, Arts of Haiti Research Project Archives.

spring. Similcar, approaching the themes from a secular standpoint, evidences advanced studies in art and knowledge of modernist composition and color.

Notably, some works by members of the Obin family of artists in Cap Haïtien calmly report on school and home. Philomé Obin, the patri-

Fig. 8.12. Philomé Obin, *School Sports Exercises* (Issa El Saieh Collection, Port-au-Prince). Photo by LeGrace Benson, Arts of Haiti Research Project Archives.

arch of this artistic family, painted several versions of children and schools, a topic of some importance to a man concerned as he was with teaching the next generation. Children line up to receive prizes for achievement, parents and local dignitaries gather to celebrate the occasion. Most years, less than half the school-age population can attend class; such a painting carries a different weight in Haiti than it would in countries where nearly all youth are in school.[16] Systematic information on how many families make significant sacrifices to send children to school, and of exactly what these entail is scarce. Anecdotal information abounds, and the observations of teachers and others directly concerned yields stories of how one child is chosen from several in a family to go to school, how school uniforms, which must be bought, are carefully tended to be passed along to a relative or neighborhood youngster. When there was a supposed epidemic of swine fever in Haiti, reports multiplied of families whose pig had to be slaughtered, thus precluding paying school fees.[17] The pig slaughter was thus a double destitution.

School is understood by nearly all to be essential, literacy is almost venerated among many poorer people as well as many who are better off, and higher education is held in the very greatest esteem imaginable. The theme of schooling and school ceremonies marking passage from one degree of learning to the next appear in many paintings from the Obin family, and also from a host of other artists. It is one of the most favored subjects, even in the tourist markets. The parents of the artist moved into Cap Haïtien from a nearby small town to find better work for the father and a school for young Philomé and his brothers. This was an artisanal family, living in a provincial city in humble circumstances. But there was enough money for education, and Obin completed *lycée* with a knowledge of accounting. At the lycée, an art instructor taught the usual lessons derived from the methods of Academie Francais.[18] Eventually he established his own atelier, with first his brothers, then his son, later other aspiring painters as members. The Obins were literate and bilingual. They also had a knowledge of Haitian history, many crucial events of which had taken place in their own province. They were members of Haiti's oldest continuous Masonic lodge and attended a Protestant church. They establish the precedents for what came to be known as the "History Paintings of the North," with many followers. The children in the paintings of this family are like the painters themselves, and the report is from one of the smallest sectors of Haitian society—the urban, settled, literate families of a modest income that they parcel out first and foremost for school.

Louverture Poisson provides another example. A scene showing a young girl reading aloud from her school book goes beyond being a painted snapshot of everyday life of a Haitian family of humble means. An infant plays on the floor and the mother sews while the youngster recites. She, like nearly all children in school, memorizes the text for the recitation tomorrow. There are objects in the picture that may be symbolic, the most prominent of which is a window just beyond the girl. A road leads as directly from this window as though it were a door, heading straight for a royal palm at the vanishing point. The palm is one of the major emblems signifying the Haitian nation. There is no way now to know if the artist so intended it, but one of the most often heard sayings in Haiti is that literacy and education is the hope, indeed the salvation, of the country.

A student of Obin's, Jean-Baptiste Jean, in the same spirit presents

Fig. 8.13. Louverture Poisson, *The Lesson* (Milwaukee Art Museum, Gift of Mr. and Mrs. Richard B. Flagg, M1979.229).

images of school children on special occasions. "Procession de la fête de l'Arbre," (illustrated in Nadal-Gadère (1986)) shows dozens of boys and girls in their bright uniforms, marching through the village streets waving branches of trees to enter the school—a large edifice standing among one- and two-room houses. Parents and other villagers look on, the local policeman surveys the scene from atop his horse, and the nuns and priests make sure everyone is in line. It is a light-hearted scene, with the reds, greens, blues, and yellows of the school uniforms placed like musical notes within the geometries of wood and plaster architecture. It is a painting that might go well on a North American wall in the dead of winter, especially with the green hills beyond the enclosure of the village furnishing a flowered landscape counterpoint to the architectonics and parade order below. Yet Jean, true to his artistic mentor's concerns, shows some children in the fields. They wear ragged clothes. They are at work.

School events appear in Haitian painting from all over the country. Education of children, as mentioned, is a preoccupation throughout Haiti, but nowhere more so than in the North. Perhaps this concern with education has something to do with the history of how slaves, many of the leaders literate, wrested independence from the French. The stories come to the lips of Haitian children as easily as a song. Every child, schooled or not, can recite a version. Perhaps Philomé Obin, who lived an influential life well into his eighties, spread his passion for education like a set of school assignments throughout the population. For whatever reason, among the revolutionary battle scenes, the depictions of the Citadel fortress against the return of the French, and the portraits of heroes so characteristic of the "School of the North," there are countless scenes of school events.

Paintings of everyday life and the ordinary lives of children appear often in works by Haitian women. In several respects, the women's paintings come out of a different experience from that of the men. First there are the obvious universal differences between female and male experiences of the entire ecology of procreation, gestation, giving birth, nurturing and rearing offspring. Second there is the fact that nearly all girls who grow up to be artists in Haiti are from the professional or upper classes. It is nearly impossible for a female youngster from the rural districts or the poor sections of cities to become a painter or sculptor. (One acclaimed exception is Louisianne Saint Fleurant of the unique Saint Soliel group. In the remote village of Soissons-la-Montagne artist-educator, Claude "Tiga" Garoute, actively encouraged everyone to become an artist. They did.) This means that nearly all the girls who wish to become artists grow up in the Francophone world, educationally oriented toward the larger world beyond their island. They go to school in French but hear Kreyol folklore from domestic servants and people in the streets and markets. Their education in the arts is of the sort typical in France or the United States, often actually imparted in academies in France or North America. Third, the women artists of Haiti, nearly without exception, complain of being shunted aside in the schoolrooms and studios where art is taught. When they overcome this difficulty, they report meeting with resistance to having their work shown.[19]

Women's worlds preponderantly encompass the go'-long and go'-long of everyday life, the sustaining activities of cooking and feeding, nursing and comforting. They recognize the matter and style of daily life as consequential by featuring it in their works of art. Nadal-Gardère and Bloncourt (1986: 185) report that artist Françoise Jean refuses to

Fig. 8.14. Marilene Phipps, *Looking In*. Photo by Marilene Phipps, Arts of Haiti Research Project Archives.

paint anything *but* children.[20] Among the more broad-ranging subjects of the works of Luce Turnier are several children and adolescents, thoughtful, even brooding. One of the original members of the Centre d'Art in Port-au-Prince, she was well-educated both academically and in studio. Her works cast a sensitive light on the reflective propensities of youngsters. So too do those of Hilda Williams, who can make of the simple fact of a little barefoot girl holding a pannier over her head against the rain a study in the tentativeness, vulnerability, and curiosity of mid-childhood.

Of a younger generation, Marilene Phipps brings to her paintings the complexities of being Haitian but living in a North American, largely academic, world. The environment of everyday as lived out by Haitians of simple circumstances but complex sensibilities is the multiform and multilingual matrix of her work. Unlike the photographers necessarily framing whatever reality is before them, Phipps reveals the world inhabited by Haitian children little by little, the painterly surfaces explaining nothing, telling all. Let those who have eyes to see, see. Her *Looking In* details a fundamental and typical activity of children all over the world—attentive observation of adults in special services and circumstances or going about their skilled work. The youngsters and adults look in upon what may be a Vodou ceremony, or perhaps a healing or a divination, involving both special service and skilled work, perhaps an exceptional cook, pulling them to the window over a trail of tasty aromas. The viewer of the work will never know, can only surmise. On the one hand, whatever is going on inside is engaging enough to capture attention, but usual enough that the two boys seated on a wall beside the windows find sights on the street more interesting. Adults and children share a few moments of everyday village life, including the public mystery behind the dark windows. It is a moment caught from the Long Conversation, antique show-and-tell from the grandmothers, great grandfather, and beyond. The artist, distanced from the night fears of *lougawous* and hunger but not from the people looking in, makes a new addition to that long show-and-tell for the essential collaborative memory book. Phipps once remarked to a reporter that that work of hers "took a lifetime." Lifetime means the ancestors, means day-to-day, means the now of a university woman and the children of this village.

The life presented in Phipps's work is miscible with that brought to light by Hyppolite or Saint Brice, Obin or Pointjour, the Saint Soliel painters or Luce Turnier: many ways of life immersed in the same transparent solution, separable only by special acts of analysis. Haitian artists pull the images out of daily lives and dream times resonant with the echoes of the Long Conversations from Brittany and the Slave Coast, Paris, Philadelphia, and Hollywood. The image of childhood in Haiti is no simple thing.

Notes

1. *Marasa* (also spelled *marassa*) are twins or triplets, the idea and images of which trace directly back to West African peoples, and continue to be frequently present as images and ideas in Haitian Vodou religion, literature, and art.

2. Although Moss and Stephenson do not use this common phrase in their article, they discuss how respect for elders continues to operate in shaping identity even among Haitians in diaspora.

3. See Lerebours (1989), in which some nineteenth-century portraits of children are illustrated. See also in Alexis (2000: 20) a portrait of two-year-old Marie Légitime, daughter of a late-nineteenth-century president.

4. See Benson (1999). Here I present the concept of "Long Conversation" as exemplified in the African diaspora. The focus is on the acts of conversation, with acknowledgement of the traditions as the "content" of the exchanges.

5. *Ezuli* is the correct spelling for this Kreyol divinity. The name is often spelled *Erzulie* in French or English writings.

6. The notion of guardian angels has a long history not confined to Christianity. However, the notion began to be prominent in Western Christianity at about the same era that the French began colonizing Saint-Domingue in the seventeenth century. It would very likely have been brought into the country as both words and images by missionaries as early as the first years of the French presence on the island of Hispaniola.

7. For historian Philippe Ariès (1962), the cult of the guardian angel is strongly associated with childhood, especially with the presumed innocence of children. He cites De Grenaille, *L'honneste garçon,* of 1642 as pointing out that while adults still have the protection of their guardian angels, this privilege derives from childhood (see 124–26). In Haiti, the notion of the two accompanying angels is associated with the individual from birth to death, and adults will speak of their personal *Ti bon anj* or *Gros bon anj* as being ever-present.

8. The artist so spoke concerning his works in a conversation with the author in 1990. He has apparently told others that they were depictions of Ezuli.

9. Rey (1999: 151–52) provides a recent description and analysis of Soulouque's use of images of the Virgin, which are legion and legendary.

10. The *"avancés"* were artists of the elite, educated sections of society, most of whom had studied art abroad.

11. *Bizango* is a secret society cult that exists outside Vodou, although some of its spiritual beings have the same names and many of the same functions of certain Vodou *lwa,* especially the Gédé family. The museum in which these works are held is the Fondation pour la Préservation, la Valorisation, et la Production d'Oeuvres Culturelles Haïtiennes. I am grateful to Marianne Lehmann, the director of the foundation, for allowing me to see and to photograph parts of the collection that were at the time not on exhibition.

12. Santa Claus is ubiquitous in Haiti around Christmas time but is to be separated from the Saint Nicholas of *Bizango.* This version of the saint curiously reverts to his oldest myths, which had to do with saving people from starvation.

13. Houlberg provides a richly detailed description and analysis of several aspects of the veneration of *marasa.*

14. The work remains on view in the cathedral.

15. William Wordsworth, "Ode on Intimations of Immortality from Recollections of Early Childhood."

16. Claude Souffrant (1991: 269) claims, "Illiteracy [among the peasantry] hasn't appeared out of nowhere. This form of blindness, affecting, in 1982, 75 percent of the rural population [apparently still true at the beginning of the

twenty-first century], was inflicted by the ruling classes, an omission made obvious in the budgetary choices of the country."

17. After 1990, budgets for public schools increased to some extent but remained insufficient to provide a free public education to all, such as is common in the United States, Canada, and other countries in the hemisphere. There is some instruction available at no or very little cost through missionary and other privately funded groups that have to establish a school as one of the legal conditions of their presence in Haiti. Before the United States Occupation in 1917, the national government gave a partial subvention to the Roman Catholic Church to support elementary and some secondary instruction. Enforcing the doctrine of separation of church and state the Occupation terminated these subventions. Public schools often lack paper and pencils, books, blackboards, desks, toilets, and potable drinking water. The cost of school uniforms, mandatory shoes, and attendance fees is beyond the means of many Haitian families.

18. Philomé Obin in interviews with art historians and others seems to have made contradictory claims about the nature and extent of his art instruction. My interview with him accords with the information provided by Michel-Philippe Lerebours (1989: 397).

19. Most books on Haitian art reflect these impediments. An exception is Nadal-Gardère and Bloncourt (1986). The United States artist and teacher, Lois Maillou Jones, who taught in Port-au-Prince and at Howard University in Washington, made special efforts to support the work of women artists and collected an archive of images from some two dozen artists. Port-au-Prince gallery director, Mireille Jérôme has strongly supported the works of women artists, including through the publication of several monographs and catalogues. The works of women artists in Haiti frequently use children as subject. The impression of widespread complaint is culled from interviews with Haitian women artists over a period of two decades.

20. Jean's "Ronde enfantine" is illustrated.

References

Alexis, Gérard. 2000. *Peintres haïtiens*. Paris: Éditions Cercle d'Art.

Ariès, Philippe. 1962. *Centuries of childhood: A social history of family life.* Translated by R. Baldick. New York: Random House.

Benson, LeGrace. 1999. Habits of attention: Persistence of Lan Ginée in Haiti. In *The African diaspora: African origins and New World identities*, edited by I. Okpewho, C. B. Davies, and A. A. Mazrui. Bloomington: Indiana University Press.

Houlberg, Marilyn. 1995. Magique Marasa: The ritual cosmos of twins and other sacred children. In *The sacred arts of Haitian vodou*, edited by D. Cosentino. Los Angeles: UCLA Fowler Museum of Cultural History.

Lerebours, Michel-Philippe. 1989. *Haïti et ses peintres de 1804 à 1980*. Port-au-Prince: Imprimerie II.

Moss, Catherine Mague, and Margaret Stephenson. 1999–2000. Adolescent identity development from a multicultural perspective: A look at the Haitian-American community. *Journal of Haitian Studies* 5/6: 113–32.

Nadal-Gardère, Marie José, and Gerald Bloncourt. 1986. *La Peinture haïtienne/Haitian Arts*. Translated by E. Bell. Paris: Editions Nathan.

Rey, Terry. 1999. *Our Lady of Class Struggle*. Trenton, N.J.: Africa World Press.

Souffrant, Claude. 1991. *Littérature et société en Haïti*. Port-au-Prince: Editions Henri Deschamps.

9

Victims, Heroes, Enemies

Children in Central American Wars

Anna L. Peterson and Kay Almere Read

This chapter explores images and experiences of children in political violence in El Salvador, Guatemala, and Nicaragua since the 1960s. We look first at children as victims, who suffer disproportionately in war and political upheaval. As discussed in chapter 11 of this book, murdered children, especially victims of political violence, are practically the only Latin America children presented or known in the United States today. Central American children have been among the most victimized, and their victimization is widely publicized. Any discussion of children in recent Central American wars must begin with the different forms of violence suffered by children themselves.

However, it would be misleading, or, in any case, of little benefit to our understanding of them, to portray Central American children only as victims. Children are also moral and political actors, important members of their communities, and the contexts in which they live are informed by sharp differences concerning their roles in society. In Central America, as in many parts of Africa and the Middle East, children have served in both government and rebel armies. In this chapter, we focus especially on children's roles in opposition movements and popular understandings of their participation. The active participation of children in revolutionary movements challenges mainstream Western views of both childhood and political action. So too does the flip side of this image: the opposition's child heroes are the government's subversives, delinquents or enemies.

While condemning violence of any sort—economic and emotional

215

as well as physical—against children, we also question the notions that children are unaware of political problems, including the causes and consequences of war, and that children cannot be responsible political actors. Without denying that children's knowledge and agency differ significantly from those of adults, it is important to see how conceptions of childhood, moral agency, and political responsibility vary from one context to another. The idealized view of childhood that predominates among affluent Westerners today never accurately portrayed, even before recent civil wars, the lives of poor children in Central America— or in much of Latin America, Africa, Asia, and the Middle East. We reject the claim that poor Third World children or children in war do not experience childhood. Rather, they experience a childhood that differs from that of affluent Westerners. One version may be better or worse in various respects, but it is fruitless to define either as the only possible understanding of childhood. Exploring alternative experiences and meanings of childhood can help illuminate interpretations not only of childhood but also of the social construction of identity, the relations between individuals and communities, the nature of moral agency, and the ways all of these figure in understandings of politics, in Central America and elsewhere.

Political Violence in 1970s and 1980s

This chapter is organized thematically rather than geographically. Before entering into the thematic questions, however, we offer some background on political violence and civil wars in Central America in recent decades. Our discussion here is brief (for more detailed analysis see, for instance, Montgomery 1995; and Ruchwarger 1987).

Three countries in Central America have experienced especially intense political turmoil in recent decades: El Salvador, Guatemala, and Nicaragua. The three share certain features. All are very poor, with low per capita incomes and quality of life indicators. Infant and child malnutrition and mortality are very high throughout the region. In 1990, 100,000 of every 850,000 children in Central America died before the age of five (Chelala 1990). These figures are usually worse for children in rural areas, although malnutrition, infectious diseases, and respiratory ailments are also rampant among the poor in cities. That children suffer particularly from poverty is reflected in the fact that infant mortality is one of the prime indicators of poverty. A society's poverty is measured in large part by how much its children suffer. High rates of infant and child mortality reflect a host of other poverty-related problems: malnutrition, lack of access to potable water, disease, shortages and poor quality in housing, and lack of public services such as health care and education. Children almost always suffer disproportionately from these problems.

Poverty is related, in Central America as elsewhere, to a highly unequal distribution of land, wealth, and political power. These inequalities have prompted many forms of protest, dating back to indigenous uprisings during the colonial period. In the 1930s, opposition movements led by Agustín Farabundo Martí in El Salvador and César Augusto Sandino in Nicaragua met with harsh reprisals: in El Salvador the 1932 massacre of thousands of indigenous peasants, and in Nicaragua armed intervention by U.S. military forces. Both Farabundo Martí and Sandino were killed, but during succeeding decades activists kept alive memories of their struggles. In Guatemala, a military coup overthrew the reformist government of Jacobo Arbenz in 1954. Opposition movements in all three countries were harshly repressed, but by the early 1970s a combination of factors had led to a rise in the popular base and militancy of opposition movements. All three countries saw the rise of guerrilla movements, which drew inspiration from the 1959 Cuban revolution and the exploits of Ché Guevara. Also important were changes in the Roman Catholic Church, which in the late 1960s began emphasizing social justice and the defense of human rights as central principles of Christian faith. Many opposition activists and leaders in Central America began their political careers with experiences in *comunidades eclesiales de base* (Christian grassroots communities), literacy campaigns, and other church-related projects.

By the late 1970s, all three countries were in chaos. Aerial bombardments and massacres in the Salvadoran and Guatemalan countryside led to the annihilation of entire villages. The survivors often fled to refugee camps, if they did not join the guerrillas. In Nicaragua, the Somoza dictatorship responded harshly to growing opposition in the late 1970s with roundups of suspected activists (mostly young people) and even bombardments of urban neighborhoods. After the 1979 Sandinista victory over Somoza, a war against the Sandinista government by U.S.-backed counterrevolutionaries quickly began. The combined death tolls in the three countries during the 1970s and 1980s numbered hundreds of thousands; many more people suffered severe injury and the loss of homes and loved ones. In El Salvador alone, about 30 percent of the population—nearly 1.5 million people—had become refugees by 1986 (Edwards and Siebentritt 1991: 18).

In these conflicts, civilians suffered heavily, and children disproportionately. This reflects a more general trend in modern war. UNICEF's 1995 *Annual Report* reminds us that more civilian children than soldiers are killed in contemporary wars. Approximately two million children have died in wars over the last decade, and four to five million have been left physically disabled. Half of all refugees in the world are children (UNICEF 1995: 2, 47).

Children as Victims of Political Violence

The disproportionate suffering of children in recent wars has prompted substantial research into the psychological and social consequences of political violence upon children, especially in Africa, the Middle East, and Eastern Europe. Much of this research has been conducted by nongovernmental organizations (NGOs), often in cooperation with United Nations agencies such as UNICEF. Further, usually written from a perspective of advocacy—on behalf of the children themselves and in support of principles of human rights more generally—most of these reports focus on the various ways that children are victimized by war. A frequent reference is the 1989 United Nations Convention on the Rights of the Child, which is included as an appendix to numerous studies (e.g., Stephens 1995: 335–52).

Documenting high rates of malnutrition and undernutrition, illiteracy, and infectious disease, NGO studies emphasize the traumas suffered by Central American children as a consequence of political violence. A report by the Human Rights Commission of Central America (CODEHUCA n.d.: 13–14) summarizes,

Central American children suffer violations to their fundamental rights from their first years of life. . . . We speak of children who live in garbage dumps in the cities, of children who lack a roof over their heads or live in shanties . . . children who lack education, health care, and adequate food. These are children who are forced to work from an early age, as an economic support for their homes . . . children who are victims of war, the consequences of which leave traumatic marks on their mental health. This includes children who are orphans, displaced, refugees, physically injured and psychologically traumatized.

The report concludes that "The large majority of these children have, in effect, no childhood. What happens is that the political and socioeconomic conditions in which they have to live make them into children with the responsibilities of adults, that is, premature adults, because they have to involve themselves in the socioeconomic activities and existential decisions that should belong only to adults."

Another study, focused on El Salvador, echoes these themes. It emphasizes that "War does not affect only children who experience directly threatening situations. It also affects the entire social reality and thus directly or indirectly affects all children. The war has caused deterioration in quality of life for the Salvadoran family; it has affected the educational system and health programs" (Marín 1988: 29). While all Salvadoran children have suffered from the war, those who suffer most, both physically and emotionally, are those whose families have been displaced. The author notes that half the refugees in El Salvador are under the age of fourteen (Marín 1988: 4) and goes on to discuss various negative effects of displacement on the education, health care, nutrition, economic stability, and physical and mental health of Salvadoran children and their families. He describes, for example, the ways that constant moves and changes in residence lead displaced children to suffer insecurity, confusion, and fear. Direct experience of violence can cause more severe effects, such as "insomnia, personality changes, and psychosomatic reactions such as headaches, as well as severe psychosis, such as schizophrenia" (25).

Further evidence of psychological damage comes from refugee children's drawings, which are dominated by soldiers, airplanes, and corpses. Marín (1988: 28) cites these as "proof that the situation of civil war in El Salvador has penetrated in the thoughts and feelings of many children." While acknowledging that children also have positive experiences in war zones, such as community solidarity and mutual protection, the report concludes that "an adequate psychological development of the child and war cannot go together" (29). This echoes the views of many NGOs and much academic writing on children and political violence, in Central America and elsewhere. The case is summarized by the title of a chapter in *The Psychological Effects of War and Violence on Children:* "War Is Not Good for Children" (Goldson 1993: 3).

This point is made forcefully, sometimes polemically, in two English-language works on children's experiences in Central American wars: *Children of the Volcano* (Acker 1986), a book of interviews with teenagers in four Central American nations, and *If the Mango Tree Could Speak* (Goudvis 1993), a documentary about children in war-torn areas of El Salvador and Guatemala. Both portray Central American children as innocent victims of violence from the political enemies of their parents and communities. Their message, as Acker summarizes, is that, "In Central America many, many children are born sick and die hungry. They do not play. Their guns are often real guns, their chores are day-long labour, and their dreams are nightmares of killing. Most of their governments ignore them, reject them, or maltreat them. They have inherited centuries of exploitation and injustice, and now they are victims of war" (11). These political and economic circumstances have made it impossible for children "to be children."

The title *If the Mango Tree Could Speak* comes from a Salvadoran boy living in a war zone. Recalling the violence he has witnessed and experienced, he insists that if the mango tree in which he is seated could speak, "it would tell the truth." The children in the film tell of losing parents and other relatives to political violence, of being forced to flee their homes, of watching communities disintegrate under the pressures of fear, threat, and mistrust. The stories in the film, like Acker's interviews and the drawings of Salvadoran refugee children, are authentic and moving. They give faces and voices to the facts and statistics: recent wars and political violence in Central America have been devastating for children. Children are, and will likely continue to be, victims in multiple senses.

The victimization of children is not only widespread but also widely utilized. In arguing that children are innocent and should be kept apart from war, various factions draw on images of suffering children. "Children are an object that sensitizes public opinion" (Moreno Martín 1991: 30). The suffering of children can be used to channel indignation toward the enemy that causes these problems and also to "exalt the justice of one's own cause." Moreno Martín writes, "the use of children is [sometimes] a political calculation, other times it is an emotional reaction that can be channeled politically" (32).

During the civil war in El Salvador, both the government and the opposition used descriptions and pictures of wounded, orphaned, shell-shocked, and dead children to support their respective causes. One example is a campaign by the Salvadoran government that plastered pictures of children injured by land mines on billboards throughout the nation and that accused the guerrilla fighters of the Farabundo Martí National Liberation Front (FMLN) of attacking innocent children. In the 1980s, these billboards were among the first images seen by visitors driving to San Salvador from the airport. Moreno Martín describes another example: a photograph of the body of a little girl, with the father crying next to her, and the message "Are these the actions that they defend? They do not want peace, their actions are of war and terror and these are their victims . . ." (32).

Opposition activists also pointed to attacks on children, especially in rural communities in zones of conflict, as evidence of the government's inhumanity. Foreign opponents of the Salvadoran regime also highlighted the suffering inflicted on children as a reason to denounce the government and support the FMLN. The death of several young children in aerial and mortar attacks upon repopulated villages in war-torn rural areas during the late 1980s and early 1990s, for example, were among the most publicized of many army attacks upon civilians.

The two sides in the Salvadoran civil war not only denounced their opponents for harming children; in defending their own positions, both also portrayed children as being among the primary intended beneficiaries of their struggles. This was perhaps especially true of leftist movements. The FMLN in El Salvador, like the Sandinista Front of National Liberation (FSLN) in Nicaragua, explained the ways revolutionary change would benefit children, which served as a partial justification for the participation of children in political and sometimes military activities. As Marín (1988: 29) puts it, the logic of revolutionary movements is often thus: "We fight for the future of children, the enemy is cruel because they kill or mutilate children, the war is just because even children are willing to give their lives for *the cause.*"

This sort of argument draws on both of the main images of children used in war propaganda: the child-martyr and the child-hero. The hero image, used mainly by opposition activists, is the focus of the next section. The martyr-victim image is more common, not only among governments fighting insurgencies but also among outsiders, such as international human rights organizations and Western academics. Sometimes these observers use images of suffering children not to support either side but rather to condemn both for waging a war that produces so many innocent victims. This reinforces a view of children as passive victims of conflicts fought by adults over adult issues. This image also suggests an interpretation of the war that appears apolitical—"we condemn violence on the right and the left"—but may reinforce the status quo and governing power by criticizing opposition movements for starting wars that take so many innocent victims.

According to this perspective, it is a tragic accident that deposits children in the midst of armed violence; they play no active role in either the political discussion or its military extension. If children have no agency in war, it must be because they have been forcibly recruited. This is one interpretation of the participation of children as combatants. Child-soldiers, in this view, are perhaps the prototypical victims of war, forced to witness, experience, and even commit brutalities in the name of a conflict that has little to do with them.

Child participation is common to many wars, in Central America and elsewhere, even though it is widely condemned. Most Central American governments have simply denied charges that minors were serving as soldiers. This was the case in El Salvador, even though both Salvadoran and international observers repeatedly confirmed that boys under fifteen were serving in the government army and that throughout the 1980s the army practiced forced recruitment. In El Salvador until 1991 and even more recently in Guatemala, the armed forces used roundups to fill ranks, taking teenage boys and young men from buses, churches, and marketplaces. The recruits were usually poor, often from the rural areas, and many were moved to posts far from home, making it harder for them to notify their families or to flee (Cohn and Goodwin-Gill 1994: 24).

Heroes and Enemies: Children as Political Actors

If adolescents forcibly recruited by the army seem clearly to be victims of war, a more complex and ambiguous picture emerges when we turn to children who fight with opposition movements. In Central America, guerrilla movements rarely relied on forced recruitment, largely because combatants' morale and commitment were crucial to the guerrillas' success. Lacking the technology, funding, and numbers of the government military, opposition armies had to rely much more on their combatants' commitment and on civilian support. Thus the vast majority of Central American guerrillas were volunteers, although many of them volunteered in circumstances that were not of their own choosing. Especially in rural areas, joining the opposition was often better than the other available options: becoming a refugee, being forcibly recruited by the army, or living as a civilian in war zones constantly threatened by aerial bombardments, mortar attacks, and army sweeps. As a peasant leader in Guatemala put it, "the guerrillas don't force anyone to kill people, except in combat" and "people can at least imagine that the guerrillas fight for the good of the people." He pointed out that volunteers could leave when they wanted (Cohn and Goodwin-Gill 1994: 34–35). Similar sentiments were echoed by former guerrilla combatants in El Salvador.

Guerrilla participation brought physical and moral benefits, especially for very poor families and communities. In El Salvador, for example, "The FMLN also provided a social support structure, validation, discipline, respect, and protection to many kids who had witnessed family members or teachers killed or ill-treated, or whose families lived in Honduran refugee camps. The clothes, basic medical attention, and food provided to young fighters were rare commodities in many homes" (Cohn and Goodwin-Gill 1994: 35). This reinforces the importance of considering poverty and political repression as the necessary context for children's participation in guerrilla armies in Central America. Especially in conflict-ridden areas such as El Salvador's eastern and northern provinces or Guatemala's highlands, young people had few good alternatives. Like adults, they were frequently safer and better fed and clothed with insurgents than in civilian life. Of course, this underlines the victimization of poor people and especially their lack of good options. The fact that participation in a guerrilla army may be better than the other feasible alternatives does not make it an ideal option, for young people or adults.

Seeing young people's political and military participation only as the least of the available evils, however, misses some important points. First, young people growing up in zones of conflict are socialized in an environment where guerrillas mingle with civilians, some of their own family members are or have been guerrillas, and the larger community frequently accords the guerrillas and their cause considerable legitimacy, even admiration. In this context, joining the guerrillas is less a huge leap than a logical next step for children and families whose everyday experiences and values are tied up with the opposition movement. Their experiences and values, further, are often profoundly shaped by the government violence against their communities and relatives.

Second, young people sometimes have intensely personal reasons for joining. In response to researchers' questions about why children as young as ten or eleven were working as couriers and lookouts and why thirteen-year-olds were carrying guns, FMLN leaders replied,

The answer is very simply because that is what they want to do. Children want the war to end and want soldiers to disappear from their lives as soon as possible. They know that their participation is important if this is to become a reality, because they see the results of their participation, and this inspires them to continue living and collaborating more, even knowing they risk their lives . . . This is something that they have grown to understand for themselves, because of the painful everyday experiences that they have faced for so long. (Moreno Martín 1991: 25–26)

It is not surprising that guerrilla leaders would give this sort of response. Yet this is not a reason to dismiss the explanation, especially because many of the children's own accounts confirm it. Central American children as young as nine or ten often express the sort of commitment described by the FMLN leader cited by Moreno Martin. Children's political commitments, like those of adults, combine political ideology and moral idealism with personal loyalties and collective memories of suffering that must be vindicated. This is the conclusion that Carolyn Nordstrom (1998: 87) has reached, based on experience in war zones in many parts of the world. She writes that while children are often seen only as being acted upon, they should instead be seen as moral and political actors whose commitments may be no less serious than those of their elders. "Children often have a well developed moral, political, and philosophical understanding of the events in their lives and worlds. . . . even very young children have profound opinions on conditions of justice and injustice, violence and peace in their lives."

Such a perspective would seem to be corroborated in interviews with Nicaraguan adolescents conducted by a Uruguayan journalist, María Gravina Telechea, shortly after the Sandinista Revolution of 1979. The young people, all of whom had participated in the insurrection against Somoza, were studying in Cuba when Gravina Telechea interviewed them. Many had begun their political activism even before entering high school, and they spoke of their experiences in light of a clear political analysis and commitment. Norman, for example, recalls, "I became politically active in school . . . what was most important was the idea that our ancestors had not achieved for us the right to develop and have fun as young people. That the time we were living in was for struggling and for winning a new homeland for the new generation. And this is what we would do, on the basis of sacrifice and constant struggle and, if necessary, at the cost of blood" (Gravina Telechea 1982: 30). Another boy, Boanerges, says, "We had forgotten the things of childhood. Like playing. We had achieved such a high morale, that we weren't children anymore. We felt ourselves rightfully to be men. We didn't think that we would be happy in parties but rather we thought about a better future, with participation, a future we would forge. A future to fight against weaknesses and vices" (Gravina Telechea 1982: 78).

The flip side of children as heroes is children as enemies. Repressive governments and armies often term all guerrillas "delinquents," a word usually associated with children and adolescents. This practice suggests the conflation of opposition activism with immaturity: only the young and irresponsible would oppose the status quo, and all young people are potentially subversive. This is echoed in the frequent assertions of Nicaraguans recalling the repressive period prior to Somoza's defeat in 1979: "It was a crime to be young." Youth itself was so closely associated with opposition activity that young people who ventured out in the evenings were frequently harassed, arrested, or even killed on the spot. The association of young people with subversion also occurred in El Salvador, extending even to teenagers involved in church activities. In January 1979, the Salvadoran National Guard attacked a religious retreat at El Despertar, a Catholic center in San Salvador. They killed the priest, Octavio Ortiz, and four teenage boys, all from the parish youth group. The government accounts of the attack called the boys "subversives" and described the retreat as a clandestine guerrilla training center—presumably the only genuine reason teenage boys would gather together.

The images of children both as heroes and as enemies suggest the possibility of political agency. This possibility is affirmed by guerrilla leaders when they claim that children who participate in opposition activities do so of their own accord, by government officials when they defend attacks on teenaged or younger children as legitimate military actions against potentially dangerous opponents, and by young people themselves, in their actions and words. The possibility of children's own agency is very rarely affirmed, however, by nongovernmental organizations and scholars, especially, but not exclusively, those outside the societies in which conflicts are located. Most NGOs and scholars issue unqualified condemnations of children's participation in political movements. Their critiques are based—explicitly or implicitly—on an assumption that children can only be victims, never victimizers; only acted upon, never actors. These assumptions provide a foundation for well-intentioned and necessary efforts to protect children from the harms of war. However, they also reinforce, often unwittingly, a culturally and historically limited vision of children's needs, interests, and capacities, and even of the nature of childhood itself.

What Is a Child?

In recent years, the general sense that modern Western notions about childhood are far from universal has been sharpened by the knowledge that contemporary children often live in conditions that diverge widely from this image of protected innocence, play, and learning. As Sharon Stephens (1995: 7) specifies, attention to the plight of children in the Third World has forced affluent Westerners to confront "a chasm between their idealized concepts of childhood and the realities of many children's lives, both in the Third World and in the heart of First World urban centers" (see also James and Prout 1990). This conceptual gap reflects real divergences concerning the conditions and meaning of childhood.

Contemporary Western views of an innocent childhood protected until many years past puberty from political and moral concerns need to be contested. This contemporary perception, we argue, extends childhood far beyond the limits that have defined it in many other times and cultures. As the number of years that children in Western societies are expected to attend school grows, the duration of "childhood" itself increases. The same expectations, however, are not held by peoples from many other cultures, even those living within the boundaries of the United States (Gardner 1982: 555). In their societies of origin, for example, Hmong people typically marry in their early or mid-teens, but Hmong immigrants in the United States have faced legal and social challenges when their teenage children have contracted marriage. Disputes over child labor often reflect similar conflicts between different cultural perspectives regarding both the age limits of childhood and the responsibilities and privileges that young people rightfully owe and possess. The common view among wealthy (especially white) people in the United States that people are still socially immature as many as a dozen years after sexual maturation is idiosyncratic, historically and culturally, and thus problematic as a basis for moral evaluations or public policies concerning other cultures, both within and beyond national borders.

The age at and process by which a person becomes an adult are central for political and ethical thinking, and particularly for ideas about moral and legal responsibility. In many Third World societies, in Western societies in the past, and indeed in many present-day African-American, Latino, and immigrant communities in the United States, children often begin acting responsibly for their family and community at a very young age. These responsibilities may include caring for younger children, agricultural work, paid work outside the home, and even political participation in the context of their own communities' "civil society." Children are cared for and also care for others in these settings. Such experiences muddy the distinctions not only between adulthood and childhood but also between the individual and the community. This is the necessary context, we suggest, for thinking about images and experiences of children in Central American political conflicts.

Recent research indicates that children develop as active moral agents from their earliest years. Children as young as eighteen months have been found to have the capacity to care about the welfare of others, and children as young as two can understand the imperative not to harm others. The "caring" response to ethical and moral dilemmas typically is followed by the development of a sense of "justice," or issues of fairness. Studies on children in both the United States and non-Western countries suggest that general patterns of early moral development are largely independent of gender, race, ethnic, and class-based factors, although by later childhood such factors play an important role in a child's capacity for ethical reasoning and moral action (Nucci 1997). This research portrays even very young children as active moral agents concerned with the common good. This is a picture not of isolated innocence but of continually developing capacities to deal with the real world and its real problems. Indeed, Norma P. Lyons (1993), drawing on the work of others and on her own study of adolescent girls in a private high school in Troy, New York, suggests that young women are more likely to become depressed the more they are protected from the world's problems and, conversely, that confronting difficulties helps promote a creative awakening that spurs responsibility and self-confidence. Unlike past imagery of the idealism of youth and its remoteness from the adult world, adolescents may in fact thrive on limited confrontations with the concrete world and some of its problems. Such research suggests that cultures that encourage children's social and moral agency may be responding to natural tendencies in childhood development. This research helps make sense of the political activism of even very young people in places like Nicaragua and El Salvador, especially in times of war.

Conclusions: Children, Community, and Political Violence

We have suggested that the images and experiences of Central American children challenge mainstream modern Western conceptions of childhood as a time of innocence, ignorance, and isolation from the moral and political conflicts of the adult world. This challenge comes on several fronts. First, the suffering that Central American children have endured as a result of war, political violence, and poverty makes it impossible for them to experience a secure and happy childhood, isolated from the cruel reality of adult problems. Further, their experiences of insecurity, loss, responsibility, and hard work are more typical of childhood in most of the world and throughout most of history than is the contemporary affluent U.S. and European image of childhood as devotion to learning and play in a safe and secure environment. This reality overturns the notion that there is a single universal experience of childhood lived by children in wealthy Western societies. (It is important to note further that many children in the United States and other wealthy societies do not have safe, secure, or protected lives.)

Second, recent Central American experiences suggest that mainstream Western interpretations fail to recognize that children can have and may want agency and do make decisions. Carolyn Nordstrom (1998: 81) emphasizes this point in an essay on girls in war-torn societies:

In the war zones I have visited, girls are actors in the drama and tragedy of war along with adults. They are targeted for attack, they devise escapes, they endure torture, they carry food to the needy, they forge a politics of belief and action. [However] in general accounts of war . . . I look for children actors, and usually find none. Girls, children, are acted upon; they are listed as casualties—they do not act. They are not presented as having identities, politics, morals, and agendas for war or peace.

Countless Central American children, like those that Nordstrom studied in Mozambique and elsewhere, do indeed have political and moral convictions and agendas upon which they act in ways that might be quite reasoned and knowing.

This highlights a third important claim: the options and reasoning of children—or at least of adolescents—often do not differ much from those of the adults in their communities. We are better off viewing children's and adults' world views and behavior as part of a continuum rather than as a dualism separated by a sudden leap into adulthood at a specific age. As children develop, they are socialized into larger communities. In the process, they absorb and sort through different world views, values, histories, and goals. They do not simply accept every aspect of their inherited cultures, but neither do they remain somehow isolated from them until some magic age, be it fourteen or twenty-one, when they suddenly become fully autonomous individuals.

Moreno Martín (1991) points out that children begin at birth to internalize all aspects of their society, including evaluations and legitimations of war and violent behavior. Without denying the extent and depth of children's suffering in war, he argues, it is "necessary to challenge the supposed marginalization of children from war." As he puts it, "These children, for whom we feel so much compassion every time the machinery of war begins to function, are they just innocent victims who have nothing to do with the course of conflicts promoted and led by adults?" He concludes that, "the response that we have to give is sadly negative"

(201). Children, Moreno Martín specifies, are not responsible for war. "It is a reality which, explicitly or implicitly, presents itself to them at the moment of birth. While they are very small, they suffer its direct or indirect effects. When they lose the protective shield of early childhood, it will be their obligation to be effective protagonists in war" (1991: 201).

This points out the arbitrary and ultimately untenable character of the effort to divide childhood and adulthood sharply from each other. It also suggests some important consequences for both scholarship and activism. First, it bears repeating that we do not suggest that children are ultimately responsible for political violence or that they are not hurt by it. Rather, we ask when or under what circumstances children's own moral agency and ability to make reasoned moral choices might become an acceptable foundation for their active participation in the potentially violent actions of their own communities. Further, what might children's multiple forms of participation in political violence mean for offering aid and upholding—even for defining—their rights? We do not suggest abandoning the notions that children are victimized by political violence, that they need protection, or that they have rights. We do contend, however, that human rights workers and those offering aid, like those studying childhood, might benefit from a more nuanced understanding of what childhood and adolescence mean within particular cultural and historical contexts. Without taking these nuances into account, it may be very difficult to uphold children's rights because we are unable to see the bearers of those rights as distinctive, thinking human beings and also as humans living within their own unique communities.

References

Acker, Alison. 1986. *Children of the volcano*. Toronto: Between the Lines.

Chelala, C. A. 1990. Central America: The cost of war. *The Lancet* 335: 153–54.

CODEHUCA. n.d. *Los niños de la década perdida: Investigación y análisis de violaciones de los derechos humanos de la niñez centroamericana (1980–92)*. San José, Costa Rica.

Cohn, Ilene, and Guy S. Goodwin-Gill. 1994. *Child soldiers: The role of children in armed conflict*. Oxford: Clarendon Press.

Edwards, Beatrice, and Gretta Tovar Siebentritt. 1991. *Places of origin: The repopulation of rural El Salvador*. Boulder, Colo.: Lynne Rienner.

Gardner, Howard. 1982. *Developmental psychology: An introduction.* Boston: Little, Brown and Company.

Goldson, Edward. 1993. War is not good for children. In *The psychological effects of war and violence on children,* edited by L. A. Leavitt and N. A. Fox. Hillsdale, N.J.: Lawrence Erlbaum Associates.

Goudvis, Patricia. 1993. *If the mango tree could speak.* 1993. Video recording. Hohokus, N.J.: New Day Film Library.

Gravina Telechea, María. 1982. *Que diga Quincho.* Managua: Editorial Nueva Nicaragua.

James, Allison, and Alan Prout, eds. 1990. *Constructing and reconstructing childhood: Contemporary issues in the sociological study of childhood.* London: Falmer Press.

Lyons, Nona P. 1993. Luck, ethics, and ways of knowing: Observations on adolescents' deliberations in making moral choices. In *Approaches to moral development: New research and emerging themes,* edited by A. Garrod. New York: Teachers College Press.

Marín, Patricia. *Infancia y guerra en El Salvador.* Guatemala City: UNICEF, 1988.

Montgomery, Tommie Sue. 1995. *El Salvador in revolution.* Boulder, Colo.: Westview Press.

Moreno Martín, Florentino. 1991. *Infancia y guerra en Centroamérica.* San José, Costa Rica: FLACSO.

Nordstrom, Carolyn. 1998. Girls behind the (front) lines. In *Women and war reader,* edited by L. A. Lorentzen and J. Turpin. New York: New York University Press.

Nucci, Larry. 1997. Moral development and character formation. In *Psychology and educational practice,* edited by H. J. Walberg and G. D. Haertel. Berkeley: MacCarchan.

Ruchwarger, Gary. 1987. *People in power: Forging grassroots democracy in Nicaragua.* South Hadley, Mass.: Bergin and Garvey.

Stephens, Sharon, ed. 1995. *Children and the politics of culture.* Princeton: Princeton University Press.

UNICEF. 1995. *Annual report.* Paris: United Nations Children's Fund.

10

August

Bruna Veríssimo

Editor's note: This chapter is divided into two parts. The first consists of journal entries by Bruna Veríssimo, age twenty-three at the time, August 1999. The second part is the transcription of an interview she conducted.

Veríssimo has lived in the streets of Recife, in Northeast Brazil, since the age of nine, where she begs, works as a prostitute, and sells her artwork (she is a talented clothing designer and painter). She never attended school but taught herself to read and write by studying street signs and culling newspapers and magazines from the trash. The journal entries and the interview were handwritten by Veríssimo, then read back by her into a tape recorder, transcribed according to standard rules of Portuguese spelling and punctuation, and, finally, translated into English.

The second part of this chapter is an oral narrative by a fifteen-year-old resident of Recife, identified here as Sussana Lima da Silva, who was interviewed by Veríssimo. The questions Veríssimo asked were not included in her written account of the interview.

The material in this chapter is included neither for its shock value nor as an attempt to summarize the state of childhood in Latin America at the turn of the century. Its author is, of course, an individual, not a class of people, and the childhood she somehow managed to survive is by no means typical. Yet some of the themes touched on here—violence, work, homelessness, hunger, sexuality, and hope despite all odds—are surely important ones for researchers attempting to understand childhood in contemporary Latin America. I also believe that if we are to leave future generations with better records about the lives of children in Latin America, new ways of gathering information must be considered, including the active participation of young people and nonacademics in research.

Friday, 10 August 1999

My day begins in a routine way. I wake up at four in the morning,[1] and [like] every day I go to the Rua da Aurora[2] to wait for Dona[3] Rebeca, a lady with a good heart who always helps me. I wait for Dona Rebeca to come down from the apartment where she lives. Whenever she can, she brings food for my little dog and for the three dogs of a lady who has been living in the street for a long time. At five thirty Dona Rebeca comes down from the apartment where she lives to walk her dog. She carries two bags, one with the dog food and another one for me, which contains things for my personal hygiene—two bars of soap, some rose-petal cream, and perfume. I walk around with her and her dog until six in the morning. As I am walking with her, she gives advice. . . .

At eight o'clock in the morning I go to the Rua do Lima,[4] to Dona Maria's house, for the breakfast she prepares for me every day.[5] Dona Maria is also a very good woman since she is very religious; she has long been charitable with people who live in the street. After we[6] finish with breakfast, we stop to listen to the word of God, which Dona Maria explains to us, since it's very important for us to know what's inside the Holy Bible. When she finishes her speech, she tells us to go and get the clothing she has for us. Next she gives us some pamphlets with the word of God, for us to read and meditate. Then each of us goes our own way.

I go to the Rua da Aurora to take a bath and wash my clothing, and when I finish I walk around a little to see if I can come up with some money for food at night, because I don't have anyone who can give me any. I go to the Praça Maciel Pinheiro,[7] because there are some people there who give me things. I go to the Matriz da Boa Vista Church, because there's a girl there who helps me. Her name is Zilda. She is the secretary in the church and she is very generous with poor people and likes to help people who live in the street. She gives me some change, which is enough for a snack.

At night, I see Dona Vera of the Livraria Brandão, who always helps me when she can. Dona Vera gives me a bag of food so I'll have something to eat. I thank her and go back to the Rua da Aurora. When I arrive in the Rua da Aurora, I sit down and start crocheting for a while, to pass the time. I distract myself to avoid the temptation to get high.

When it gets dark, I continue to walk around for a while, waiting to get sleepy. When I get sleepy, I go over to the back side of the Legislative Assembly[8] to sleep. I pick up some papers and put them on the sidewalk in front of the pharmacy that's across the street from the Legislative Assembly. And when I am sleepy I doze off, waiting for a new day to arrive and to begin my routine again.

Some time ago, life ceased to make any sense to me because I had experienced so many terrible things and I no longer felt any love for myself, so much so that I started using drugs again. When I was high I couldn't stand looking at people because I had been so humiliated. . . . There are street children who are very violent because they have suffered various kinds of violence. Some of them even threaten people who want to get close to them to offer them help. They are children who have experienced some sort of trauma from having suffered various kinds of violence, so it doesn't occur to them that there are people who might want to help them. . . .

Saturday, 11 August 1999

This morning I woke up and found myself looking onto a terrible scene. The pound was taking away my dog and the other street dogs. I felt very sorry for the dogs, but I couldn't do anything for them. Even so, I went to ask the dog catchers to let my dog go. It didn't do any good, though, because I was mistreated by the guards, who called me every insulting name, just because I was insisting that they let my dog go. They didn't like my insistence, and they even threatened to have me arrested.

When they went away, I was very sad, and then I started crying because I missed my dog and I wouldn't be able to endure the rest of the day without her because I had gotten used to her company.

Wednesday, 17 August 1999

My day started off terribly because I witnessed a very stupid and violent scene. The city [workers] and the police were beating some people who live in the Rua da Aurora and they were doing it in a very unscrupulous fashion. Not content to just beat those people, they hurt the people who insisted they should be able to stay where they were. They remained there in the Rua da Aurora until two o'clock in the afternoon, watching to see if anyone came back to the park where people had been living for a long time, but which was now undergoing a process of renovation. What shocked me most was when two policemen beat a pregnant woman. They did not respect her pregnancy and were very violent with her.

I couldn't stand to watch all that barbarity and I went up to the two policemen. I told them that the woman was pregnant, but even so he [one of the policemen] didn't stop hitting the girl. I told him I was going to report him on the radio, but it didn't do any good. He got very irritated with me, and then he let the woman go and struck out at me. He hit me twice in the face and told me to disappear from that place. I was very afraid and I went away. The passersby were horrified by what they were seeing, but they couldn't do anything to help the poor lady to get out of the clutches of the police.

When they were finished beating up the other street girls they went away but they threatened to come back at night, to settle scores with me and with the other girls who hang out around there. I was crying for almost an hour because there was no one who could help us. I was very sad because the girl lost the baby she was expecting. So I got to thinking, why is it that no one wants to come forward as a witness of what they saw? Maybe the people who saw the banal act of the police are afraid of what might happen to them, so they don't want to get involved.

Thursday, 18 August 1999

On Thursday I got up at eight o'clock in the morning and went to the Rua da Aurora to take a bath.[9] When I finished, I went to the Rua do Lima, to Dona Maria's house for breakfast. After breakfast, I went to the Praça Maciel Pinheiro to get some money so I could buy some cleaning products, because my clothing was dirty. I went to the Matriz da Boa Vista Church, because there's a girl there who helps me, who is the secretary at the church. I got the handout she had for me and then I went to the Livraria Brandão to see the owner, because she likes me a lot and helps me whenever she can. I spend a few hours talking with her and when it's noon she gives me some spare change so I can buy myself something to eat. I thank her and continue on my way.

It was four o'clock in the afternoon when I arrived at the Rua das Ninfas. I sat down on the sidewalk in front of a store, crocheting to pass the time. I crocheted until eight o'clock at night. When it was eight thirty, I got up and went to the Rua da Aurora to sleep because I was very tired and had a headache. I went to the place I normally sleep, behind the Legislative Assembly. I sat on the sidewalk under the awning and since I had a headache it took me a long time to fall asleep. Since I had spent the afternoon crocheting, I decided to stop. I took out my notebook to draw and I drew until three o'clock in the morning.

Since I was afraid, because of the threat from the police on Wednesday when I saw them beat up a pregnant woman who lives in the street, I couldn't fall asleep. All of a sudden a police van passed by and the policemen were chasing two street girls. I got up and [hiding in a tree] observed them from a distance, to see what they wanted with the girls. Two policemen grabbed them and made them go down to the edge of the river. When the girls went down there, two more policemen came along. They ordered them to take off their clothing and started having sex with the girls. They ordered them to practice oral sex and while the girls were doing that one of the other policemen penetrated her from behind.

I was unlucky because the branch I was sitting on and witnessing that barbarity from broke. When the policemen realized that someone was watching what they were doing with the girls, they ran after me and grabbed me. They asked what I was doing there and because I didn't have an alibi I made one up. I told them I was waiting for my boyfriend. But it didn't do any good because they didn't believe me and they hit me and shoved me inside the van, saying they were going to take me to the police station. But they didn't take me there. They took me to the overpass in Coque.[10] When we got there, they opened the door and told me to get out. When I got out, they started beating me up. Then they ordered me to perform oral sex on them. I was very scared because one of them was pointing a gun at my head and when I finished doing what they had asked me to do they hit me a few times and ordered me to take off my clothing. Then they ordered me to run in my underwear and since they had beaten me up I did what they told

Fig. 10.1. Bruna Veríssimo, *Iemanjá* (the Afro-Brazilian goddess of the sea).

me to do. I ran, in a panic, wondering, What are they going to do with the girls . . . ?

I ran, I ran a lot, and when I was tired I stopped in front of a house and picked up some pieces of a newspaper that was on the ground and covered myself up. I stayed there in front of the house until six in the morning. I was lucky because the lady of the house came up to me and asked me if I had been there for a long time. I told her I had been there since three in the morning. When she asked me why I was dressed like that, I didn't mince my words (*eu não fiz ironia*). I told her what had happened to me. Thank God, the woman understood me. She was very shocked by the things I told her, because she had a son who was a policeman and it was difficult for her to believe that the police are so unscrupulous with people who live in the street. To make a long story short, she asked if I was hungry. I told her I was. She went into her house for a cup of coffee and two pieces of bread and she also gave me a pair of shorts and a T-shirt. She asked me if I had bus fare to get back to the city and I told her I didn't. She gave me two reais, which was a good thing for me. I thanked her and went to the bus stop. . . .

An Interview in the Street

My name is Sussana Lima da Silva. I left home at the age of ten to live in the streets of Recife. Previously, I had lived in Água Fria[11] with my mother and my three younger brothers. My family was poor. My father was dead and my mother was an invalid, so she couldn't work to support us. I was the oldest child in the family, and since I was the oldest, I would go out every day to beg to support my family. I couldn't stand seeing the hunger and desperation my mother and brothers were experiencing. I would leave the house every day to look for someone who could help, but I hardly ever found people with a good heart who would help me.

As each day went by I became more and more angry because I couldn't stand seeing how my family was suffering. That's why I decided to go and live in the city, but whenever I came up with some money I'd take it home. I went through a lot of terrible things because I wasn't used to living in the street. The worst part was the nights because I didn't have a safe place to sleep and I was afraid of running into someone who would hurt me. I was so afraid because I was new to the street, but I still managed to get by.

I was shocked by the things I would see every day. There were a lot of people living in the street: women, children, old people, girls. Every day I would go to the Praça do Diario and spend the day there. One time I noticed a lot of girls there who were about my age and who prostituted themselves in order to survive. That's when I thought to myself, since my mother and my brothers are hungry, now I know what I have to do to get money to take home. So I decided to do what the other street girls were doing, because every time I remembered how my family was suffering, I would suffer.

That was when I decided to prostitute myself. I joined the other girls who were turning tricks. When the first client showed up and invited me to go out with him, I didn't think twice. I followed him. We went to a motel. The only thing I was scared about was the fact that I was a virgin, but when I remembered the troubles of my family I could only think about the money I would be able to take home. I went with the man to the motel. When we got there, he paid for our time and we went to a room. I asked him if I could order something to eat because I was very hungry. I called the motel waitress and asked her to bring me lunch. Two minutes later, the girl knocked on the door and delivered the food. Since I was very hungry, I started to eat, but I was still really nervous because it was the first time I was going to have sex with someone. The man noticed my nervousness and asked me why I was so afraid. I explained why I was so nervous. He understood and said that I didn't have to have sex with him and that he only wanted me to masturbate him. And he said, "Sussana, since we aren't going to have sex, I won't give you the thirty cruzeiros[12] we had agreed on, I'll only give you fifteen."

But when I remembered how my family was suffering, I felt braver by the moment. . . . And so we went into the bathroom and took a bath and when we finished we went over to the bed. The man asked me to lie down and then the ritual began. . . . I asked him to do it slowly because I was afraid of the pain I was going to feel. But thank God the man was careful and he did everything gently and I didn't feel as much pain as I thought I would. It didn't take him long because the man soon had an orgasm and felt the pleasure he wanted to feel. I bled a little. I went to the bathroom to wash myself and when I left the bathroom the man was putting on his clothes. He took out his wallet and gave me forty cruzeiros, he kissed me, and told me to be careful because there are a lot of men who just want to take advantage of girls like [me].

So as I remembered how hungry my mother and my brothers were, I began losing my fear. Every second that went by, I became braver in going out with men. Sometimes the men approached me, they called me over and offered me money. . . .

I suffered a lot, but I got used to it quickly. It was hard for me because it wasn't just penetration. It hurt because I had never been penetrated before but I got used to it. The pleasure I felt with the men wasn't the pleasure of sex or having an orgasm, but the need I had for money, because of the hunger and misery my family was experiencing.

I spent a lot of time in the street and then I went back home, happy because I had managed to bring in money. When I arrived in the house, my mother asked where I had gotten that money from and I told her that I cleaned a house and that the lady had given me some change. But my mind was heavy because I thought I shouldn't lie to my mother. But when an aunt of mine showed up at the house and she started helping at home I decided to go back to the street, to continue with my daily routine.

Every day I went to the Praça da Independência to practice prostitution, and up to a certain time I continued living in the street, until the age of fourteen. After that I found a guy with a good heart and we got together. I had a son with him. I spent a year living in Santo Amaro and now, recently, I started living in Encruzilhada. I wash clothing and I don't need the street any more for prostitution.

Notes

The text in this chapter was transcribed by Jandyra Guerra and translated by Tobias Hecht.

1. The author's notion of time corresponds only in a very flexible way to that recorded by clocks.

2. A street in central Recife lined by a number of tall apartment buildings. The street is flanked by a long, narrow park frequented by many homeless people and prostitutes.

3. "Dona" is a term of respect often placed before the first name of women.

4. A nearby street.

5. "Every day" probably means "frequently during recent weeks."

6. Presumably the author and other homeless people who have come for breakfast.

7. A square in central Recife.

8. The building where Pernambuco's state legislature meets.

9. By hauling a bucket of water to the river's edge and washing herself hidden among the mangrove trees.

10. A violent *favela,* or shantytown.

11. A working-class neighborhood of the larger Recife metropolitan area. The other neighborhoods mentioned are likewise very poor.

12. A currency formerly used in Brazil.

11

Children and Contemporary Latin America

Tobias Hecht

Perhaps because they inherit the world their elders leave them, children figure prominently in adult concerns about the future. In contemporary Latin America, poverty, unemployment, environmental devastation, malnutrition, drug wars, corruption, "readjustment" packages, and the cultural and linguistic weight of living under the shadow of the United States make for an uncertain future. What is left for the children? For residents in cities from Lima to San Juan, Mexico City to São Paulo, no problem seems to augur worse than violent crime. And it is little wonder. Taken together, the categories "Homicide and injury purposely in-flicted" and "Other violence" rank as the fifth leading causes of death in Venezuela, the third in El Salvador, and the first in Colombia—ahead of even heart disease or cancer (UN 1999). Impoverished children, some of whom are perpetrators of the violent crime that has swept the region, have come to be vilified to such an extent as to prompt one anthropologist to liken them to "folk devils" (Márquez, 1998: 114).

Contemporary popular knowledge of Latin American children is mostly limited to the murdered and murderous. Children in Latin America are at that uneasy crossroads of "pity and fear," to use the terms so aptly paired by Lewis Aptekar (1988). A reading of all *New York Times* articles about Mexico published in 1997 will uncover only three that mention children; in each of these, children are discussed in rela-tion to a massacre in Chiapas. These are examples of murdered Latin American children considered from time to time worthy of note. Mean-while, recent years have seen both widespread violence against street children and global protest over their treatment. Unattended urban children, especially dark-skinned ones, are easy targets for those trying to rein in a runaway world; poor children are widely blamed for crime, but their suffering also reminds us that no society murdering its own children can hope to survive.

And yet there is another sort of murder of Latin American children that receives virtually no attention at all. Four hundred and forty-six thousand Latin Americans under the age of five died in 1998, according to the United Nations Children's Fund (UNICEF), figures that reflect only recorded deaths; almost all of these children perished from diarrhea and other preventable or easily treatable diseases in combination with hunger.[1] The nearly one-half million children who died that year alone surpassed the toll of all combatants and civilians killed in armed conflict in Central America during the entire twentieth century; it was approximately one hundred and fifty times the number of all adults killed in the attack on the Twin Towers in New York in September, 2001.

Children are as scarce in contemporary writing about Latin America as women were three or four decades ago. Sometimes children are mentioned in relation to extraordinary events (such as the case of Elián González, the young boy who survived a shipwreck in 1999 on his way from Cuba to Florida, only to become involved in a custody battle with all the entertaining power of a transnational soap opera), yet they rarely figure in larger discussions of economic and political processes in Latin America. But consider the difficulty of making sense of, say, the economies of Latin America and the Caribbean without taking into account the role of child labor. Across the region, more than 23 percent of people live on less than one dollar per day (World Bank 1998: 4). My own ethnographic work (Hecht 1998), though very small in scale, would suggest that at such levels of deprivation, children's productive contributions are vital to household strategies of survival. Yet child labor has become so enmeshed in the First World conundrum of how it can best be eliminated that there is little room left for seeking to understand its meaning for the majority of Latin American children or households, who happen to be either poor or extremely poor. Why is it that in this still-Freudian age, in which we tend to hold that the adult can only be understood with reference to the childhood he or she once lived, that the early years of life continue to attract such scant attention from students of political, economic, and social realities?

The Uruguayan essayist Eduardo Galeano (1998: 12–13) has observed that, "In the most diverse cities and in the most far-flung parts of the world, privileged children resemble one another in their customs and practices, just as shopping malls and airports—detached from time and space—all look alike." Today, children's shoes, clothing, music, and toys are marketed globally and the little ones' computers mostly run on a single type of software. According to an undated letter sent in 2002 as part of a direct mail campaign by *Harpers Magazine,* consumers across the planet—most of them children and their obliging parents—have spent four and a half billion dollars on licensed Star Wars merchandise since 1977. They may not all speak the same language, but children now inhabit a global society in a way no previous generation has. If we know little about the lives of poor children in Latin America, we know even less about the lives of middle-class and rich ones. The children in Latin America that really pique the curiosity of journalists are the tiny minority who live in truly extraordinary circumstances—on the street or in brothels, for instance; yet some of the most insidious lessons about race and class and gender are being taught to the children of the privileged, the very same children who may some day be in charge of their countries. Surely inequality across Latin America has something to do with what rich (mostly white) children are taught and the childhoods they live.

Marx and Engels drew attention to the remarkable cultural differences evident under capitalism between members of the working class and the owners of capital. Something similar is being expressed today about the rift between middle-class children and adults in Latin America. In the introduction to her second collection of essays about the history of childhood in Brazil, Mary Del Priore (1999: 7) writes, "In today's world, children have gone from being monarchs to dictators. Their attitudes often seem incomprehensible to us. Hostile even." At the same time that the generations lead increasingly separate and culturally distinct existences, children—as well as the rest of humanity—are presented with institutions, laws, and cultural artifacts endowed with an ever more global reach. One of these cultural artifacts concerns ideas about the nature of childhood itself.

In rich countries and among the rich in poor countries, children tend to be highly differentiated from adults: they dress distinctively,[2] and they enjoy discrete leisure activities. Childhood is closely circumscribed by the home and school (Ennew 1995), and children's spatial mobility depends largely on the goodwill of adults, who must ferry them from one place to another. Childhood is widely seen to consist in a state of innocence in matters of sexuality, and child rearing to involve considerable sacrifice—financial and otherwise—on the part of parents. Children and adults occupy complementary but discrete positions in the capitalist economy, the distinction here being not between those who control the means of production and those who sell their labor, but between which group contributes to production and which group consumes without producing. Privileged children are economic parasites.

It is difficult, and of little merit, to reduce any conception of childhood to its bare essentials, but these broad characteristics clearly have taken on a global relevance and been enshrined in international conventions and through the initiatives of policymakers and nongovernmental organizations (Boyden 1990; Burman 1996). In the same way that sixteenth-century Iberians, for whom Christianity was the only legitimate world religion, looked to children as vital adherents of the faith, contemporary processes of globalization depend in part on the appeal to and the forging of a universal culture of childhood. For a banal example of how globalized certain attributes of childhood are becoming, consider the fact that Mickey Mouse surely has greater name recognition around the world than any political leader, living or dead. Disney World and Disneyland are so popular in Latin America that the theme parks, particularly the one in Orlando, are the most important destination in the United States for visitors from a number of Latin American countries with the means to vacation abroad. Many flights from Brazil, Paraguay, and other South American countries have Orlando as their first point of entry in the United States. Were the Disney corporation not peddling a sort of fun based on something as purportedly universal and natural as a carefree childhood, it is doubtful the theme parks would command such wide popularity.[3]

Yet the attributes of childhood that are so widely taken for granted and the practices and tastes that resonate so broadly are very much a thing of our moment in history. Even in the First World, it is only recently that children have come to be accepted as an inevitable financial burden on their parents. In his history of U.S. children of newly urbanized, working-class families during the first two decades of the twentieth century, David Nasaw (1985: 41–42) writes "There was nothing new or extraordinary about asking children to go to work. Only recently has childhood become—almost by definition—an age of irresponsibility." Viviana Zelizer (1985: 11) argues that by the 1930s, changes in the social value of children in the United States had consolidated to the extent that children came to be seen as economically worthless but emotionally priceless. Children became an "exclusively emotional and affective asset [that] precluded instrumental or fiscal considerations. In an increasingly commercialized world, children were reserved a separate noncommercial place."

Similar changes have taken place in Latin America. In archival research on a study of early-twentieth-century custody cases in the southern Brazilian city of Porto Alegre, Claudia Fonseca (1989: 122) finds that "the files suggested that the central question was who would have the right to direct the upbringing of the child and to enjoy the services of the child. . . ." The difference between North America and much of Latin America is that whereas children are economically worthless— even burdensome—for the rich, for the majority of the poor in Latin America children are far more than an affective asset. Thus, so much of what is now seen as universal and natural about children is not only historically peculiar but also fictitious. Whereas it may be true that the children of the Latin American elite increasingly resemble one another and their middle-class peers elsewhere in the world, the children of the poor in Latin America tend to have little in common with rich children who may live only a stone's throw away.

Poor children in Latin America can be heard to voice attitudes about work and responsibility that are something like the inverse of the ideas about childhood that are taken for granted in the First World and among the rich in the Third World. In contrast to the coddled offspring of the rich, whose consumption patterns are dependent on the possibilities and largesse of their progenitors, poor children are likely to take pride in working and bringing in resources for the household. Rather than being a bottomless pit of expenditure for their parents, they carry out many essential tasks within the household, such as minding younger siblings, and in urban areas they do what they can to bring in money, be it by begging, selling candy, stealing, boot blacking, or any other means.

One of the most curious consequences of this double rift—between the generations, on the one hand, and between rich and poor children, on the other—is that the majority of young people in the region, who happen to be poor, lead lives so divorced from the expectations of the middle-class Latin American and First World observers who describe them that they are sometimes said not to have a childhood at all. Philippe Ariès (see discussion in the introduction to this volume) was criticized for basing his argument that there was no concept of childhood in medieval society on the rather unsurprising observation that there was no concept of childhood that matched the contemporary one. Yet surprisingly few studies of childhood in contemporary Latin America consider the possibility that there may be multiple forms of childhood coexisting and competing with one another at a single moment and that the terms and limits of these socially constructed notions are partially set by children themselves. For example, a study of children in a shantytown in Rio de Janeiro that also makes reference to children in Northeast Brazil suggests that "in Brazil, childhood is a privilege of the rich and practically nonexistent for the poor" (Goldstein 1998: 415). Likewise, in an analysis of working children in her country, a Brazilian scholar (Campos 1993 [1991]: 151) laments that for so many of her young compatriots, there is no separation between "work and childhood." As a result, these child laborers are "unable to fully live their childhood."

Lately a few historians have begun reexamining some of the most intensively investigated periods of history through a consideration of the lives of children. For instance, in *The Children's Civil War*, James Marten (1998: 5) portrays a side of this devastating war in the United States through the experiences of children, arguing that young people "saw themselves not merely as appendages to their parents . . . but as actors in their own right in the great national drama." William M. Tuttle Jr. (1993) studies World War II in a similar spirit.

This volume has likewise sought to explore how a consideration of the roles of children reinvigorates the study of the Latin American past and how the history of children cannot, in fact, be conveniently separated from what we think of as history in a general sense. Scholars of contemporary Latin America clearly have a similar opportunity.

Notes

1. In 1992, the American anthropologist Nancy Scheper-Hughes published a controversial ethnography of mothering in a shantytown of a city in Northeast Brazil. Attempting to get at the rates of child death, the author studied official statistics—which she found to be inaccurate and incomplete—interviewed local health officials, examined documents in the civil registry, and observed the work of the municipal coffin maker and the frequent burials at the local cemetery. She arrived at the conclusion that it was impossible to come up with anything like a reliable infant mortality rate for the city as a whole. Nonetheless, in bringing together a sample of seventy-two women in the shantytown aged nineteen through seventy-six, she found that of a combined total of 688 pregnancies (9.5 per woman), of which 579 were carried live to term, only 308 babies survived to the age of five. Even more than the astounding number and rate of deaths in this sample, what reportedly most puzzled the ethnographer "was the seeming 'indifference' of Alto women to the deaths of their babies and their willingness to attribute to their own offspring an 'aversion' to life that made their deaths seem wholly natural, indeed all but expected" (270).

Scheper-Hughes argues that infant mortality has come to be perceived in two radically divergent ways in the modern world. On the one hand, for those in the First World and those who enjoy a privileged status in the Third World, the death of a child, now a very unlikely event, is viewed as one of the worst tragedies that can befall a parent. On the other hand, those who live in conditions where the possible imminence of death is a reality attending every birth evidence a certain reluctance to become attached to their young offspring until they are reasonably certain their children will survive. Scheper-Hughes goes on to cite "prejudicial forms of infant care" as one factor "consign[ing] children to an early grave" (273).

Whereas the book has been criticized for seemingly blaming the victims (see, for example, Lassalle and O'Dougherty 1997)—the impoverished mothers—the argument is not so simple. Nonetheless, it is clear that the relationship of political economy to pervasive infant and child mortality in contemporary Latin America has been largely ignored by scholars.

2. In *The Language of Clothes*, Alison Lurie (1981) argues that by the nineteenth century children's dress in North America and Europe was distinct from that of adults, with the emergence of such styles as unisex sailor outfits and the Fauntleroy suit for boys.

3. For a fascinating treatment of the Disney theme park within the sociological study of childhood, see Hunt and Frankenburg (1990).

References

Aptekar, Lewis. 1988. *Street children of Cali*. Durham, N.C.: Duke University Press.

Ariès, Philippe. 1962. *Centuries of childhood: A social history of family life.* Translated by R. Baldick. New York: Random House.

Boyden, Jo. 1990. Childhood and the policy makers: A comparative perspective on the globalization of childhood. In *Constructing and reconstructing childhood: Contemporary issues in the sociological study of childhood,* edited by A. James and A. Prout. London: Falmer Press.

Burman, Erica. 1996. Local, global or globalized? Child development and international child rights legislation. *Childhood* 3 (1): 45–66.

Campos, Maria Machado Malta. 1993 [1991]. Infância abandonada: O piedoso disfarce do trabalho precoce. In *O massacre dos inocentes: As crianças sem infância no Brasil,* edited by J. de Souza Martins. São Paulo: Hucitec.

Del Priore, Mary. 1999. Apresentação. In *História das crianças no Brasil,* edited by M. Del Priore. São Paulo: Contexto.

Ennew, Judith. 1995. Outside childhood: Street children's rights. In *Manual of children's rights,* edited by B. Franklin. London: Routledge.

Fonseca, Claudia. 1989. Pais e filhos na família popular (início do século XX). In *Amor e família no Brasil,* edited by M. A. d'Incao. São Paulo: Editora Contexto.

Galeano, Eduardo. 1998. *Patas arriba: La escuela del mundo al revés.* Mexico City: Siglo XXI.

Goldstein, Donna M. 1998. Nothing bad intended: Child discipline, punishment, and survival in a shantytown in Rio de Janeiro, Brazil. In *Small wars: The cultural politics of childhood,* edited by N. Scheper-Hughes and C. Sargent. Berkeley: University of California Press.

Hecht, Tobias. 1998. *At home in the street: Street children of Northeast Brazil.* Cambridge: Cambridge University Press.

Hunt, Pauline, and Ronald Frankenberg. 1990. It's a small world: Disneyland, the family and the multiple re-representations of American childhood. In *Constructing and deconstructing childhood: Contemporary issues in the sociological study of childhood,* edited by A. James and A. Prout. London: Falmer Press.

Lassalle, Yvonne M., and Maureen O'Dougherty. 1997. In search of weeping worlds: Economies of agency and politics of representation in the ethnography of inequality. *Radical History Review* 69: 243–60.

Lurie, Alison. 1981. *The language of clothes.* New York: Random House.

Márquez, Patricia C. 1998. *The street is my home: Youth and violence in Caracas.* Stanford, Calif.: Stanford University Press.

Marten, James. 1998. *The children's Civil War.* Chapel Hill: University of North Carolina Press.

Nasaw, David. 1985. *Children of the city: At work and at play.* Garden City, N.Y.: Anchor/Doubleday.

Scheper-Hughes, Nancy. 1992. *Death without weeping: The violence of everyday life in Brazil.* Berkeley: University of California Press.

Tuttle, William M. Jr. 1993. *Daddy's gone to war: The Second World War in the lives of American children.* Oxford: Oxford University Press.
UN (United Nations). 1999. *1997 demographic yearbook.* New York: United Nations.
UNICEF (United Nations Children's Fund). 1998. *The state of the world's children.* New York: Oxford University Press.
World Bank. 1998. *1998 World development indicators.* Washington, D.C.: International Bank for Reconstruction and Development/World Bank.
Zelizer, Viviana A. 1985. *Pricing the priceless child: The changing social value of children.* New York: Basic Books.

The Children's Rebellion

Cristina Peri Rossi

Editor's note: The reader is reminded that unlike any previous chapters, which are all very recent, this prophetic, dystopian tale was written in 1971, that is, two year's before the consolidation of the military coup in the author's native Uruguay. The author clarifies, "Had I published it then, it would have seemed implausible, insane. . . . But the political events in my country and in neighboring countries turned what might have passed for frenzied imagination, delirious invention, into tragic reality. It isn't my fault."

The translation of this short story is slightly abridged.

We met by chance at an art exhibit, on the ground floor of the building. The exhibit, organized by the Center for Youth Expression, consisted of a collection of experimental objects we had made in our free time or during craft sessions; according to the latest theories of Applied Psychology and Rehabilitation through Work, nothing is better for us lost sheep than devoting ourselves fully to self-expression through sports, handicrafts, or manual labor.

To give the affair an atmosphere of genuine spontaneity, the pieces were not subjected to any kind of previous screening; each of us was allowed to present whatever we wanted and no conditions were imposed—except, of course, those governing any activity in the Republic, conditions intended to protect us from chaos, disorder, or subversion masquerading as something so apparently inoffensive as art, whereby, under the guise of experimentation or creative license, the seeds of family breakup, institutional degeneration, and social corruption are frequently sown. All that in a single canvas.

I had found an old chair in the garage belonging to my family (I don't know if I should use the term "family," but since language is the result of convention—a partial renunciation of my solitude, of my individuality—I don't see any compelling reason not to, given that, if I were to use some other, unconventional term, like *goro, apu, bartejo, alquibia,* or *zajo,* no one would understand and the invention of language would be pointless because mothers wouldn't have to teach their little children anything. And when the day comes that parents cease to be intermediaries, transmitting conventionality from one generation to the next, who knows what will happen to the concepts of authority, respect, private property, inherited wealth, society, and culture). I removed the wicker from the chair, stripping it down to the bare frame. I did leave a few tattered shreds of fabric from the cushion, like old skin or stigmata from *a life in the gutter.* I can thank my family for that nice saying. They use it in a vulgar way but there's something beautiful about it. Whoever invented the expression, who knows how many years ago, must have been a poet or something like that, one of those people with great intuition. But society appropriates those sayings for its own purposes and the images lose intensity, effect, and beauty; even though they still allow a whole bunch of primates to communicate with one another, it's not the same. I repeated the phrase several times, closing my eyes until I completely forgot the way I had come to understand it, and this led me to imagine other things. *A life spent in the gutter* ushered in fantasies so rich in colors, shapes, and climes that I decided I'd use the expression in all sorts of ways.

In the gallery, people milled around among the different pieces, asked questions, consulted the catalogs. Shiftless, bored, those of us who had our work on display were aimlessly roaming the corridors and gallery rooms. Some visitors had come from other places to see the exhibit. If they liked what they saw, they would probably replicate the idea where they were from, so that other States, other children, other societies, other oppressors and oppressed people could learn the formula. In practically every activity, or at least in practically every language, things are resolved by means of invention or imitation. Little children—like my brother—begin inventing symbols until the oppressors force them to accept a ready-made language available in any guidebook or dictionary, like ready-to-wear clothing at a department store. I used to like clipping the pictures from the London-Paris catalog. The London-Paris store had several departments and my mother would take me there, dragging me up and down the elevators, through the crowds. I was afraid of elevators because once I got stuck in one with a black man. I was very little and he was the first black man I'd ever seen in my brief life. I wasn't ready for the surprise. The London-Paris catalog, published annually, was divided up into different sections and I still remember the smell of the paper where the prices, the designs, and illustrations were printed. Expensive imported clothing, just what you'd expect in a colony. English subjects, a further flood of immigrants from Europe, gentry, a mixture of races and nationalities; it's impossible to find a trace of the Indian after so many voyages in search of gold in the New World.

My little brother's first words were *"baal-doa, doa,"* which was an excellent invention. To express himself, he didn't need all those phonemes we're taught to use; he could make do with five vowels and a few fricatives. But like any oppressed person, he had to accept the language of the fittest, and before long, for *"baal-doa, doa"* he had to substitute "Papa-Mama" (which, frankly, doesn't say much for the imagination of whoever made that one up). By the age of three, my brother had ceased to use his imagination. He had appropriated a lot of widely used linguistic symbols. He could understand almost everything people said and communicate things fairly easily. He had been assimilated.

You were wearing knee-high black leather boots. I wanted to understand the language of your clothing and experienced a number of hallucinatory sensations: a secret feeling of complicity, an inner shudder. From your boots sprouted dark lilac-colored pants more suggestive of catamount than of corduroy. The feline sensuality of a catamount, a mountain cat, penned at the zoo, subjugated yet still salacious. The froth at the lips. A discreet, suggestive, licentious walk, part power, part seduction. Your coat, long and shapely, reached the floor and I was afraid of stepping on its tails, of turning you to stone, of myself turning to stone, forever prisoners in an exhibit. If nearly everything is language, it must be that we are devilishly exhibitionist. We display ourselves all the time, exceed our limitations, attempt to communicate, to reveal, to transmit. Ring-ring-riiiing. Ululaaations. Ah-AHH-ah. Tarzan of the Jungle, the schooner lost in the fog, the train in the tunnel, it's all related; she relates her unease, walks along the beach, the swimsuit is skimpy—to reveal or to conceal? She couldn't decide between subtle provocation and the terrifying simplicity of nakedness. We're all a bunch of lousy provocateurs.

With the lights glinting off the piece you were exhibiting, off the piece made with your hands, that came from deep inside you, I couldn't make out the color of your coat. Using fragments of glass (shiny, iridescent glass so similar to the color and texture of your skin) you had made a playful waterworks that splattered just about everyone. This was the best part of the exhibit. Whenever some elderly gentleman would come over to inspect the contraption, curious to know how it worked, a splurt of dirty water would suddenly wet his face, his collar, his shirtfront, his tie. No one quite got angry and we, the exhibitors, enjoyed the spectacle. None of us had come up with anything that good. Take my chair, the skeleton of a chair. It was fairly unimpressive. Although I tried to upholster it with old newspaper clippings, it didn't look like something you would want to sit on. It really just made you want to look at it. I was careful in selecting which clippings I would display. Since our guardians don't allow us to collect information, I went to the National Library and combed through a lot of newspapers from the past two years. Our guardians have faith in the rapid decay of memory, a process they encourage by forbidding us to register or document our impressions. Of the present, we will remember only what memory wants to preserve, but our memory is not free; it is subject to certain conditions, oppressed, fragile, laid up, and lulled to sleep, vanquished. Although I've tried different exercises to improve my memory, the results haven't been very good. If writing had never been invented, I'm sure our memories would be better. In reading the old newspapers, I realized the incredible number of things I had forgotten during the course of those two years. Things so important I thought I could never forget them. And this was over the past two years alone. It's hard to imagine how many things I must have forgotten from the time I was born. Assassinations. Catastrophes. Presidential inaugurations. Strikes in the mines. Plane crashes. Wars. Protests broken up by the police here and there. People dousing themselves in gasoline and setting themselves alight. Of every one thousand children born across the continent, six hundred and forty-six die of treatable diseases. Babies born without heads. Astronauts. Demonstrations for peace. Bombs detonated in the Pacific—for experimental purposes. "Accidents" in the prisons, leading to the deaths of workers

and students. But with everything remaining the same. Wars declared
and wars covered up. Napalm falling from planes in the sky. International beauty pageants. Political intrigues. Ambushes, collective crimes,
massacres, torture, martyrdom, torment, jails, "confessions," exile, trials,
violations, injustices, revolutions, proclamations, speeches, declarations,
scandals, sacrifices, selflessness. And a lot, a whole lot of sporting events.

After carefully selecting the material that interested me, I clipped
different pictures. That's what I used in upholstering one part of the
chair. One picture showed a napalm-singed baby in Vietnam. The picture was obviously taken from close up, with a powerful lens, and then
enlarged until it was the right size for the newspaper. Soldiers like to
display their trophies, exhibit their talents. I also selected a shot of a
demonstration in Cordoba, just at the time it was being broken up by
the police. There was a mushroom of gas in the air and the cottony
smoke stretched over the demonstrators, who were trampling one another. Elsewhere I included a large picture of Charles Bronson in a
vaguely feline pose, his drooping mustache, his air of muscle-bound vi-
rility that women love—old women, that is, women over thirty. Next I
found the amount in dollars (which I underlined with a red marker)
that Alain Delon earns for every movie he acts in. I also clipped and
pasted on several speeches delivered by generals and other characters
in charge of running countries. I used a blue pen to underline the words
and phrases they repeated, which made it look like they'd all been written by the same person or else copied from the same instruction manual.
Entire sentences repeated. It was really funny. Then I added the picture
of two naked women kissing each other on the mouth and touching one
another's breasts. That picture wasn't actually from the newspaper. It
was a pornographic postcard featuring two very pretty women with
tender, light-skinned bodies. Gentle curves. There was nothing shocking
about it. The publisher must have made a mistake. They wanted a picture that aroused the senses, but that one aroused the sentiments. The
speeches were even more interesting. A number of fellows stood in front
of the chair to read them. The phrases repeated in almost every speech
were mostly the ones that could be defined only vaguely without opening up a lot of debate: "The well-being of the nation," "in defense of
freedom," "safeguarding the interests of society," "protecting public institutions," "law and order," "progress and development," "the Republic's pursuit of happiness," "the sacrifice and dedication of the Armed

Forces," "the arduous struggle against foreign enemies," "foreign influences," "salutary nationalism," "military honor and integrity," "dark forces undermining the nation," and all kinds of things like that written in the worst kind of prose, official prose.

Your waterworks was beautiful. I would have liked to have had one like it in my backyard at home. I especially liked the colorful glass. Your hands were a little roughened up from the metalwork. I realized right away that it was very important to you. Collecting different materials, pieces of wood, iron, glass rods, pottery shards, so you could eventually give shape to your imagination. You explained to me that in your workshop section there was an engine, an oxygen tank, a soldering iron, and it was easy for me to picture you there, delicate, thin, moving among the sheets of metal and car parts. Rummaging through that junk, all that stuff that had been thrown away, until you found the things, the shapes, the materials you needed to finish your piece.

"What are you doing?" she asked when we'd made our way through the throngs of people, to one side of the garden. I was thinking about her waterworks.

"Nothing," I said, which was one of the most serious answers I'd ever given in my life of fourteen years. We sat at the edge of a fountain, in the garden, away from the gallery, among linden trees so dark, like guards positioned for ambush, that you couldn't see them. She didn't seem to be paying much attention to the landscape, then or at any other moment during the evening. She accepted the landscape, but it was unclear whether that was because she thought it was nice, harmonious, or whether, on the contrary, it was so far beyond repair that it wasn't worth mentioning.

"And how do you manage that?" she asked. "For the last twelve years I've been trying to do nothing but I haven't been able to yet. Things are always going through my mind and before I know it my hands are getting into something. Do you think I should tie them up?"

"You're more than twelve years old," I protested. I didn't want our conversation to be built on a shaky foundation.

"Of course I am. I'm fourteen, like you. But during the first two years I was forced to do certain things, learn to walk, to speak, to read newspapers, things like that. So they don't count. Those years were wasted. People should be born knowing how to do those things, so they can spend all their time doing nothing."

I really liked her. In the distance, I saw the lights in the gallery, the people, dark, moving among the objects, and a lone attendant picking up extension cords outside the gallery, among the linden trees, which were also dark. He seemed to be concerned only with following the serpentine trail of the cord through the moist leaves, the wind, the scattered seeds, the fence posts, the placards.

"How do you know I'm fourteen?" She already had the upper hand in the conversation and I had to be careful.

"I read your entry in the catalog. Your chair is unremarkable. It lacks originality."

"I'm not pretending to be an artist," I said, a little upset. "The culture of letters is disappearing, giving way to a civilization based on images, so I register my protest on the golden rims of chairs," I argued, my hands in my pockets, my eyes downcast. Like anyone, it bothers me to be questioned. At that precise moment a linden leaf fell on my head. Annoyed, I brushed it off, but the little accident didn't stop her.

"Artistic protest lacks meaning in the context of mass culture. Just like chewing gum or reproductions of *Guernica,* protest can be mass-produced, neutralized. In the universe of submissive masses guided by the ideologies of the owners of computers, an artist's chair is less important than the leg of a fly rebelling against the inhumanity of the system," she stated.

I hadn't wanted to discuss such deep topics. In fact, depth gives me vertigo. That's why I had decided not to think anymore: to avoid falling. The smallest thing—thinking about a little piece from an automobile engine—leads me, by means of tangential associations, to other thoughts, and from those to yet others, so that that little piece from the automobile engine becomes the center of a puzzling universe from which vertigo itself falls, like a ripe piece of fruit. And like a piece of fruit I fall into the well, a well I'm afraid of. Other people don't have wells or they've filled them in. If I had enough sand, I'd fill mine in, but I don't think all the sand I've seen at the beach would do, and in any case that sand is dirty: it has trash from boats, bathers, lovers. Love also leaves its traces, its refuse, its residue, and sometimes the wind, the sea, the breeze doesn't want to sweep them away. The day I manage not to think, no one will notice, because most people I know have decided to do the same thing. It's simpler and promises freedom; the forms of freedom we can have, in any case, so that State security won't be endangered. And if I do manage to do it and the authorities realize, they might award me a medal for good behavior or for service to the nation, which would allow me to live off the interest. And who could imagine anything better, enjoying unearned income without thinking? Someone told me that that was the American dream, someone who'd been abroad (abroad is all that evil beyond our borders) and saw the work of a guy named Albee, or something like that.

"I didn't intend to rebel against the inhumanity of the system," I insisted. "The chair is the chair, that's all there is to it, it's just that instead of resting his ass on beautiful plush green upholstery, anyone who uses it will have to plunk his behind onto Vietnamese mud, colonialism, class inequality, organized repression, *The Colossus of Maroussi*, the Armed-Forces-that-Protect-the-Nation. For those who still believe in the existence of sexual instinct I pasted on a picture of Charles Bronson and of a lesbian couple, depending on consumer preference."

"Both of those things seem a little naïve for someone who's fourteen," she said, looking at me straight on. It was difficult to face the harshness of her green eyes, their sparkle of intelligence and lack of sensuality. "But taking into account that the average age of visitors is about forty, I think you chose the right motifs. Let's sit here," she said, when we were at the edge of another fountain. We had walked part way down a path of cypresses she hadn't even noticed. In the fountain there were two large angels astride a big fish. Water dribbled in all directions from the moss-covered angels, which symbolized something or other, something of interest to the State.

"Try to keep your clothing dry," I told her. "The art of our grandparents is oozing all over the place."

"That kind of art is all washed up," she said, unwrapping a piece of candy, placing it in her mouth with evident pleasure, and offering a piece to me.

That was a good thing we had in common: we both loved candy. We spent some time filling our mouths with a lot of different flavors: chocolate, cherry, milk, banana, honey, plum, orange, pineapple, lemon. We chewed on the candies, sucked the liquid they released, and looked at the dark, placid night. She told me I could call her by whatever name I wanted. I decided to call her Laura, after a poem by Francesco Petrarch that had just popped into my mind: *"Donna, non vid'io"* (*Ballata I, Accortasi Laura dell'amore di lui, gli si mostra severa*). We read Petrarch because he's from way back when, so there's nothing dangerous about him. She had already collected a variety of names, aside from the truly prosaic ones her parents had given her and that weren't good for anything but filling in official forms. Someone had decided to call her Brunilda; a twelve-year-old who had fallen in love with her named her Yolanda; her cousin, with whom she first dabbled in the ceremonies of sex, christened her Anastasia; and a close girlfriend with whom she learned about love and poetry called her Gongyla. She remembered that she had a grandmother named Gertrudis, and a grandfather, Nicanor.

"I'll call you Rolando," she said, kissing me on the forehead solemnly, austerely. "I always wanted to have a brother. I think I still feel the scars from that childhood trauma. Have you ever wanted to have a sister?"

"No," I lied, lowering my gaze and kicking at a little red stone, which was round and stuck out through the leaves on the ground. How could I tell her that at that very moment I had the cursed desire for her to be my sister. If I'd had a sister I would have fallen hopelessly in love with her and lived a Western, Christian drama because in me incest brings out feelings of reverence, tenderness, respect, sensuality, and pleasure. I don't know if it was her lilac-colored pants, her black boots, or her auburn hair falling across her shoulders that made me think of her as an incestuous sister. Her fine hair had a hard time reaching her shoulders and by the time it got there it is was hesitant, dispirited. To banish those thoughts I looked at the ground and asked, "Where are your parents?"

I knew that all the students from our year had a similar story. Our parents had been caught: a lot of them had died in the armed uprising of 1965, others, it was thought, disappeared during the months of the civil war, or else they were locked up in the State's penitentiaries, jails, or military barracks, paying for their revolutionary dreams. We, their offspring, had been placed in the custody of the country's best and most patriotic families, families that, to nip in the bud any subversive tendencies we might have inherited, like an illness lodged in the darkness of our genes, had graciously volunteered to watch over us, reeducate us, teach us in accordance with the system, unbreed us, keep us, and, in a word, assimilate us into *their* society. Some, with greater or lesser luck, depending on how you look at it, had remained in the hands of the State, which placed them in its institutions, orphanages, or shelters,

where they awaited rehabilitation, which might take a lifetime. As everyone knows, the State has the constitutional obligation to provide a roof,
shelter, and food for *all* of its sons and daughters, regardless of their
birth, race, or skin color. What can make a difference is the color of
ideas, because the state won't provide a roof, shelter, and food for those
who wickedly undermine its institutions, plot its destruction, soil its
name. That was precisely what happened with my brother, Pico, and
me: to prevent us from being subversives, scheming together and threatening national security, they separated us from one another. I had the
honor of going to live with one of the country's most blue-blooded families whose faithfulness over the last fifty years to the institutions-that-
be (as if they themselves were the institutions) was as steadfast as their
will to exorcise me of any spore from the past. Pico, on the other hand,
who was younger and less rebellious, ended up in a reformatory. He
was still being reformed, last I knew. This is what I was told by a boy
I spoke with in the park and whose brother is in the same reformatory.
The boys invented a relatively safe and effective system of communica-
tion. It seems a little complicated at first, but once you get the hang of
it, it's efficient and simple. They communicate by means of postage
stamps they trade back and forth. Up to now, no one has realized what
they're doing, and the boy volunteered to send Pico my messages by
means of this system. I accepted but quickly realized that I don't have
much to say to Pico. Pico is only seven years old and, as a matter of
fact, when my parents died in the 1965 uprising (in our comfortable
two-story house, summarily shot as they listened to a piano concerto by
Franz Liszt) he was only three, which is why I still didn't know much
about him. But our separation was very painful because neither of us
wanted to go where we were sent, I to the new family in charge of
redeeming me nor he to a reformatory, likewise meant for rehabilitation;
I don't know which one of us is better off because both systems have
their pluses and minuses. To console us, they said we were lucky the
revolution hadn't been successful because in that case children would
have been sent to Siberia, which, as everyone knows, is very cold and
full of bears. But I don't think my father wanted to send anyone to
Siberia or that he would have separated any child from his family because he liked children and families; in any case, in the name of family
unity, they separated us from our families.

I sent Pico a message with the boy. It said, "Dear Pico, how are you?"

He replied two days later with a text that, when decoded, read: "I'm more or less all right, or not all right, depending on how you look at it. And you?"

A few weeks went by and I had nothing to tell him until I finally sent a message that said, "I live with a rich family and I'm pretty clever. If you need anything, let me know and I'll try to send it to you."

His reply came in the form of a long list of requests, which I tried to satisfy right away: "Since you have offered, we are short on cigarettes, pencils, stationery, knives and other sharp instruments, chocolate, books, magazines, combat manuals, picklocks, cotton, ether, scalpels, and blowtorches. There's a guy here who wants to know whether you could find a discreet way of sending him a chemistry book. I would like a colorful fish but I'm afraid they might take it away during inspection. I couldn't stand to have them take it away after I'd had it."

I was busy for a while, trying to get what Pico wanted, which wasn't easy given the rigid measures of control we live with. I had no trouble supplying him with cigarettes. All I had to do was take some packs from my new ancestor, a very rich man with influence in the administration of things public. He deliberately leaves them on his desk or nightstand, to tempt me. They're first-rate cigarettes, American, filtered, and they come in beautiful packages. I thought Pico would like the pictures on them even if he doesn't smoke. The pencils, on the other hand, proved more difficult. Anything that allows us to express ourselves is strictly controlled, so we won't express things that wouldn't be appropriate for us to express. So, in exchange for some used-up pencil ends and a few bits of chalk, I had to swap some of my best stamps (stamp collecting, an inoffensive hobby, is encouraged by the State, by reeducation centers, and by the cooperating families). It's unbelievable how expensive pens are, the few we've managed to get our hands on and hide, that is. Getting hold of sharp instruments proved completely out of the question. Since my parents died I haven't seen anything with a sharp edge and I've been told that instead of blades I should use an electric razor to shave these beginnings of hair on my face. Beards are forbidden, they make us suspect. At the same time it would be impossible to take apart one of those machines used to cut vegetables, meat, or the lawn without anyone at home noticing, reporting us, and our receiving the maximum sentence, which wouldn't be light, since matters of national security would be at stake. I was able to send Pico a lot of chocolate, even Swiss and English bars, which my adoptive mother receives as gifts from foreign companies, along with perfumes, lotions, canned goods, liqueurs, extracts, prebath creams, afterbath creams, creams for using around the house, creams for the morning, for the afternoon, for the night, creams for discreet dark interiors, creams for gala and other sorts of celebrations that I can't remember but that I'm sure exist. (She also has a cream for removing facial cream and another one for removing cream from the body.) Choosing the magazines was very difficult. I don't know what Pico or his companions like and he didn't specify what he wanted to read. The magazines that circulate freely are those meant to awaken our sexual instincts; becoming obsessed with that sort of thing would presumably stifle any dangerous ideas we might have, which is why we never lack colorful, entertaining material for our leisure time. But I have no way of knowing what sort of sexual literature Pico might like. I also have no way of knowing whether he's decided on a particular sexual orientation or whether he would rather be fully informed before making up his mind. Uncertain about his preferences, I decided to send him different sorts of pornographic magazines. Some were strictly heterosexual and their in-your-face content struck me as unappealing: what normal person could be interested in male–female copulation, regardless of how amazing the position or the manipulations of the specially designed camera that can enlarge the organs and suggest sensations that never actually occur in bed? Only if he had never experienced heterosexual copulation, which was unlikely, would Pico feel enticed by that sort of magazine, and then only if his imagination was very poor. So I included a number of issues dedicated to other sexual activities: zoophilia, necrophilia, homosexuality, onanism. Because they're forbidden, I couldn't get magazines about electricity, auto mechanics, politics, history, philosophy, or sociology, and out of respect I didn't want to send him anything about sports. I know that in his community (which is what they call his shelter), one of the harshest forms of punishment for someone who has committed an offense against good brotherhood is to make him read about sports. I also sent him a lot of drawing paper. His other requests proved impossible. Practically every book was banned, for one reason or another; every day boats chock-full of them set off for the high seas where they dump their cargo and where the fish might be inspired to rise up, if they haven't already lost their instinct for rebellion. I once saw an important guerrilla warfare manual, but that was a long time ago, when my parents were still alive. Back then the book was also forbidden, but a lot of people found ways of circulating it clandestinely. Once the uprising failed, though, I never heard of any way of getting a copy. The people who survived didn't need the book anymore, since the military was there to protect us; everyone else was either dead or put away for life (or should I say, for death) in State prison camps. I did send Pico the colorful fish. It was a beautiful little red fish, shapely, nimble, with delicate fins, a round body, elegant movements, and a pair of eyes that, unlike those of so many other fish, were restless, excited about life.

A little while later, I received a final message from Pico, which read, "Thank you for the little fish. It's named Ugolino. We all love it a lot, especially me. The monitor took it away last night and flushed it down the toilet. It was still alive when it was dumped in the sewer."

I haven't heard anything further from Pico. Either he has nothing new to tell me or his messages were intercepted. The boy I used to meet up with in the park, supposedly to trade postcards with, told me something terrible had happened at the shelter. He doesn't know what, though. To avoid trouble, his own brother has stopped communicating for a while. The boy thinks they've been transferred somewhere else, maybe because it was discovered that someone had been communicating with the outside world or else some serious offense was committed. Anyway, once again we're left without news.

"My parents are in jail," Laura answered finally, sucking the taste of candy off the tip of one finger. "'Life sentences,' a military judge ruled: 'Treason against the constitution,' 'seditious assembly,' 'complicity after the fact,' 'conspiracy,' 'criminal concealment,' 'incitement of violence,' 'insult to the Armed Forces,' 'assassination,' 'possession of explosives,' 'high treason.' Isn't it surprising that one person can commit so many crimes simultaneously? Nine hundred and fifty-five years in prison, all told. I don't think they'll be able to complete the sentence. They'll die first, which will be their revenge," Laura observed as she tried to clean off a bit of lichen that the angel had splattered on her lilac-colored pants, at about knee level. As I leaned over to help her, wetting the green stain with saliva, some of her auburn hair caressed my forehead. My naked forehead. My hair was cut when I joined the new family unit. Sometimes I miss it, my soft brown hair that used to cover my forehead and that reached the back of my neck, but the authorities don't allow males to have long hair. I don't think they like it.

"I haven't seen them again," Laura mumbled in a low, steady voice.

It would have been tactless to ask if it hurt her to say that. What good is it to miss things and people we're not allowed to miss? A useless rebellion.

"The spot's gone," I told her, gently caressing the fabric, her knee, her bone, her skin. My finger moved slowly, like a timid boy exploring a city deserted but full of soldiers.

"I think you're a little sentimental," she told me, disappointed. She lit a cigarette and held out the pack.

"Not now," I said. "I'm tired of making smoke."

The attendant was moving in the distance, winding up cables that ran to the gallery. Someone was probably giving a speech in there, distributing ribbons, venerating the world, ranking the works, extolling the virtues of order, of our order, of the imposed order. But we were silent. A little sad, listless, unmoving among the shadows of the garden, we were together, she smoking and looking at the fallen leaves on the ground, I looking at her, at her lilac-colored pants. Lilac. Laura. Lilaceous. Ligeria. The linden leaves. Laura as light, as lilaceous, as lilac as the linden leaves.

"What kind of trees are those?" she asked, and I knew she was referring to the trees all around us. Like dead, embalmed relatives. Like relatives dead amid the sadness.

"Linden. Linden trees," I answered.

"You make me feel a little melancholy," she told me, gently crushing the cigarette end against the wilted leaves on the ground.

"That's not true," I told her. "It's the statues, and the linden trees."

Classical statues, wild lindens. We fell silent again, but without moving away from one another. In our silence a bond united us, like siblings in the same den of iniquity, womb, or dungeon. Maybe because she was tired, she allowed one of her lilac-colored legs to gently fall against me, as if by accident. She let it rest there, as if it weren't attached to the rest of her. I brushed a few strands of hair from her forehead—conspirators, drunken argonauts.

"Do you think they'll ever be allowed to see each other again?" she asked me suddenly, her voice quivering. "Maybe across a partition or a fence, over a wall," she continued. "Just once over the years?"

"Maybe," I lied. To lie like that I had to light a cigarette and appear lost in thought as I looked at the wisps of smoke that rose toward the tops of the linden trees.

"No," she said, resolutely. "They're separated, a long way from one another, each in a different cage, somewhere remote, kilometers down dirt roads, across fences, partitions, posts, barbs, and sirens, behind gigantic walls that stretch as far as the eye can see. They may have lost their memories, lost everything they knew, he knowing only that he is a man and she that she is a woman, all other knowledge gone from their minds, spilled along with the blood lost in captivity, when they were imprisoned, separated from one another, alone. Maybe neither remembers the other. It would have been better if they had died," she concluded somberly.

I remained silent, motionless.

"If they haven't killed themselves, it's out of discipline," she declared. "Revolutionaries don't kill themselves, because they love life."

"I would have killed myself," I said, firmly.

"How would you have managed that?" she asked, curious. I went on smoking, out of habit, not principle.

"How would I know?" I said. "I would have shot myself or something."

"Suppose you hadn't been armed at the time, that they'd taken away all your weapons. How would you have done it then?"

"I would have run, that's it, run. I would have run in front of them until they were forced to shoot me."

"But that's impossible," she mumbled, disappointed by my answer. "Between five or six of them, they've tied you up and thrown you inside a cell. You've spent days and days incommunicado, without eating or drinking, in a state of utter, silent, terrifying loneliness. Entire weeks without speaking, without hearing the sound of another human being, a voice; entire weeks in pitch-black darkness, without air or light, without hearing the singing of birds or being addressed by another person, touching nothing but cold urine, smelling nothing but your own excrement piled up on the floor; once a day, as if to an animal, they toss an old piece of bread and a piece of worm-infested meat through the iron window that's otherwise always shut. And after weeks of darkness, blackness, cold, and madness you long for someone to hit you, for the prison lackey to yank at your growing beard."

She had me cornered. I was feeling besieged by her questions, with salvation an increasingly remote possibility. The sirens were wailing nearby, time was running out; terrified, I was running through the wet streets; the dogs about to catch up with me, I was running, running, behind me the masters, the pursuers, but I didn't want to go on living without you, without you, without you . . .

"I would have thought of that beforehand and kept one of those handy sudden-death pills hidden behind my ear. The moment I had my hands free, pop, it would be in my mouth and I'd be as good as dead."

"That wouldn't work, dummy. With the first punch, the capsule would have been lost forever or else it would have fallen inside your ear. You would have been left pretty hard of hearing for a while, but that would have been about it."

I had exhausted all the options. Hemmed in, surrounded by the dogs, pursued by the sirens, running down a dead-end street, I would never see you again, hear anything from you, look into your eyes or touch your knees, see you alive. I think she had given up too because she said, "Next time, you'll have to think this through carefully."

Once that was settled and we were feeling pretty depressed, we walked down a path that led back to the gallery, where by then they were calling us over the loudspeakers.

"What will you do with your prize?" I asked, certain she would win first place.

"You'll see," she said, with a malicious, conspiratorial glance.

We arrived just as the center's president was announcing that the jury had finished its deliberations. Like docile soldiers, Laura and I took our respective places, assigned previously during rehearsal. Identified by numbers, we were displayed like monkeys before the distinguished ticket-purchasing audience, which was expecting to be amused with clever tricks. They do the same thing with prisoners, except that with them no one knows their names, not even the jailers: they are forever the number assigned them by a judge. I thought that her parents, Laura's parents—mine if they had been alive—would have numbers, numbers for identifying and not identifying them, numbers so they could occupy their cells, numbers to sit down to eat a reheated stew, worm-ridden meat, and once they had lost their memories, once time had gone by, they would be reduced to that: a three- or four-digit number. No one would remember their names, they wouldn't even remember their own names; a number at roll call, on the warden's list, in statistical tables, in the registries, in the history that someone will someday tell about this period—although who knows if the person telling the history will know anything more about them than their identification numbers, and who knows if the history they will tell is the true one or whether they, those in charge of telling it, will be telling a history that doesn't correspond to the true history. Would memory be obliterated? It occurred to me that the *story* in the history we were taught was not really an intentionally made-up one, or even a story written with good intentions but undermined by a lack of memory, by oblivion, by anonymity, by forgiveness. Because it's the winners who write history. That's what I was thinking when, docilely, I settled into my designated spot. It didn't bother me to be docile about something like that, it even struck me as an amusing concession. From a distance, Laura cast me conspiratorial glances, which I answered soberly, feigning the seriousness appropriate for the occasion. But deep down I was rejoicing. Against the conspiracy of the gorillas we had a conspiracy of intelligence. That was when the ceremony began.

The right honorable president of the Arts Circle, donning his Supreme-Simian-Pontiff-of-the-Primates, Master-of-Ceremonies, Grand-Organizer sash, ambled solemnly toward center stage. The anthropoid toyed with the microphone for a moment until he had it right in front of his snout. We were all motionless, silent. Motionlessness and silence—as opposed to movement and words (factors that, as everyone knows, contribute to political subversion, instability, and disunity)—were the basis of our moral, social, and civic education.

The ceremony began with a reading of the list of pieces that for one reason or another had been disqualified. Mine, considered hostile and unappealing, was one of the first to be mentioned. Clearly, no one of good birth would want a chair like that in their home, it wasn't pleasing to the eye; it's important to keep in mind that everything in our society is supposed to give us a feeling of well-being when we're sitting down, the position most propitious for State security. One by one, the pieces were either eliminated or discreetly praised. The list was long. Finally, with obvious pride (as if he were the true creator, as if the piece—given its form, dimensions, and meaning—were the most faithful reflection

of the desires and thinking of the authorities), the Maximum Monkey,
the Erectile Anthropoid, declared that the waterworks made by Laura
had won first place. Great jubilation. Congratulations. Unanimous ap-
plause from all those assembled. The primates clap and devour bananas.
They've come down from the trees and set themselves up in houses
with doors and windows. They drive automobiles. They manufacture
washing machines and jails. Donating their vines to museums, they
move about the streets, walk the pavement in new low-cut boots. When
they see one another they say hello, as if they all belonged to the same
family. The monkeys, united. . . . We also applaud, in accordance with
our new education. We have evolved and know when we're supposed
to applaud.

After extolling the virtues of the winning entry—its usefulness, malleability, functionality, and colors, which, taken together reflect all the
qualities favored by the system—the right honorable president invited
the winner to come forward and receive her prize. She did so with great
poise. Both her face and her stride were angelic. Her gaze softened and
her eyes moistened a little from the emotion she was obviously feeling.
The right honorable president of the Arts Circle had her step up onto
his dais, which, as was appropriate for a monkey higher up in the hierarchy, was elevated slightly above the platform we were on; he congratu-
lated her warmly (in other words, the immense honor of presiding over
the ceremony had made him perspire). With a solemn air he handed
her the award. In the midst of a silence as vast as the entire gallery,
the garden of sad linden trees, and the memory of our ancestors taken
together, he placed in her hands a beautiful gold medal decorated with
patriotically colored ribbons. Next, ceremoniously—as if he were vest-
ing in her the weight of the icons of former times preserved in the city
thanks to the bravery and daring of soldiers who with blood and fire
had triumphed over the barbarian invaders, the enemies from within
and without, over cunning, wicked, devastating conspiracies—he
handed her a trophy, the symbol of the propagation and conservation
of the species, of the triumph of good over evil, of order over chaos, of
institutions over anarchy; and she, the winner, the repository of the future in whose lap the coming generations will seek warmth, protection,
and sustenance, she, the visionary, the vestal to whom the future of the
city and the keys to the kingdom were entrusted, received the bust of
the nation's Commander General, the hero of 1965 who crushed the

uprising, saved the nation, the children, the youth, the adults and old people, the grandmothers and grandfathers and grandchildren, and who, in evidence of his infinite spirit of sacrifice, his love for the fatherland, gave up his private life and forwent his well deserved rest to thenceforth govern our proud nation, to worldwide—or is it universal? (I don't remember which)—acclaim.

Clearly moved, Laura received the greenish bust of the general (I've noticed this color is characteristic of all busts of generals, living or dead) and brought it lovingly to her breast, as any decent citizen and future mother of the homeland would. Then, to bring the ceremony to a close, the president invited the winner to set her invention in motion, so the distinguished guests and all those assembled could appreciate its full splendor. Pressing against her breast the bust of the Commander General of the Nation, Laura went over to the waterworks and calmly twisted one of the wing nuts hidden below the iridescent glass. Suddenly, a deluge showered the room. The crazed jets began to spin, to spray in all directions, like a terrified father fleeing a soldier who has just struck him over the head with a cudgel, a father leaving a trail of blood behind, his head sagging from a limp neck, the blood gushing like rivers bursting their banks; the jets spun circles, spewing from their furious hoses a rain that inundated the gallery, geysers that sent the audience crashing against the doors, against the walls, like during the protests of 1965 when the water cannons on military trucks sent people somersaulting across the ground, left them to crawl along the sidewalks, blinded by the liquid, pushed on by the water. The jets fired their liquid torrents at the crowd, the furniture, the walls, round and round the room, smashing things, sweeping the floor, climbing the walls, ricocheting off the ceiling. The crazed, panic-stricken audience, blinded by the force of the liquid against their faces and bodies, the fury of the downpour, scurried in vain to find the exits. Invariably, when people would reach the doors or windows, a burst of liquid, like a gale-force wind, would send them smashing into the walls, crashing into one another, twisting, turning, falling.

I had jumped out the window the moment the fun began, and from outside, from out in the garden of sad linden trees, of fountains decorated with nymphs, where the memories of our ancestors swung from tree to tree, from fountain to path, from path to branch to nearly memoryless children, from the dark, silent, sad garden, I threw a burning torch inside the gallery, just as Laura had instructed me. Amid the linden trees, calm, at ease, indifferent to the landscape, she was waiting for me. She was also indifferent to the spectacle of the gasoline spewing from the jets, bathing the gallery, feeding the ferocious blaze.

When I could see that everything was burning, I made my way down the agreed-upon path. In the distance, the flames illuminated the dark sadness of the linden trees.

"Rolando," Laura said, as we set off, "get this spot off my pant leg. Another angel has splattered me with something."

Glossary

Contributors

Glossary

adulterino the offspring of adulterous unions in which one parent was married to someone else.

agente fiscal crown's attorney; somewhat like a modern prosecutor.

ama wet nurse.

andeyo the countryside, in Haiti.

audiencia *see* "Real Audiencia."

Bizango a Haitian cult that exists outside Vodou, although it shares some of the spiritual beings from the Vodou religion.

cabildo in colonial Spanish America, town council and court of first instance.

cacique as used here, an indigenous lord.

casta a term referring both to individuals of mixed racial background (usually of free status) and to a system of classifying individuals based on color, class, and social status.

curador ad litem a court-appointed legal representative for minors of age.

Cuzqueño a resident of Cuzco, Peru.

dolo wrongdoing.

espurio the children of Catholic priests.

Ezuli (also *Erzulie*) the most important female spirit in the families of Haitian Vodou, patroness of love of every variety.

filiation as used in this book, one's birth status as legitimate or illegitimate.

FMLN Farabundo Martí National Liberation Front, the armed wing of El Salvador's Revolutionary Democratic Front (FDR), which fought against the government in the 1980s.

FSLN Sandinista Front of National Liberation, which lead the Nicaraguan revolution against Anastasio Somoza and governed the country from 1979 until 1990.

hidalgo untitled noble.

hounfo the place of worship for most Vodou communities.

houngan male spiritual leader in the Vodou religion.

273

hijos naturales the offspring of single parents who were technically able to marry.

huehuetlatolli speeches delivered by Aztec elders.

justicia ordinaria literally "ordinary justice." Referred to the policing and judiciary function of the *cabildo*.

juvenency youth as a stage of life.

Kiskeya the name the native Taíno used to refer to the ideal version of their land, Ayiti (Haiti).

Kreyol the language of Haiti, based on French but with many African and New World influences.

Limeño inhabitant of the city of Lima, capital of the Viceroyalty of Peru.

limpieza de sangre purity of blood; in colonial Spanish America, the extent to which one's blood was "untainted" by racial and ethnic attributes, a specific religious heritage, or a particular birth status deemed undesirable.

lougawou werewolf, in Haiti.

lwas in Haiti, complex spiritual beings who guide, protect, demand fealty, insure blessings, and mediate both social discourse and healing.

marasa twins or triplets, the idea and images of which trace back to West African peoples and continue to pervade Haitian Vodou religion, as well as Haitian literature and art.

mestizo person of mixed European and Amerindian ancestry.

moreno a racial classification used in many Latin American countries to refer to people who are dark skinned, though not very dark.

pardo a racial classification used in many Latin American countries to refer to people who are dark skinned but not of exclusively African descent.

patria potestad legal term referring to the power of a patriarch over his children and members of his household.

plaza mayor main square in a town or city.

procurador a legal adviser.

Real Audiencia in colonial Spanish America, a combined executive advisory board and high court.

restavek this Kreyol term derived from the French *rester avec*, to stay with, refers to a child who is sent to live with relatives or another family because his or her own family is too poor to offer adequate food, clothing, and education. Although there are many instances of generosity toward these youngsters, the more typical case is exploitation under conditions of virtual slave labor. There is such stigma attached to being a *restavek* that even children in orphanages are often observed to refuse such association.

sala de crimen literally "crime room." Refers generally to the judges who sat on the high court and heard criminal cases. In Lima, referred also to an actual room where interrogations were taken and scribes recorded statements.

torno where babies could be abandoned anonymously and left to the care of a foundling hospital.

viceroyalty the largest jurisdictional and administrative unit in the Spanish American colonies until the end of the eighteenth century.

Contributors

LeGraçe Benson is Director of the Arts of Haiti Research Project and Professor Emeritus at the State University of New York. She has published extensively on Haitian art and is currently writing a book entitled *Art from Paradise: How the Sun Illuminates under Cover of Darkness*, which discusses the arts of Haiti in terms of "long conversations" over time and across lands and oceans.

Carolyn Dean is Chair of the Department of Art History at the University of California, Santa Cruz. Her book *Inka Bodies and the Body of Christ: Corpus Christi in Colonial Cuzco, Peru* was published by Duke University Press in 1999. She recently won a Pew Charitable Trust Collaborative Grant to study Christianity in the colonial Andes. She has published many articles on Latin American art of the colonial period.

Ondina E. González recently received her Ph.D. from Emory University, where she wrote a dissertation on children in colonial Latin America. She is an Assistant Professor of History at Reinhardt College.

Donna J. Guy is Professor of History at Ohio State University. She specializes in Argentine and women's history and is the author of *Sex and Danger in Buenos Aires: Prostitution, Family and Nation in Argentina* (University of Nebraska Press, 1991) and coeditor of *Sex and Sexuality in Latin America* (New York University Press, 1997). She is currently researching Argentine state policies toward street children.

Tobias Hecht is the author of *At Home in the Street: Street Children of Northeast Brazil* (Cambridge University Press, 1998) and translator of *The Museum*

275

of Useless Efforts (University of Nebraska Press, 2001). A recipient of a National Endowment for the Humanities award for independent scholars, he received his B.A., M.I.A., and Graduate Certificate in Latin American and Iberian Studies from Columbia University and his doctorate from the University of Cambridge. With a grant from the Harry Frank Guggenheim Foundation, he is currently writing a book about one of the contributors to this collection, Bruna Veríssimo.

Sonya Lipsett-Rivera, Professor of Latin American history at Carleton University, received her doctorate from Tulane University in 1988. She is coeditor of *The Faces of Honor: Sex, Shame, and Violence in Colonial Latin America* (1998) and author of *To Defend Our Water with the Blood of our Veins: The Struggle for Resources in Colonial Puebla* (1999), both published by University of New Mexico Press. She has published many book chapters and articles, including one that was awarded the Tibesar Prize.

Nara Milanich is a graduate student and Mellon Fellow in Latin American History at Yale University. Her dissertation, *"Los Hijos del Azar:* Culture, Class and Family in Chile, 1850–1930," explores relations between poor families and the state. Her previous research focused on infanticide in rural Chile.

Cristina Peri Rossi was born and raised in Uruguay but has resided in Spain since she went into exile in 1972. She has published more than twenty books—novels, poetry, short stories, and one collection of essays—and been awarded numerous literary prizes, including the Premio Benito Pérez Galdós. Her fiction and poetry have been translated into a dozen languages.

Anna L. Peterson is Professor in the Department of Religion at the University of Florida. She is the author of *Being Human: Ethics, Environment, and our Place in the World* (University of California Press, 2001) and *Martyrdom and the Politics of Religion: Progressive Catholicism in El Salvador's Civil War* (State University of New York Press, 1997), and is coeditor of *Christianity, Social Change, and Globalization in the Americas* (Rutgers University Press, 2001). She received her M.A. and Ph.D. from the University of Chicago Divinity School and her A.B. from the University of California at Berkeley.

Bianca Premo, Assistant Professor of History at Emory University, specializes in Spanish colonialism and Peru. She received her M.A. from the University of Arizona and her Ph.D. from the University of North Carolina at Chapel Hill. She is currently revising her dissertation, "Children of the Father King: Youth, Authority and Legal Minority in Colonial Lima," for publication.

Kay Almere Read is an Associate Professor in the Department of Religious Studies at DePaul University. Her research interests include pre-Conquest religious traditions of Mesoamerica, comparative ethics, and religious imagery. She is the author of *Time and Sacrifice in the Aztec Cosmos* (Indiana University Press, 1998). Currently she is working with Jason J. González on *A Handbook of Mesoamerican Mythology* and *An Encyclopedia of Mesoamerican Mythology* (both for ABC-Clio Press). She holds degrees from the University of Chicago (Ph.D., M.A.), the University of Colorado (B.A.), and the University of Illinois (B.F.A.).

Irene Rizzini received her M.A. at the University of Chicago and her Ph.D. in Sociology from the Rio de Janeiro Institute of Research (IUPERJ). She is currently Director of the Center for Research on Childhood of the University of Santa Ursula and Professor at the Department of Social Policy at the Rio de Janeiro State University. She serves as the Vice President of the Advisory Board of Childwatch International Research Network, coedits the journal *Childhood,* and is the author and editor of many books and articles about children in Brazil.

Bruna Veríssimo has lived in the streets of Recife, in Northeast Brazil, since the age of nine. Although she never went to school as a child, she learned to read and write on her own by studying street signs. She is also a self-taught artist. With support from the Harry Frank Guggenheim Foundation, she is currently working on an ethnographic research project about life in the streets of Recife.

Living in Latin America